WEB NAVIGATION
DESIGNING THE USER EXPERIENCE

WEB NAVIGATION
DESIGNING THE USER EXPERIENCE

Jennifer Fleming

O'REILLY®

Beijing · Cambridge · Farnham · Köln · Paris · Sebastopol · Taipei · Tokyo

Web Navigation: Designing the User Experience
by Jennifer Fleming

Copyright © 1998 O'Reilly & Associates, Inc. All rights reserved. Printed in the United States of America. Published by O'Reilly & Associates, Inc., 101 Morris Street, Sebastopol, CA 95472.

Editor: Richard Koman

Production Editor: Jane Ellin

Printing History:

September 1998:   First Edition.

ISBN: 1-56592-351-0   [12/00]
[I]

CONTENTS

Foreword   ix

Preface   xi

1 GETTING STARTED   **1**

Movement in space   1

Understanding the user experience   4

Putting yourself in users' shoes   6

Recap   11

2 TEN QUALITIES OF SUCCESSFUL NAVIGATION   **13**

Principles of successful navigation   13

Recap   27

3 DESIGNING FOR USERS   **29**

Defining your audience   32

Moving toward user-centered design   34

Getting started with user testing   38

Recap   44

4 SITE ARCHITECTURE   **45**

The quest for order   45

Organization defines content   48

Building your infrastructure   51

A closer look at process   58

Recap   62

5 INTERFACE AND INTERACTION DESIGN   **63**

Visual messages   63

Show and tell   68

The psychology of design   71

Recap   74

6 LOOKING AT PROCESS   **75**

Process: A six-phase approach   75

Phase 1: Information gathering   78

Phase 2: Strategy   84

Phase 3: Prototyping   91

Phase 4: Implementation   96

Phase 5: Launch   99

Phase 6: Maintenance & growth   101

Recap   103

7 NAVIGATION DESIGN FOR SHOPPING SITES   **105**

Laying the groundwork   106

Outlining specific goals   110

Who's doing it right: Amazon.com   113

Who's doing it right: Garden Escape   118

Who's doing it right: FAO Schwarz   122

Recap   125

8 NAVIGATION DESIGN FOR COMMUNITY SITES   **127**

Laying the groundwork   128

Outlining specific goals   134

Who's doing it right: sceneServer   138

Who's doing it right: Firefly   143

Who's doing it right: Café Utne   146

Recap   148

9 NAVIGATION DESIGN FOR ENTERTAINMENT SITES   **149**

Laying the groundwork   150

Outlining specific goals   154

Who's doing it right: Urban Diary   156

Who's doing it right: Riven Journals   160

Who's doing it right: Crimson Empire   162

Recap   164

10   NAVIGATION DESIGN FOR IDENTITY SITES   **165**

Laying the groundwork   166

Outlining specific goals   169

Who's doing it right: Razorfish   170

Who's doing it right: IBM   174

Who's doing it right: powazek.com   179

Recap   181

11   NAVIGATION DESIGN FOR LEARNING SITES   **183**

Laying the groundwork   184

Outlining specific goals   189

Who's doing it right: DigitalThink   191

Who's doing it right: National Geographic   198

Who's doing it right: The Annenberg/CPB Project   200

Recap   204

12   NAVIGATION DESIGN FOR INFORMATION SITES   **205**

Laying the groundwork   206

Outlining specific goals   211

Who's doing it right:MSNBC on the Internet   213

Who's doing it right: Lycos   216

Who's doing it right: Computers.com   220

Recap   222

A   TECHNICAL TIPS   **223**

B   GLOSSARY   **231**

C   NETOGRAPHY   **235**

D   BIBLIOGRAPHY   **247**

Index   251

FOREWORD

Until recently, most of us thought clean code and pretty graphics were the key to a successful site. Now we're realizing that unless we also create navigable interfaces, all our hard work could result in an unusable failure. Anyone interested in communicating effectively on the Web must recognize the importance of navigation and seek to master its many facets. This will mean learning some new skills and ways of thinking, since the skills that apply to coding or visual design are very different from those needed to design navigation that works.

Web Navigation: Designing the User Experience provides a methodical approach to arriving at answers that are right for you—not for some mythical, one-size-fits-all web site. Beneath the useful structure and methodology is an effective system designed to help you outline your own goals and find personalized solutions for meeting them.

As you read this book, you'll find many new concepts—such as designing for multiple audiences, building community, conducting user testing, or planning for commerce—demystified. Jennifer Fleming presents each subject in an extremely accessible manner and offers many exercises to help you identify which navigation approach is appropriate for your type of site.

Kudos to Fleming for her excellent research, approachable tone, and generosity of information. If you're looking for help in giving your site's visitors a more positive experience than they get today, this book is an excellent place to start. It provides ideas and direction, not preachy rules that apply to someone else's site.

The Web needs more books like this if it is to evolve to the next level. I believe this book can help you make your site a better place, regardless of whether your purpose is community-building, commerce, education, entertainment, information, or hobby. It's written in such an enjoyable, conversational tone that you may have trouble putting it down; I certainly did. I wholeheartedly recommend it for all web publishers.

—Lynda Weinman,
Author, trainer, columnist
http://www.lynda.com

PREFACE

There's a cartoon I like, drawn by an artist named Rich Tennant. It shows a frazzled-looking man standing in front of a web design shop, the storefront covered with neon signs and arrows and all manner of blinking things. The caption reads, "Where's the dang door?"

The best humor has an element of truth in it, and I'd say there's a healthy dose of it in this cartoon. Navigating web spaces, it turns out, is not as simple as it seems. Designing navigable web spaces can be downright difficult at times.

That's why I wrote this book—because I needed it. I needed to know why it was so hard to get around on the Web in the first place, and what we developers could do to make it easier. I needed to know how we could use knowledge gained from users to inform navigation design. And I needed to know what other developers were already doing.

Hopefully, this book will begin to answer some of those questions. There are many questions I can't answer, however. I can't tell you whether frames are better than a sidebar, whether a search box is better than a site map, or whether Dynamic HTML is the one true path to navigation enlightenment. Navigation is more complex than that. There are as many approaches as there are developers, and a good many of these approaches will work on the Web. The problem is that they may not work for your situation.

This book focuses on how to find out what will work for you, for your audience, for your content and purpose. I've interpreted navigation design broadly, since I believe it's much more than just the study of buttons and sidebars. It's the study of movement in space, of inter-actions, of user goals and how to facilitate them. It's as much about removing barriers as it is about constructing roads.

What you'll find in this book

In the first half of the book, we'll look at concepts and principles behind navigation. How does architecture affect navigation? What can we learn from interface and interaction design? What steps in the development process have the greatest impact on navigation? Do sites with successful navigation show common traits? These first six chapters offer a foundation for navigation design.

Chapter 1, *Getting Started*, offers some basic thoughts on what navi-gation design is really about. It also outlines this book's approach to navigation design: a holistic approach that focuses on the "user expe-rience," not just on buttons and bars.

Chapter 2, *Ten Qualities of Successful Navigation*, presents common traits shared by sites with successful navigation. Each trait is explained and supported by examples from site designs.

Chapter 3, *Designing for Users*, looks at understanding and designing for your audience (or audiences). Who are these users, and what do we know about them? How should you incorporate their preferences into the design process? This chapter also offers tips on user testing.

Chapter 4, *Site Architecture*, explains the role of site architecture in navigation design. How information is organized—or, in a sense, what sort of space you create—reflects how people move around within it.

Chapter 5, *Interface and Interaction Design*, explains how visual communication design can affect movement through a site. What do you need to know about visual hierarchies such as color or move-ment? Concepts from interface and interaction design are offered in this chapter.

Chapter 6, *Looking at Process*, describes the development process and outlines important areas for navigation design. Each step, from brain-storming to launch and beyond, includes a note on "how to do it."

In the second half of the book, Chapters 7–12, we'll look at sites that are doing it right. We'll also look at designing navigation that works for your site's purpose and goals. How do you get people to needed information as quckly as possible? How do you design for commu-nity-oriented sites? What should you know if you're planning e-commerce? The case studies in these chapters show how other sites have solved some of these problems.

In each of these chapters, typical user goals and expectations will be outlined. There are three tiers of goals which will be discussed: basic, purpose-oriented, and topic- or audience-oriented. Basic goals apply to all sites; these are typical navigation questions such as "Where am I?" or "Where can I go?" Purpose-oriented goals are specific to broad site types: a shopping site won't have the same navigation issues as an entertainment site, because users' goals differ. Topic- or audience-oriented goals are the final, most specific level of user goals. They have to do with your site's audience (such as kids) or topic (such as selling books). Here's what a completed goals and expectations chart would look like for a site that sells books:

First Tier (general navigation questions)	Where am I? Where can I go? How will I get there? How can I get back to where I once was?
Second Tier (purpose-oriented questions)	How do I know my financial information is secure? How can I protect my privacy? How can I find the item I want? What if I'm not sure exactly what I'm looking for? How can I preview products to see if they're right for me? What if I have problems or returns?
Third Tier (product- or audience-oriented questions)	How can I find books by a particular author? How can I find books that are similar to books I like? How do I know what the reading level of a book is? Where can I get reviews or recommendations? How do I find out about new releases and awards?

In each chapter, we'll go into these goals in greater depth and offer ideas on how to discover your audience's goals and expectations.

Chapter 7, *Navigation Design for Shopping Sites*, takes an in-depth look at the navigation issues commerce sites face, including trust and security issues. Case studies presented in this chapter are Amazon.com, Garden Escape, and FAO Schwarz.

Chapter 8, *Navigation Design for Community Sites*, explores how some community-oriented sites are approaching the design of shared spaces. Case studies include Café Utne, sceneServer, and Firefly.

Chapter 9, *Navigation Design for Entertainment Sites*, offers navigation concepts important to web entertainment design, such as avoiding distracting problems and creating immersive spaces. Case studies include the Riven Journals, Crimson Empire, and Urban Diary.

Chapter 10, *Navigation Design for Identity Sites*, features issues that designers of identity sites (both personal and organizational) should understand, including sending the right message to users and using "fish food" to pull people in. Case studies include IBM, Razorfish, and powazek.com.

Chapter 11, *Navigation Design for Learning Sites*, looks at important concepts for learning sites, including handling different learning preferences and building in opportunities for people to test their skills. Case studies include DigitalThink, National Geographic, and the Annenberg/CPB Project Exhibits Collection.

Chapter 12, *Navigation Design for Information Sites*, offers navigation concepts that information sites should understand, from building in shortcuts for speed users to handling storage and delivery needs. Case studies include Lycos, Computers.com, and MSNBC.

In the appendixes, you'll find tips and resources to help you in designing navigation. Appendix A offers brief technical tips, including how to optimize graphics and target frames. Appendix B is a glossary of development terms that relate to navigation. Appendix C is a "netography" of related web resources, while Appendix D is a bibliography of related books.

There is also a full-color insert in the middle of the book. Figures that appear in this insert are labeled as "Figure C-x."

Accompanying this book is a CD-ROM that I'm hoping will act as more than just a handy drink coaster. Just open the *start.htm* file in your web browser. It offers links to the resources mentioned in the book, and provides a quick tour (in full color) of the case study sites. It also features trial versions of software tools, including Macromedia's Dreamweaver and BoxTop Software's Image Vice. The CD-ROM was designed by Nathan Kendrick (*nkendric@risd.edu*).

Acknowledgments

Web Navigation: Designing the User Experience would not have been possible without the help of quite a few people. Special thanks to:

- The many site designers interviewed in this book, who made time to share their thoughts and ideas despite hectic schedules.

- Richard Koman, my editor at O'Reilly, for his help, patience, and encouragement. Thanks also to all the talented O'Reilly production folks who made this book a reality: Jane Ellin, Robert Romano, Edie Freedman, Nancy Priest, Claire Cloutier LeBlanc, Nancy Wolfe Kotary, Nicole Gipson Arigo, Ruth Rautenberg, Seth Maislin, and Sheryl Avruch.

- Lou Rosenfeld and Marc Rettig, both of whom answered many foolish questions with unfailing kindness and insight.

- Lynda Weinman, for writing the Foreword (and numerous excellent web design books).

- Nathan Kendrick, who designed a cool (and useful) interface for this book's CD-ROM.

- Andrew Chak and Teri Smith for being advance readers.

- My family and friends for putting up with my complete insanity during a lengthy writing process.

- My students at the Massachusetts College of Art and Naugatuck Valley Community-Technical College. Their questions and insights helped shape this book.

- Sara Fleming, Carrie Arnaud, Dave and Mary Gould, Ed Piou, Nancy Fleming, Lisa Joubert, George Cumming, Kim Smith, Joe Curro, Ruth Ann Gurecki, Mike Kaltschnee, Linda W. Braun, Natasha Jafri, Asha Kilaru, Wambui Mwangi, Katie Goodrow, Peter Beaven, and Ginetta and Juan Candelario-Romero for their valuable input at various stages in the process.

Many of this book's strengths are due to the help these people offered. Where faults remain, they are entirely my doing. I'm looking forward to hearing your thoughts on navigation design. Thanks for your interest in this book.

—Jennifer Fleming
jennifer@squarecircle.com
Summer 1998

## CHAPTER ONE

GETTING STARTED

It's not rocket science.
It's social science.
—Clement Mok

In this chapter

- Movement in space
- Understanding the user experience
- Putting yourself in users' shoes
- Recap

N avigation is about verbs. Searching, choosing, shopping, chatting, downloading, backing up, charging ahead: what we do on the Web is based on action.

Skeptical? "Clicking hardly counts as action," you might argue (ignoring the nagging carpal tunnel in your wrist). But the Web is by nature an active medium, and like it or not, we are forced to interact with it. You may be a couch potato while watching TV, which requires little more active participation than the periodic twitching of your finger on the remote, but passive viewing on the Web is a much trickier proposition.

What makes the Web an active medium? It begins with how we perceive it: as a space to move around in, an environment we can change, a place where we can get things done.

Movement in space

There is a shared hallucination that happens routinely on the Web—and not solely because we're all staring into the light of a cathode-ray tube, though that might have something to do with it. What I'm talking about is an illusion, a trick of the mind that few Web users recognize but most of us experience: knowingly or unknowingly, we perceive the Web as a space.

Look at what we demand of the Web: freedom of movement, clearly marked paths, personalized service, quick delivery, immediate answers. These are things that someone designing a library, theme

Clement Mok, Studio Archetype

park, or department store might worry about. Your enjoyment of a store or museum depends in part on the ease of moving through it without unnecessary complications. It's no different on the Web. Your enjoyment of a site is linked to how successful you are in moving across pages and among files—in essence, through the space.

We think of web spaces as "virtual" because they can't be touched, smelled, or tasted, but they feel real enough when we're mucking around in them. They feel real enough to annoy us when things go wrong, or are too slow, or aren't as we expected them. They feel real enough that we expect the same level of service from a web store-front as we do from the local shops. They feel real enough that we expect to get things done without unnecessary and frustrating barriers.

If you need more evidence that the Web is an active space, look again at the vocabulary of the Web. We talk about dead ends and dead links. We worry over who is visiting and try to track how long they stay and what they do. We provide site maps, "Go!" buttons, shortcuts, fast paths, and alternate routes. If users aren't moving around in Web space, what's behind this active vocabulary? If users aren't moving around in Web space, why are so many of them hope-lessly lost in it?

For most people, navigation is about purposeful action, about moving toward a final destination or goal. It's a means to an end. It's not an end in itself. After all, Columbus didn't risk his life and reputa-tion because he thought sailing by the stars was fun.

If navigation is really about goals, then the way we've been thinking about designing navigation is wrong. We worry about the act of navi-gating as if it could be detached from the more important goals of our users. How do I make a pull-down menu? Should I try frames? Can I use a database? These are valid concerns (which we'll talk about later in this book), but they don't really address web users' pressing problems.

To begin solving these pressing problems—user frustration, disap-pointment, and confusion—we need to begin thinking about this medium in new ways. Instead of obsessing over new gimmicks and digital doodads, we should focus on removing long-standing obsta-cles between users and goals. Instead of focusing on clicks or hits, we should focus on the entire *user experience*.

Clement Mok: "It's about wayfinding"

Clement Mok is the founder of the well-known design firm Studio Archetype (formerly Clement Mok designs), author of several books, and one of the creators of NetObjects Fusion. He is also one of the Web's finest design minds, and was willing to share some of his experience and insight into designing navigation systems.

"Navigation is about wayfinding," Clement explains. "You can't treat it as separate because many other things run parallel with it. If you look at studies in wayfinding, everything from exhibit design to building the cathedrals, it's about creating a complete system. It's about looking at the whole."

Web developers with backgrounds in software development and those who have come in from the print world have very different approaches to the screen, Clement points out. "If you are coming in from the world of application design, the Web is seen as less about communication and more about functionality. In application design, they really don't have a concept of navigation. They see it as a tool that appears and functions on a page. Why would one need to have navigation for an application? That's a new thought.

"The intent in each case is also fundamentally different," he adds. "In the application world, it's about making things efficient, useful, and functional. In a strange way, it's very binary. It works or it doesn't work. In the world of communication design and the world of print (and as you translate and adopt this on the Web), the intent is to create narratives. It's about suspending reality and taking you to places. It's operating in a world of fantasy.

"If you suspend reality, then all of those usability tests and functionality tests that you measure in application design get thrown out the window," he says. As to how these two different approaches might come together, Clement suggests, "I think that these two opposing areas of communication design and application design will create tension, as well as debate, about what's good and what's not."

Clement also suggests that we begin to look at the Web in a new way, rather than simply as something we can access through a computer screen. "If we see the Web as *multimodal* (that is, accessible on a PDA, a telephone, and so on), we have to look at things very differently. If things are multimodal, it means having more than one sort of navigation system. I honestly believe that at the end of the day, in 10 years time, the way we will look at the Web is going to be multimodal and multidimensional. We'll access it through television, computer screens, PDAs, even the phone."

With new technologies meaning new modes for communication, a focus on the end result is essential to developing appropriate and meaningful navigation. "Richard Wurman looked at this in the most logical way," Clement says of the author of *Information Architects*. "It's not about one way to do things. It's really about the end goal. If we start to look at the Web as multimodal and focus on accommodating the end, that's probably the best way to move forward."

Studio Archetype's site features selections from Clement's book *Designing Business* as well as links to other interesting resources. See *www.clementmok.com*.

"Knowingly or unknowingly, we perceive the Web as a space."

Understanding the user experience

Nordstrom's repeatedly wins retail customer service awards. Why? They understand that keeping visitors happy is the key to gaining loyal customers. Likewise, Disney allocates vast time and resources to the problem of ensuring that their theme park visitors are immersed in a fairy-tale world. Disney, like Nordstrom's, understands the value of creating a positive experience, start to finish.

If we look at the average web user's experience, it might be quite different from the controlled, immersive experience that Nordstrom or Disney has in mind:

> Jim wants to check how his stocks are doing. He dials into his ISP from his home computer and waits while he's connected. He feels lucky to get in. Jim opens his web browser and enters the URL for a new investing site a friend told him about. Unfortunately, he types it wrong. He gets an error message. He gets flustered. Jim retypes the URL and thankfully gets it right this time. He waits for what seems like forever as the page loads over his 28.8 modem. He shuffles papers. Taps his feet. Fiddles with the mouse. The page finishes loading.

> So many choices! Jim can't tell where to begin, and it doesn't help that he can barely read the small type on screen. He clicks on a link to investor information, and follows it a few pages in. It isn't what he thought it was, but he can't find a way to go back, so he hits the Back button several times. He selects another link and is prompted to enter his username and password for a subscribers-only service. He hits Cancel and gets another error message. Again, he backs out.

> Back on the main screen, he spots a link to a Java stock ticker. He doesn't know much about Java, but figures a stock ticker is what he needs. He selects that link and a new page loads. It's taking forever. Jim loses patience and tries to back out. He clicks the Back button a few times, but nothing seems to work. He's crashed.

Sound familiar? Unfortunately, this scenario is all too common.

Jim's not likely to go back to that site. Why would he? He didn't get what he wanted there, he could barely read the text, and he probably thinks it'll crash his computer again. His entire experience at the investing site was a lesson in frustration, and he's not about to repeat it any time soon. If this were the only stock quote service online, chances are he would muddle through it to get the information he needs. Fortunately for Jim, the site probably has plenty of competition. He doesn't have to stick around.

Jim's goal was clear: he just wanted to check his stocks. Why didn't he succeed? A number of unnecessary obstacles stood in the way, many of them things that could have been avoided.

If we look at designing navigation as the process of planning for user goals, then we need to become more sensitive to obstacles that might stand in the way. Doing that means looking not only at users' goals, but at their behaviors, preferences, and resources. You can't know everything about every user, but there's a lot you can find out about them without too much extra effort.

In general, most people need to know some basic things in order to orient themselves. This is true whether they're navigating a building or a web site. These basic navigation needs include answers to the following questions:

- Where am I?
- Where can I go?
- How will I get there?
- How can I get back to where I once was?

Where am I? On the Web, before you can evaluate where you might want to go, you need to know where you are. In life, it's easy to take this sense of location for granted. We're surrounded by clues about location—signs, maps, sounds, smell, color, climate. On the Web, however, you can get very lost very fast. There's little sense of "you are here," which even your average mall tends to provide. Without this basic sense of location, it's very difficult to plan routes.

Where can I go? If I'm planning a trip to Harvard Square, and I'm planning to do it by subway, one of the first things I need to know is whether the subway goes to Harvard Square. I can get that information by looking at a subway map or by calling for more information. On the Web, if I want to get from the front door of a site to any point within, I also need to know the possibilities so that I can weigh the alternatives.

How will I get there? Let's take the subway example again. If I'm planning that trip to Harvard Square, it's important that I know 1) where I am now and 2) whether I can get to the Square on the subway. But I also need to know which connections to make. What's the route I'll need to take? Route planning is pretty underdeveloped on the Web. People often march down a path without a real sense of the connections they'll need to make along the way.

"Where am I? Where can I go? How will I get there? How can I get back to where I once was? People need to know these things in order to orient themselves."

For example, imagine browsing through Yahoo!'s subject categories (*www.yahoo.com*). Take a wrong turn and you'll end up farther from your goal than you were when you started. Being able to search for relevant categories—which reveals not just categories but paths to information, as shown in Figure 1-1—helps visitors plan routes through Yahoo!'s subject tree. It's no wonder Yahoo! is consistently ranked a popular and user-friendly search site.

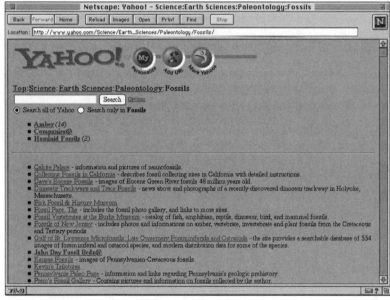

Figure 1-1. *Yahoo!'s visible pathways help make it a popular and user-friendly search site.*

How can I get back to where I once was? Once I'm in Harvard Square and my business there is done, I still have to find my way home. The same goes for web users. Many people feel hopelessly stranded a few layers into a web site. Without the ability to leave breadcrumbs in their wake, they depend on having the right navigation tools on hand. A meaningless link to some vague "back" location is not the kind of guidance they need. A clear path and descriptive labels will help visitors backtrack without needless frustration.

Putting yourself in users' shoes

If all web users were the same, and all of their goals consistent, we could probably stop our planning at the basic needs level. Thankfully, we're not all the same. We want different things, and for different reasons. In navigation design, then, we have to go beyond basic needs and look at specific end goals.

In web development, we're accustomed to analyzing company goals. Often, our paychecks depend on it. More importantly, it's part of being a responsive and effective designer.

That loyal analysis of company goals can sometimes get us into trouble—unless, that is, we also take the time to examine the goals of the site's intended users. Lumping client goals with user goals is a serious blunder, since they are often very different things. Designing for clients without calculating for end users is one quick path to an unnavigable site.

Take the example of a typical shopping site. A developer signs on to help a record store set up a web storefront. In the early stages of discussion, the developer quizzes the client on their mission and goals, their needs, and their concerns. In service to the client, the developer then spends three months creating a site that will meet every one of these needs and then some. The client is thrilled at the result. When the site premieres, however, the client receives a flurry of email from disgruntled consumers. From server logs, the developer can tell that customers are not making it very far into the site. Sales are practically nonexistent. Six months later, the client abandons the web storefront, convinced that web shopping is a terrible farce.

What happened? No one stopped to consider the *users'* goals, and how they might be different from those of the *company*.

The seller and the buyer can sometimes have radically different goals. The following chart shows the different goals that might be held by a record store and a user.

Site	User
Wants to make money on the Web.	Wants to purchase securely.
Wants to find out about customers.	Wants to retain privacy.
Wants to offload 6,000 overstocked copies of Sheena Easton's last record.	Wants to buy the new Smashing Pumpkins CD.

If the storefront design proceeds with only the client's needs in mind, what's going to happen? The following chart gives an idea.

Site	User
Requires users to pass through an "On Sale Now!" screen that promotes the discounted Sheena Easton records.	Is annoyed with having to look at a promotional screen. Just wants to find the Smashing Pumpkins CD!
Rushes shoppers to the checkout and locks them into the ordering process.	Panics on entering the checkout process, since questions about security still haven't been answered and there seems to be no easy way to change one's mind.
Asks for personal information on preferences, buying habits, and income.	Is infuriated by the request for personal information. None of their business!

"Designing for clients instead of users is one quick path to an unnavigable site."

"User profiles are like a character study in acting or literature. They help you put yourself in someone else's shoes."

What's the likely end result here? *No sale.* A lack of understanding and communication is this site's main problem—it's not some vague fault of web commerce. But what does this have to do with navigation?

Everything, really. The user in search of the new Smashing Pumpkins CD had a primary goal, and that goal should have been driving the process. The developer and the client should have sat down (with users if possible) and thought through what people might want and expect from the site, and how they would behave. Avenues designed to help shoppers meet their goals quickly and easily could have then been created.

Without this focus on shoppers' goals, there are unnecessary (and often insurmountable) obstacles in the paths of visitors. What's more, when users can't meet their goals, the client is the one who ultimately suffers the most—in lost sales, lost customers, and a sometimes substantial lost investment.

If you accept the premise that you need to understand user goals and design accordingly, the next question is: How do you do that? This is a question we'll keep coming back to in the book, but there are two methods you can start with: creating profiles and thinking in scenario.

Creating profiles

Imagine you've come up with a terrific idea for a site: an online matchmaking service. You've spent some time exploring possible technologies and you know you can make it work. But what would people really want from a matchmaking site? What are their goals, besides getting hitched? Coming up with some user profiles can help fill in the gaps.

User profiles are brief studies of the sort of person who might visit your site. They're a little like a character study in acting or literature, in which you try to put yourself into someone's shoes in order to understand them better. They aren't meant to replace focus groups or user testing. Instead, they act as guides throughout the design process, and help keep human factors at the forefront.

Taking the example of the matchmaking site, you might brainstorm profiles for two fictional users who represent part of your target audience.

Profile #1: George

George is in his early 40s. He works full-time at an insurance agency and has recently divorced. He's definitely leery of jumping back into the singles scene. He lives in a small, tight-knit community, so he's also very worried about privacy. He's interested in finding a match who shares his religion, and he doesn't want to have to relocate. He loves opera and travel and wants to find someone who shares his interests. George will access the site from his home computer, which is a couple of years old and has a slow Net connection.

For the last three months, George has been trying more traditional dating services, without much luck. He complains to friends that it's difficult to select a date based on a video segment or brief description, and he's had a few embarrassingly bad dates as a result. He wishes there were a better way to find out about people before meeting them face to face. George is not sure that a Web matchmaking service will work, but he'd rather do that than go barhopping.

Profile #2: Natasha

Natasha is 21 and in her last year of college. She heard about the matchmaking site from a friend and thinks it would be a fun thing to try, since academics don't leave her much time to meet people. She's not really interested in a serious relationship, and location is not important to her since she'd be just as happy talking with someone by email as in person. But she's definitely leery of getting mixed up with a weirdo, even though she's pretty savvy about the Web and uses chat services frequently.

Natasha will access the site from her college's computer lab, which has a high-speed connection but does not allow students to install browser plug-ins. By default, Java is turned off in the lab, and security software deletes any unauthorized files (including cookies) from the computers every night.

The profiles of George and Natasha may seem very different, but even from sketching out these two very basic profiles, you can already see shared concerns, which demonstrate the type of patterns you should look for. In this case, both George and Natasha are worried, to some degree, about privacy. Natasha wants to be sure she can avoid "weirdos," and George would be horrified at the idea of his community finding out he was looking for love online. Privacy, then, should become a central issue in the design of your matchmaking site.

You can also predict other things from these profiles. For example, you may need to build in search capabilities for things such as religious affiliation or location. You may decide to avoid using certain technologies or plug-ins. Or you may decide to put your mind to a particularly interesting problem—such as George's wish that there were better ways to find out about someone before meeting them in

"Starting with scenarios gives you a better sense of the landscape of your site, and the routes you'll need to build within it."

person. User profiles can help you predict people's problems, but even more importantly, they may also lead you toward surprising and innovative solutions.

Thinking in scenarios

Thinking like your site's users is harder than predicting New England weather, but scenarios can help. Scenarios, or possible situations, can offer you a view of the navigation process as a whole. Thinking in scenarios also fits the view of a site as an active place for people to move around in. You'll be surprised at what you can learn if you take the time to sketch out some scenarios.

For example, let's take the user profile of George, created earlier. If we have this fictional (but representative) user, how would he move through the site? What barriers might he encounter along the way, and how can we remove them? Add predictions about action to a user profile, and it becomes a scenario.

> George is ready to give the matchmaking site a try. He connects to his ISP on his home computer and goes to the site. He's a little nervous about the whole process. Right away he looks for some instructions describing how this works, and he wants to be able to try the service before he signs up. He's also looking for some sort of reassurance about privacy.

If George doesn't find all of these features very close to the front door, he may not continue. Assuming George can find them (since you now know you'll need to build them in), let's keep going with this scenario.

> George signs up as a trial member. He's able to pick an alias, which helps him disguise his real identity until he feels confident about meeting someone. He didn't have to give a credit card, but was able to take a tour of how the service works. He's feeling pretty good so far. Now he can focus on finding a match. He figures the best place to start is with the things that are most important to him: religion and location.

Again, if George doesn't have the ability to search the way he wants to search, he may become frustrated with the service and go elsewhere. You'll need to build flexible search capabilities into your matchmaking site if you want to please George. Let's assume you go one step farther, and build in some interesting personality searching.

> George does a search by location, and then is able to modify those results by religion. He's left with 150 possible matches who share both his location and religion. That's a lot of results to wade through. George notices another search feature that

allows him to modify results by other factors such as personality and interests. He selects some personality traits he values, and then views his results. It's down to 60 possible matches. Finally, he modifies his search so that only opera lovers appear on the list. Now he has a manageable list of 18 possible matches. He begins clicking on their aliases to find out more.

Reading the first few matches, he finds several he'd be interested in meeting. He stops to scribble down these aliases on a scrap of paper near the computer.

If George were able to store possible matches on the site somehow, he might have an easier time of it. Scribbling aliases on scraps of paper isn't exactly ideal. Let's assume you build in the ability to tag and store possible matches, plus a few extra perks.

George tags five of the possible matches to contact later when he has a bit more time to explore. He's relieved to see that there are reassurances about the privacy of his choices. He also notices that if he becomes a full member, he can check to see if anyone has tagged him! He won't be able to see who, but he thinks this could be a lot of fun.

George quits for the evening with a pretty positive outlook. He may not have such a smooth time of it when it comes to actually meeting someone, but so far, so good.

Working through this scenario, you've probably learned several new things about how to design your matchmaking site. Starting with scenarios has given you a better sense of the landscape of your site, and the routes you'll need to build within it.

Recap

Navigation is goal-centered and action-oriented. It occurs within a space, though it may not be a "real" physical space. Understanding these key concepts is the first step in understanding navigation design. Rather than designing sidebars and menus, you're designing spaces and interactions. In short, you're crafting the user experience.

Scenarios and profiles are a helpful first step in understanding the whole experience of a site from a user's perspective. Interviews and tests with users, along with other research, complete the picture. We'll talk about these methods in more depth in later chapters.

Find out more

Carroll, John M., ed. *Scenario-Based Design: Envisioning Work and Technology in System Development.* Wiley, 1995.

Dinucci, Darcy, Maria Giudice, and Lynne Stiles. *Elements of Web Design, 2e.* Peachpit Press, 1998.

Lefkon, Wendy, ed. *Walt Disney Imagineering: A Behind the Dreams Look at Making the Magic Real.* Hyperion, 1996.

Mok, Clement, ed. *Graphis New Media 1.* Graphis, 1996.

Waters, Crystal. *Web Concept and Design, 2e.* New Riders, 1997.

## CHAPTER TWO

TEN QUALITIES OF SUCCESSFUL NAVIGATION

Bad navigation is like a roach motel.
Users go in, but they can't get out.

—Doren Berge, Lycos

In this chapter

- Principles of successful navigation

- Recap

With so many software programs promising a site in a box, it's easy to believe there are quick formulas for success. But this isn't Minute Rice we're talking about (regardless of how good our tools get). There are no simple recipes for navigation design. Two parts Magical Mouseover Beans mixed with one part Interactive Image Map doesn't necessarily add up to anything. There is no *Joy of Cooking* for the Web.

Principles of successful navigation

Looking at successful navigation, however, can shed some light on qualities that are consistently shared. These don't add up to a formula, but they can help us understand the principles behind our design choices.

Navigation that works should:

- Be easily learned

- Remain consistent

- Provide feedback

- Appear in context

- Offer alternatives

- Require an economy of action and time

- Provide clear visual messages

- Use clear and understandable labels
- Be appropriate to the site's purpose
- Support users' goals and behaviors

Navigation should be easily learned

Your content might be wonderfully mysterious, but getting to it shouldn't be. If your visitors have to spend time learning how to use a complex navigation device, they won't have much energy left to absorb your content. What's more, they're not likely to bother trying—not for long, anyway.

People who have sunk $500 into a software tool will usually take the time to learn it, even if (like Adobe Photoshop or Microsoft Excel) it's famous for having a bit of a learning curve. The same is not true of the Web, however. Visitors don't feel the same sort of ownership of a web site that they feel about a software tool, so there shouldn't be a learning curve—users won't put up with it.

In navigation design, then, it's best to avoid burdening your users with a steep learning curve. Take on the extra challenge of making your system easy to learn—making it transparent and obvious to your users. In Figure 2-1, for instance, MetaDesign's *(www.metade-sign.com)* icons are straightforward and clearly labeled. If the noble pursuit of user-centered design is not enough, then simple business sense should be: people won't stick around if you don't serve them well, and you have only one chance to make a first impression.

Navigation should be consistent

If you develop a navigation scheme that works, users will come to rely on it. Make sure your approach to navigation is consistent, or you may unwittingly confuse your visitors. The ability to predict where navigationals will be found is an important first step in making choices.

People will put up with quite a few navigation quirks as long as you're consistent in your offerings, their placement, and their appearance. It's the Hansel and Gretel factor: nobody likes to feel lost, and the quickest way to make someone feel lost and disoriented is to take away something they were relying on for direction. Sweep up the bread crumbs, and the fairy tale tykes are lost. Move or change the navigation scheme from screen to screen, and your users are lost.

One common error on the Web is the disappearing navigational, a menu option or button that seems to appear or disappear as it pleases. Often this is intended to be helpful: some designers remove

Figure 2-1. *MetaDesign's icons are simple, clear, and easy to learn. The icons are labeled on the introductory screen, so they're not mysterious hieroglyphics.*

an item from a navigation menu when users are on the page it corresponds to. The intent is good, but the result is poor navigation design. Users confronted with a menu that seems to change from five choices to four, or ten options to twenty, will become disoriented. They'll lose their trust in the navigation aids, and, eventually, in the site.

Instead, developers who want to be more responsive about location should consider shading out the current position, making it visible but not clickable. This maintains consistency without needlessly confusing users.

It's also important to keep things in the same place across your site. Your main site navigation menu might be at the top, for example, with subtopic navigation to the right. If you suddenly decide to put your subtopic navigation on the left, you'll throw off your users. They're expecting to see it where they saw it last—and that's where you should put it. Shown in Figure 2-2, Amazon.com is a model of consistency.

Another threat to navigational consistency is what I think of as the breakdown point. Every developer has probably encountered the breakdown point—the magical point where navigation breaks down due to poorly planned architecture, an overcrowded screen, an overabundance of information, or other factors. It's a frustrating point,

Figure 2-2. *Amazon.com provides consistent navigation headers and footers on every page. Important features—such as the shopping cart—are always available.*

and some developers respond by tacking on an extra bunch of links or just continuing to add menus and lists willy-nilly.

Rather than letting chaos rule three or four layers into your site, work it through. Find a solution that is consistent with the choices you've already made, and work with a good site architect to delve into those troublesome buried layers. Consistency is a guideline not just for your top-level screens, but for every area of your site.

If a certain section or piece of content can't be kept consistent with the rest of a site (for example, if the content requires some sort of special navigation), consider building a subsite. A subsite is a separate area of your site that has its own look and feel and usually its own approach to navigation. A subsite can sometimes be the best solution to managing a very large, information-rich site with numerous departments. IBM (*www.ibm.com*), for example, uses multiple subsites that are tied together with a few standardized layout elements (including the familiar logo).

Navigation should provide feedback

We're conditioned to expect reactions from things (and people, too). Push a button, a doorbell rings. Turn a knob, the music changes. Getting through our everyday interactions is based on evaluating feedback. It's the same with navigation. Feedback is often the only way we can tell whether we've been successful—whether we have arrived.

Designing navigation feedback includes creating controls that are responsive (ideally, in the way that many of life's knobs and buttons are responsive) and in providing information about location. Both types of feedback are essential to users, since both help them judge their success or failure in moving through a site.

Rollovers (or mouseovers) are one good way to provide responsive controls. With a rollover, passing your mouse over an object on the screen causes it to "react"—by revealing a set of instructions about that image, animating, or simply lighting up. This is good human factors design, assuming it's used to show active items and isn't just an indiscriminate gimmick.

A sense of location can be established with something as simple as a second version of a navigation image, darkened or lightened to show that "you are here." Studio Archetype and MetaDesign do this to great effect (see Figure 2-3). Other methods include using an arrow or pointer to show the current position, or, if a text menu is being used, making the current position unclickable. These are simple methods, but can be crucial to users' success.

Navigation should appear in context

To complete tasks, people need the right tools at hand. To make decisions about movement, they need to see possible routes. Navigation should always be available when it's needed, since people shouldn't have to rely on browser features or guesswork to move around.

Part of understanding context is understanding the uselessness of most "back" links. Users are accustomed to the browser's Back button—it takes them back to the last page they saw, regardless of where that page lies within the site plan. With users coming into your site from the front door and following a set path in and out of your site, "back" might nicely correspond to exactly what they think it will. But this is a dream world, since most visitors are unpredictable, come in from the side or bottom as well as the top, and may not follow a military march through your site. Taking these things into consideration, "back" begins to sound a bit hazy.

With proper context and explanation, a back link can work. "Back to the such-and-such-page," for example, is not so bad. "Go to the such-and-such page" might be even better for some situations, since it doesn't imply any particular starting point. "Start game over" might be

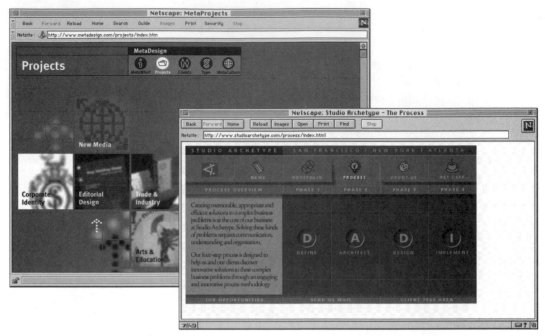

Figure 2-3. *Both MetaDesign (left) and Studio Archetype highlight navigation options to show "you are here." It's a simple method, but very effective.*

a descriptive solution for a gaming site. "Go to the lobby" could work if you're using that metaphor. Being descriptive and avoiding highly relative terms like "back" or "top" is the best approach, unless you have a completely linear presentation.

Another part of providing navigation in context is understanding where people will be when they finish doing things. When they finish reading a long article, for example, will they need a link back up to the top? When they click on an image to see a larger view, will they need a link back to the thumbnail? When they download a piece of software or fill out an online form, where will they end up when it's over? Considering these questions helps you design navigation that is available when it's needed. For instance, Figure C-1 (see color insert) shows how @tlas magazine *(www.atlasmagazine.com)* makes links accessible and obvious.

Navigation should offer alternatives

Users are different, from their computer equipment to their personal preferences, so you may need to explore navigation alternatives. Incorporating alternatives such as low-end site versions, site maps, or search boxes can help match various user behaviors. Be careful to balance this with clutter management, though—too many options is as confusing as too few.

Providing alternatives has a lot to do with accessibility. Often "accessibility" is thought to be synonymous with disability, but it's much more far-reaching than that. It's as important that you try to meet the needs of a blind visitor as it is to meet the needs of someone who doesn't have the Shockwave plug-in. Whatever the specific reason for being locked out of content, the effect is the same.

There are some basic techniques for promoting accessibility that don't require much extra work. Avoid locking important content, especially navigationals, in a proprietary format (such as a Flash movie or JavaScript rollover that can't be viewed in Internet Explorer 2.0). The same goes for images—locking in content without using ALT tags is unnecessarily restrictive.

In some cases, using browser or object detection can help make sure things go smoothly. Detecting for a certain plug-in, for example, could help reduce the chance that someone was later bombarded with insulting error messages. This usually means building several versions of your site, though as the Web becomes more and more object-oriented, it should just mean building templates. For the time being, though, the best approach if you desperately need to use a proprietary component is to construct an alternative version of a site. Constructing an alternative version that simply says, "Sorry Charlie, but your browser/equipment/connection/life stinks," is not a workable solution for a professional developer—and it certainly isn't workable for the people who are faced with it.

The added benefit of detection is that often new users don't know what sort of equipment they have. In some cases, people may not know what browser they are using (I've watched it happen more than once). Offering them the chance to pick their route—"high-calorie" or "lowfat" are popular choices—is often a puzzling cross-roads. Amazon.com is more straightforward. As shown in Figure 2-4, they offer a "text-only" mode and a "graphics" mode. And if you've opted for a particular navigational scheme, it can be useful to offer alternatives. In Figure 2-5, for example, @tlas lets users click through the images in a photo gallery either linearly or by clicking on thumbnails. Offering control to users is always a good idea, but where it could get confusingly technical, it's best to offer guidance instead.

Navigation should require an economy of action and time

In cars, planes, or on the Web, people lose interest on long trips. Remember all those car trips you took when you were a kid? The

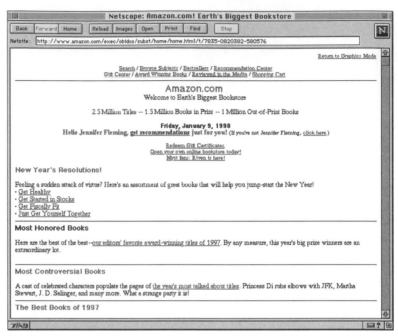

Figure 2-4. *Amazon.com provides a text-only version of their site—no small feat for a large and complex site that is updated daily.*

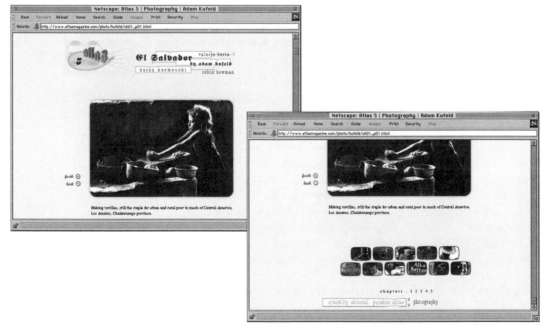

Figure 2-5. *In some of their photography pieces, @tlas Magazine offers users the ability to either browse in a linear fashion or jump to a specific photo using thumbnails.*

scientific term for this delicate condition is "Are We There Yet?" syndrome, and it's roughly synonymous with acute frustration.

A site structure that features layer upon layer of subcategories with many levels to click through can induce "Are We There Yet?" syndrome. So can a situation in which there are a ridiculous number of steps to complete before any serious content can begin (such as a prolonged login process or time-consuming shopping cart). Forms, especially long forms, are a source of frustration for many users, since they are perceived as not only a potential threat to privacy but a potential waste of time. Forms are an obvious barrier you can place in front of users, especially if you put them right at the front door.

Forms that go across pages are also potentially troublesome. Users may not know how many screens they will need to complete, how many more questions or steps the process entails. Because of these uncertainties, many people retreat when faced with a form. You can make their lives easier, though, by being selective and focused in what you ask of them, and in communicating how long it will take people to complete the form, why the information is valuable, how they might benefit, and what the rest of the process will entail.

Without navigation shortcuts, "Are We There Yet" syndrome is almost sure to kick in. Navigation shortcuts—whether in the form of a site map, index, contents list, or pull-down menu—are especially essential for complex sites. The deeper and wider the site, the more likely it is that users will protest at having to burrow through numerous. intermediate pages. Allowing users to jump quickly from one corner of a site to another—as Computers.com (*www.computers.com*) does with their recursive menu (see Figure 2-6)—is a part of maintaining an economy of action and time

Navigation should provide clear visual messages

Interface design is not just about beautifying. It's visual guidance. How you present navigation options is closely tied to how usable they are. If they're hidden, difficult to find, look too much like text, look too much like other images, or are otherwise visually confusing, your users will have trouble getting around.

Visual hierarchies are one way to provide this guidance. Movement, color, position, size, and other factors help people judge items and make choices.

There is an ongoing debate over whether we have a "visual vocabulary" or set of conventions we can use on the Web. In other media, such as book publishing, we have conventions such as page

"Movement, color, position, size, and other factors help people judge items and make choices."

"A site structure that has many levels to click through can induce 'Are We There Yet?' syndrome."

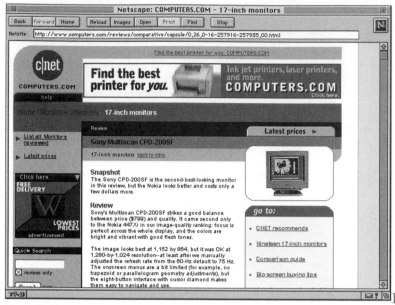

Figure 2-6. *Recursive categories (such as those used by CNET's Computers.com) make it easy to jump back to different category levels.*

numbering that help us to orient ourselves. In travel and tourism, we have icons for restrooms and restaurants and gas stations. We do have some web conventions, such as underlining text links. Generally, though, almost everything has been up for grabs.

This can make it difficult to get around on the Web. As Clement Mok, founder of Studio Archetype, points out, "If you're coming in from the world of print, navigation is implicit. You already have a vocabulary that you've learned over and over again, a variety of conventions that help people get from one part of a book to another part. Pagination, structure, a table of contents: these implicit structures carry over, and we take them for granted. That set of conventions does not hold as true on the Web. One has to go out of the way to make it clear."

"Right now, in the absence of web conventions, we're relying on crutches," he continues. "The house icon is about home, and so on. This situation is partly the result of technical limitations in giving the physical sense of space in three dimensions. The minute you have that, I think some of the more lame conventions of underlining and 'home' will probably go away. At some point, it will become very implicit, but there is no set convention at this point in time."

Despite the underdeveloped visual conventions of the Web, we are still subject to a larger cultural visual vocabulary. Whether we intend it to or not, there is visual meaning in much of what we create. For example, a graphic might look like a navigational button because it appears to be three-dimensional. A clickable word, created as a graphic, might appear to be just plain text rather than a link. Visual messages communicate ideas about tone, purpose, or audience that are essential to how we perceive a site.

For example, take a look at the Remembering Nagasaki site (*www.exploratorium.edu/nagasaki/*) in Figure 2-7. Where do you think you should begin? The size of graphic elements provides clues. On interior pages, such as the one shown in Figure C-2, a high-contrast red is used to show links that are "hot" and a somber gray is used when something is "cold" and has been clicked on. Reversing this color scheme would send the wrong messages to users   .

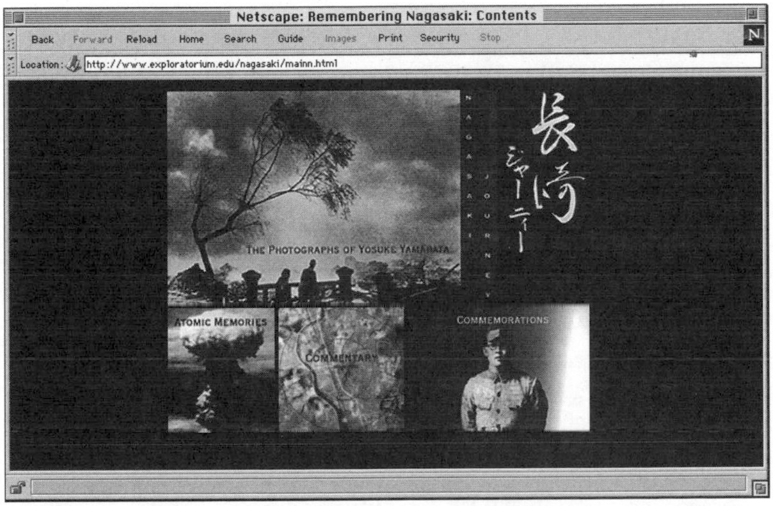

"Never use a big, clumsy word if you can use a small, clear one. Never choose to confuse if you can clarify."

Figure 2-7. *Remembering Nagasaki sends clear visual messages using layout.*

Navigation should offer clear labels

Navigation labels—like the ingredients labels that prevent you from swallowing something you really shouldn't—are an important part of communication. Good labeling is more an art form than a science, since it's based less on a standard thesaurus of usable words than it is on common sense and customer sensitivity.

Andrew Chak, chief information architect at Quadravision (*www.quadravision.com*), relates a story that shows how as developers we sometimes take labels for granted. "We once designed a site that had a restaurant finder in it," Andrew explains. "Within the navigation bar, we had a link for the 'site map.' In this particular context, users thought that the site map was an actual map to the restaurant (its geographic location), not a map for the web site. The term seemed reasonable to us as developers, but it wasn't for these users in this context."

In selecting labels, it's best to use the terminology of your users, not cool hieroglyphics, office shorthand, or organization-speak. Dead ends and misunderstandings are a waste of time for your users, but they're all too common when terse one-word labels leave so much open to interpretation.

What's the difference between "clients" and "projects," for example? Or "home" and "top"? Or "help" and "FAQ"? Many of these unnecessary ambiguities could be avoided by better, more precise, and more descriptive labels. Not all misnomers and ambiguities are foreseeable, but some you can predict.

Often, ambiguity or confusion exist because no label is present at all. Icons are common in navigation design, but most have various interpretations. What does a question mark icon mean, for example? Does it imply you can search? Read a FAQ? Submit questions? Is it a help screen? The icon itself has many possible meanings, and there is no reason your users should need a pocket Rosetta Stone to use your site. Adding text labels to icons is a simple and effective solution, as shown in Figure 2-8, assuming the text label doesn't introduce further ambiguity.

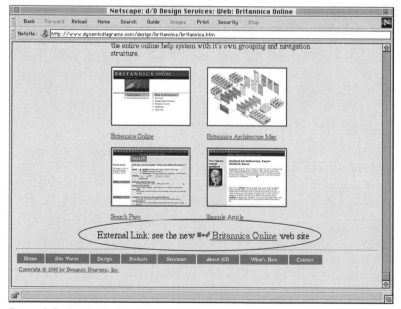

Figure 2-8. *Dynamic Diagrams (www.dynamicdiagrams.com) labels external links (links to other sites) with text and an icon.*

What about the "cool" labels designed to pique our interest and prove how funky the site is? The artful use of linking and labels gets to be a bit tricky, since when it's done well (such as Suck's linking out mid-sentence to point at some interesting factoid; see *www.suck.com*), it becomes part of the story. When it's done poorly or inconsistently, though, it's maddening—much like listening to two people share an "in" joke. What is the difference between mystery and frustration? It's often a very fine line. Getting reactions from users can help you understand if you've crossed it.

Another common web quirk is the carryover of ridiculously inappropriate organization-speak into web communication design. Coming up with navigation labels that seem as if they're peeled from someone's office door or copied from an org chart is a pretty sure-fire way to lose your visitors. Why say "Department of Targeted & Interstitial Marketing" when you could say "Ad Sales"? One of my favorite professors in college used to say, "Never use a big, clumsy word if you can use a small, clear one. Never choose to confuse if you can instead clarify." Insider jargon, especially organization-speak, can be a serious barrier to communication. Figure 2-9 shows a page admirably free from organization breakdowns. The links at the top of the page simply state "Who We Are," "What We Do," etc.

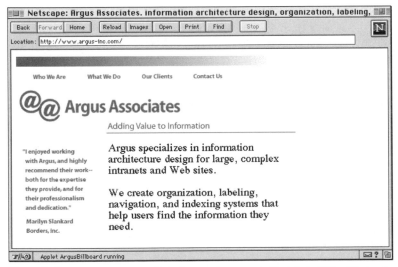

Figure 2-9. *Argus Associates offers clear and approachable labels: "Who We Are," "What We Do," etc.*

Navigation should be appropriate to the site's purpose

Your navigation approach will depend a lot on what your goal is and on what your users will expect to accomplish. A shopping site will not necessarily have the same sort of navigation solution as an information site, for example. If your main focus is moving visitors comfortably through a shopping process, your approach may be quite different from a site that needs to provide fast, up-to-date computer virus information.

Mismatches between the site's purpose and the navigational approach can be a cause for user confusion. A good match will mean that the site's navigation reinforces the site's purpose and is integrated with the overall experience. Using a mysterious icon-based navigation approach for that virus information site will keep people from getting what they need. They're not looking for a game or a puzzle. Chances are they're preoccupied with figuring out why all their Word files are suddenly written in Greek, and they're probably not in the mood for laughs.

On the other hand, using a mysterious iconic navigation approach was perfect for the Riven Journals (*journals.riven.com*), an entertainment site where solving puzzles is part of the game plan, as shown in Figure C-3. The mood of the navigation, which is both pleasantly mysterious and very usable, supports the entertainment purpose. Designing a buttoned-down navigation scheme that allowed Riven users to go directly to the answer would definitely have spoiled the fun.

Navigation should support users' goals and behaviors

If you read the previous chapter, you already know that navigation is about supporting users' goals—in particular, your users' goals. What will people want to do? How might they behave? Understanding these goals and behaviors is the most important step in designing navigation that works. For example, Amazon.com offers a recommendation center, shown in Figure 2-10, that helps individuals find books they're likely to be interested in.

How can you know how users will act, though, and what they really want? You can use scenarios, which were covered briefly in the last chapter. Focus groups, ethnographies, observation, and interviews are also immensely valuable. User testing at several points in the process is essential. We'll go into these methods in the next few chapters, since they represent the most valuable source of knowledge you

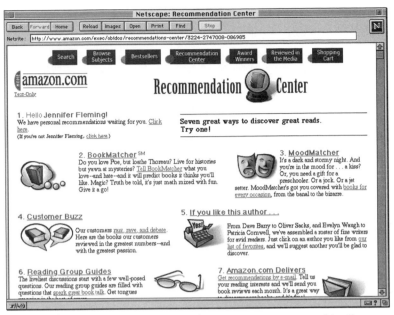

Figure 2-10. *Amazon.com's Recommendation Center is a customer-friendly approach designed to match the way people want to find books.*

Find out more

Flanders, Vincent and Michael Willis. *Web Pages That Suck: Learn Good Design by Looking at Bad Design.* Sybex, 1998.

Gloor, Peter A. *Elements of Hypermedia Design: Techniques for Navigation and Visualization in Cyberspace.* Springer Verlag, 1996.

Veen, Jeffrey. *Hotwired Style: Principles for Building Smart Web Sites.* Wired, 1998.

have—more important than what your clients can tell you, more important than survey data. They're the key to successful navigation design.

Recap

There are no easy answers where navigation design is concerned. It's a difficult area, and one that requires a lot of planning and forethought. What works well for one site may be all wrong for another. If there are no simple formulas, how do you know where to begin?

The answer is in understanding not which navigation solutions work, but why. The design principles in this chapter are based on the need for feedback, accessibility, alternatives, and other important considerations. Balancing these principles with the needs and goals of your audience will help you design navigation that works.

## CHAPTER THREE

Designing for Users

*Do not do unto others as you
would they should do unto you.
Their tastes may not be the same.*

—George Bernard Shaw

In this chapter

• Defining your audience

• Moving toward user-centered design

• Getting started with user testing

• Recap

It seems obvious that we should design for users, not for ourselves. But in the thick of the development process, it's easy to forget this fact. Many developers mistakenly assume that they're part of the intended audience for the site. Unfortunately, this is seldom the case.

Most web users are not nearly as technically savvy as most web developers. Most users aren't quite sure how to install a plug-in, never mind a whole new browser. Most web users don't find quirky web sites an interesting puzzle to solve. Instead, they beat a hasty retreat.

In the early days of TV, you pretty much had to be a geek to get things to work. Now even kids can switch on the tube with few problems, and the rest of us geeks get to play with the Net instead. It sounds funny to describe a TV set as a technological challenge, but those early TV sets caused people almost as much frustration as computers do now—which is to say, a lot.

In training new web users, I've watched people stare in confusion at the items on screen, trying to interpret what was a "clickable" thing and what was a pretty picture. I've watched people try to use the mouse like a TV remote, or grapple with what a page was and how it got there. I've listened to people become agitated over sites, browsers, and the whole shebang. Technology just isn't all that fun when you're starting out.

Ease of use never came easy

For an amusing look at the early days of television ownership, see Don Steinberg's column "The Digital Funhouse," at *www.cnet.com/Content/ Voices/Steinberg/042397/*

You'd be surprised at how many people are reduced to tears by things that are relatively easy to fix. If you don't remember what that feels like, try to keep it in mind the next time you work on a buggy new script, learn a new language, or set up a new piece of equipment. Then multiply your frustration by a factor of ten, throw in a liberal helping of fear and self-doubt, and you'll have a better sense of it.

In teaching people who have already had some computer and Internet experience, things are not radically different. People have trouble typing URLs, get frustrated with slow downloads, panic over error messages, and are often completely confounded by what to do with a cookie or site certificate.

Last year, I started asking students in my beginning web design classes what bothered them about the Web. Nothing more than that. No prompting or secret agendas. Just a simple question about what bothered them, a room full of students ranging from complete newbies to programmers who were retooling.

What happened wasn't scientific, but it was surprising. I asked one class, and got a list of about half a dozen core complaints:

- Delays/speed
- Lack of trust
- Dead ends
- Easy to get lost
- Need for plug-ins
- Hard to read

Then I asked another class. They listed virtually the same half dozen or so complaints, with some differences of interpretation or wording. So I asked several more classes, and the outcome was almost exactly the same. This may be only anecdotal, but it was a real eye-opener. What it suggested to me was that there aren't a hundred small unrelated problems that hamper the Web's growth. Instead there are a handful of big challenges—speed, trust, and so on—that we need to solve collectively, with the assistance of equipment manufacturers, software developers, and anyone else who can help. What we'll have when those barriers are removed is tantalizing to imagine.

For now at least, we still have some pressing problems, and it may get worse for users before it gets better. More and more new users are joining the ranks every month, many of them with only rudimentary computing skills. There is now a great pool of people we might call "casual" users of the Web, based on their light use at work or at school. Increasingly, we'll need to be teachers and caretakers, not just developers.

I don't want to suggest that we serve newbies at the expense of repeat visitors or experienced users. Experienced users don't want hand-holding, and repeat visitors don't need guided tours. Both tend to want shortcuts, power features, and freedom to move as they please.

It's an odd quandary we're in, then, assuming we don't always have the resources to create four or five versions of a site. Meeting the needs of newbies and pros, and most of the people in between, is no mean feat, but I think it's doable if we keep in mind what each group needs. Balancing guidance and freedom won't be simple, but it's likely to pay off in loyal customers.

The best way web developers can keep in touch with ordinary users is to talk to them, spend time with them, and listen to their questions and worries. But most of us also have deadlines, so we can't hang out in cybercafés all day (though I for one would really like to). Though it's no substitute for human contact, keeping up with Internet user surveys can help fill in the gaps.

These surveys are not without their flaws and biases, but there's still a lot we can learn from them. Probably the most well known surveys are those done by Georgia Tech's Graphics, Visualization, and Usability (GVU) Center. The GVU surveys are done roughly twice a year and they're usually a treasure trove of industry information. Take a look at some of the results from the survey completed in October 1997 (about 10,000 people responded to the survey):

- More than 1/3 of the Internet users who responded had gone online for the first time in the last year.

- Close to 60% of the people who responded to the survey connect to the Internet by modem at 33.6 kbps or less.

- More than 20% were unsure of their connection speed. Nearly 40% had no idea what their monitor resolution was. Nearly 30% had no idea what their monitor bit depth was. About 25% had no idea what a cookie was.

- Respondents were asked if they had ever had a "dissatisfying experience" at a shopping site that had caused them to leave. A majority said this had happened to them, and the top three reasons for leaving were that pages were slow to download; that the site was disorganized and confusing; and that they could not find what they were looking for.

- When asked to select "the single most critical issue facing the Internet," survey respondents ranked navigation third in importance, behind only privacy and censorship issues. Europeans and respondents over 50 years old ranked navigation on a par with censorship. Women and men, while disagreeing over whether

Top ten requests that scare the heck out of most ordinary users:

10. Please identify your browser.

9. Please download this plug-in/upgrade/doo-dad.

8. Please turn on Java/JavaScript.

7. Please resize your window and remove your directory buttons.

6. Please accept/decline this certificate.

5. Please accept/decline this cookie.

4. Please verify that you have requested an insecure page.

3. Please enter your username and password.

2. Please tell us a little bit about yourself.

... and the number one request that scares the heck out of users ...

1. Please enter your credit card number now.

"Your audience will probably be made up of many distinct groups, each with different concerns and interests."

privacy or censorship was more important, agreed in their ranking of navigation. Experience level had little effect on the ranking of navigation.

So what does this tell us? Since this was an online survey, the people who responded were already skilled enough to get on the Web, find the survey, and complete it successfully. A little over 40% of these people had also, at one time or another, created a web page. That makes it even more revealing that so many of them knew so little about their monitors, connection speed, or other technologies. It's worth thinking about the next time you suggest that people alter their color settings for better viewing, or resize their browser.

We can also see that modem users dominate, and that there are a lot of new users out there. But hearing directly from users that a "dissatisfying experience" is enough to make them leave a site may be the most interesting finding of all. It makes the need for user-centered design seem suddenly very pressing.

Defining your audience

To stay on our toes and better serve clients, it's important to understand ordinary users. But here's the bad news: despite the time you just spent reading the last section, most of you won't be designing for this broad audience. The most heavily visited sites (such as the large search sites) may need to grapple with how to serve this dauntingly wide range of users. Most sites will serve a smaller, more targeted audience.

Narrowing the field

So how do you know who your audience is? It's trickier than you first think. If you're planning an online toystore, you might guess that parents are your primary audience. But "parents" is a pretty large group. Are you targeting wealthy parents? Parents who work? Montessori advocates? U.S. citizens or parents worldwide? Depending on what you're selling, and who you expect will want to buy it, your approach could be quite different.

For example, if you're selling brand-name toys at bargain prices, you're going to want to focus on working parents with tight budgets. What do those parents worry about? It might go beyond simply getting toys at a discount. They may believe that safety or durability is a concern for bargain toys, or worry that they'll need to pay extra to order additional parts. They're busy, too, so they won't have a lot of time to spend browsing for toys. Understanding the specific concerns of this narrow audience can help you build a site that is responsive to their concerns. Without a clear picture of your audience, it's almost impossible to predict what they'll need.

Multiple audiences

In reality, though, your audience will probably be made up of many distinct groups, each with different concerns and interests. Take the toy store example again. The store selling brand-name toys at discounted prices may find that while working parents are the primary audience, there are a number of additional audiences being served.

Teachers, for example, might visit the site to research ways to get the most for their overstretched classroom dollars. There may be a swift business in birthday or holiday gifts mailed from relatives or friends. There will probably be some kids coming to the site, too. How should each of these additional audiences be handled? They won't approach the shopping process in the same way, and you won't want to treat them all the same.

You might decide to come up with an approach for each audience, and design tailored paths just for their interests and needs. Table 3-1 gives some examples of how issues, and approaches would differ for different audiences.

User surveys

GVU User Surveys
*www.cc.gatech.edu/gvu/
user_surveys/*

NUA Internet Surveys
www.nua.ie

Jupiter Communications
www.jupiter.com

Relevant Knowledge
www.relevantknowledge.com

Nielsen Media Research
www.nielsenmedia.com

Table 3-1. *Sample audiences, issues, and approaches*

Audience	Issues	Approach
Parents	Cost Safety Durability Time spent shopping	Provide a store tour outlining how discounts are possible and commitment to safety. Include kid-tested durability rating on toy screens. Design fast purchase paths for busy parents, and provide opportunities to layaway items electronically.
Teachers	Cost Safety Educational value Curriculum ideas	Create a teachers' or educational corner of the site. Offer "success stories" from other teachers who've built a large toy collection by buying discounted toys online. Add a forum for teachers to exchange ideas, and archive it. Provide a safety and educational value rating on toy screens, and allow searching by these fields.
Relatives and friends	Gift ideas Age level Shipping time and cost Gift wrapping	Offer "Gift Central" for tips and ideas on purchases. Include age level on toy screens, and also make it possible to search by age and interests. Provide a purchasing FAQ to answer questions on shipping and gift wrap before people head to the checkout.
Kids	Fun value Trendiness Related collectibles Payment permission	Design a "Just for Kids" area with original editorial content—reviews and toy ratings by kids, for example. Create an area to showcase new toys. On every toy screen, provide links to related items. Address the issue of how kids can or cannot buy online, which also helps ease parental concerns.

What you'll probably end up with are various corners of your toystore that are designed specifically for each audience. What you know about the behavior, concerns, or equipment of each of these audiences can help you design paths and shortcuts that work.

Moving toward user-centered design

Why spend so much time learning about users just to do a navigation design? In related fields, such as architecture or exhibit design, quite a lot of time is spent understanding user behavior and preferences. Think about the color of a classroom, the height of a bank window, the paths through a museum hall, or the way a mall is laid out. By better understanding users, we can build environments that support desired behaviors. It's no different when we're looking at the active nature of site navigation. If anything, taking the time to understand these behaviors might be even more important on the Web, where users have little patience with problems.

The challenge, then, is to make your site as easily learned as possible. This doesn't mean dumbing down content, just anticipating problems and providing for them beforehand. The first thing you'll need to do is dumb yourself down: your own in-depth knowledge of your site can make it difficult to understand a visitor's perspective.

I'm OK, you're OK

Web users are a diverse bunch, and not just in computer skills. Each of us has a different—and very personal—way of approaching the world. And unlike computer skills, these differences are unlikely to change.

People tend to have unique approaches to learning, for example. Some people prefer to absorb information visually, by way of maps, icons, movies, or other images. For many others, information is most easily understood by reading or listening. Still other people have what's called a kinesthetic approach: they tend to learn by touching, trying, experimenting, or charging ahead. Most of us use all of these approaches at one time or another, depending on the task we're facing, but we tend to favor one approach over others.

As a developer, then, one of my challenges is to go beyond the visual tools I want to build and try to see what other alternatives might be needed. I might decide to add a table of contents, search box, or other tools. I might need to consider that some people surf with images deliberately turned off, as a matter of preference as well as a need for speed. If I take the time to build in alternatives, there will be less chance of stranding someone without the tools they need to proceed.

The "disease of familiarity"

For most people who are experts on something, it's awfully hard to remember what it was like not to know it. Richard Saul Wurman, a respected designer and author of *Information Architects*, calls this "the disease of familiarity." For example, try to remember what it was like the first time you used the Web. Remember what confused you royally? Remember what your first web search was like, or how long it took you to work out the mysteries of a URL? Most of us forget these things relatively quickly, just as we have no memory for pain.

I remember taking a class on programming in BASIC (yeah, that was a while back). The instructor sent us home with a weird assignment: write, from start to finish, how to make a peanut butter and jelly sandwich. Most of the instructions we came up with looked like this:

1. Spread peanut butter on a slice of bread.

2. Spread jelly on another slice of bread.

3. Smush them together and eat.

As the instructor pointed out afterward, the tricky thing about programs is that they need more detailed information on processes. A better set of instructions might be:

1. Walk to cupboard.

2. Open cupboard door.

3. Get peanut butter jar from middle shelf.

4. Put peanut butter jar on counter.

5. Get strawberry jelly jar from middle shelf.

6. Put strawberry jelly jar on counter.

7. Get loaf of whole wheat bread from bottom shelf.

8. Put loaf of whole wheat bread on counter.

...and so on. Providing guidance for users is much the same. What's obvious to you may not be quite as apparent to your site's users, so the more you can guide them through your home on the Web, the better their experience will be. The better their experience is, the more likely they are to become *return visitors*.

Usability engineering

To push ourselves even farther beyond the "disease of familiarity," there's an area of study that can help: usability engineering. With roots in the software industry, the field of usability comprises a growing body of research on user expectations, behaviors, and preferences.

"People have trouble typing URLs, get frustrated with slow downloads, panic over error messages, and are often completely confounded by what to do with a cookie or site certificate."

Jakob Nielsen, Sun Microsystems

In usability engineering, a number of methods can be used to determine whether a product or interface is "usable" by the people it's intended for. User testing is one method, but there are others. Jakob Nielsen, a consultant and author of several books on usability, describes a method based on using a predefined set of heuristics (guidelines) as a benchmark test for usability. By having a small set of users rate a product in each of these areas, a good general picture of the product's usability emerges. Nielsen recommends these ten heuristics:

1. *Visibility of system status.* The system should always keep users informed about what is going on, through appropriate feedback within reasonable time.

2. *Match between system and the real world.* The system should speak the users' language, with words, phrases, and concepts familiar to the user, rather than system-oriented terms. Follow real-world conventions, making information appear in a natural and logical order.

3. *User control and freedom.* Users often choose system functions by mistake and will need a clearly marked "emergency exit" to leave the unwanted state without having to go through an extended dialogue. Support undo and redo.

4. *Consistency and standards.* Users should not have to wonder whether different words, situations, or actions mean the same thing. Follow platform conventions.

5. *Error prevention.* Even better than good error messages is a careful design which prevents a problem from occurring in the first place.

6. *Recognition rather than recall.* Make objects, actions, and options visible. The user should not have to remember information from one part of the dialogue to another. Instructions for use of the system should be visible or easily retrievable whenever appropriate.

7. *Flexibility and efficiency of use.* Accelerators—unseen by the novice user—may often speed up the interaction for the expert user such that the system can cater to both inexperienced and experienced users. Allow users to tailor frequent actions.

8. *Aesthetic and minimalist design.* Dialogues should not contain information that is irrelevant or rarely needed. Every extra unit of information in a dialogue competes with the relevant units of information and diminishes their relative visibility.

9. *Help users recognize, diagnose, and recover from errors.* Error messages should be expressed in plain language (no codes), precisely indicate the problem, and constructively suggest a solution.

10. *Help and documentation.* Even though it is better if the system can be used without documentation, it may be necessary to provide help and documentation. Any such information should be easy to search, focused on the user's task, list concrete steps to be carried out, and not be too large.

Nielsen's heuristics

You can find Jakob Nielsen's ten usability heuristics on his site, Use It. Reprinted with permission.

www.useit.com/papers/ heuristic/heuristic_list.html

While these heuristics were first designed for software usability inspection, they can also be used in web design. Combined with other methods, such as user testing, focus groups, and participatory design, these heuristics are an essential part of a developer's toolbox.

Participatory design

How can you get past your own biases? Try as you might, it's not always easy to do. Usability guidelines are a great help, and testing is essential. Participatory design goes one step farther, actively involving members of your site's intended audience in the design process—not as visitors, but as team members. Michael Muller, who's written and studied participatory design for several years, puts it this way:

> Through participatory design, users move out of roles such as observer, approver, "knowledge repository," or "component of the system," and into roles such as peer co-designer, design co-owner, expertise contributor, and self-advocate ... from "other person as problem" into "other person as partner."

It's a tantalizing idea, and has had some successes. Mainly it's been used in the software industry or in corporate workplaces, but its applications on the Web are already being explored by a few forward-thinking companies.

How do you make the most of participatory design, considering factors such as deadline pressure, roles, and client relations? In the early stages of a project, designers "participate in users' worlds"— doing ethnography, interviews, and observations. As ideas are hashed out and early prototypes begin to take shape, the focus shifts. Now users are participating in design activities. An intense prototyping period allows team members to explore the best possible solutions, with the flexibility of being able to go back repeatedly to the user co-designers.

Jakob Nielsen: "Focus on tasks"

Jakob Nielsen has been a voice for usability since before the Web's inception. He has written numerous books and articles on the topic, and maintains a web site called "Use It," a clearinghouse of usability resources. Jakob offers some thoughts and tips on designing user-centered navigation.

"Web navigation is a challenge because of the need to manage billions of information objects," Jakob explains. "Right now, the Web 'only' has a few hundred million pages, but before the end of the decade, there will probably be ten billion pages online that can be reached from any Internet-connected device. Current user interfaces are simply not well suited to dealing with such huge amounts of information."

Jakob offers some ideas on what might need to happen in order to improve web navigation as the medium grows. "We obviously cannot represent every single information object in a navigation UI, given that there are so many. Thus, we will need a variety of methods to reduce the clutter. Some useful methods are aggregation, summarization, filtering, and elision- and example-based representations."

He describes *aggregation* as "showing a single unit that represents a collection of smaller ones," a sort of chunking of information. "The very notion of a 'site' is one useful level of aggregation," he explains.

In *summarization*, a large amount of data is represented by a smaller amount. "This might include the use of smaller images to represent larger ones, or the use of abstracts to represent full documents," he says. "We need ways of summarizing large collections of information objects."

Filtering is getting rid of information that the user (or a group of users) doesn't care about. "I personally believe quite a lot in collaborative filtering and in quality-based filters," he explains, giving as an example the ability to show only things that other people have found to be valuable.

With *elision- and example-based representations*, instead of showing everything, you show a few examples and indicate that there are more available. For example, a user might be able to see representative examples of a type of information and then be told that 1 million more items were available.

Jakob reminds designers to keep the user in mind when creating navigation systems. "There is always one principal issue to remember: the user's task. Think about why the user is at your page and what the user is likely to want to do. Then include links that are likely to help users accomplish that task."

You can find Jakob Nielsen's Use It site at *www.useit.com*. He also writes the popular Alertbox column on Web usability, which can be found at *www.useit.com/alertbox/*.

Getting started with user testing

Your average overworked web developer tends to believe that user testing involves a discouraging investment of time and money. While that might sometimes be true, it doesn't have to be. There is low-cost research and testing that can help you design a site that works for users.

Web users will often torture-test your site (and inform you of their conclusions) whether you set up formal opportunities or not. You may get complaints via feedback forms or scathing personal attacks via email. Though some feedback is remarkably detailed, many of these unhappy visitors may not describe their experience beyond a generalized statement that "your site sucks." Without the observation and interview process inherent in user research, you may never know exactly why it sucks.

Getting started with user testing is not nearly as hard as it's cracked up to be. Most developers do ad hoc, informal testing of their coworkers in between coding, on lunch breaks, or as people pass their desks. You probably have most of the basic equipment (a computer, some paper, a pencil). The next sections describe what you need to know to get started.

When should you test?

Some developers like to begin with pre-design testing or focus groups. Focus groups, as Jakob Nielsen points out, are more helpful in developing a broad site approach than in gathering any kind of detailed information about preferences or behaviors.

People often don't fully understand how they will react in a situation until they are in it, and with navigation design this is extremely important. If you asked a group of people to describe how they would navigate through a building and then spied on them while they actually did it, chances are there would be real discrepancies between their intent and their behavior. Focus groups are best for brainstorming, where they can be a valuable and exciting tool.

Pre-design testing can also be done with "blank slate" dummies or paper mock-ups. Jim Faris of Alben+Faris (*www.albenfaris.com*) once described a technique he used in industrial design, in this case a device similar to a personal digital assistant but used by technicians for entering important airline maintenance information. The prototyping began with showing technicians a blank box and asking them to suggest the placement of buttons and other tools. This might not be an efficient way to design every web site, but it would certainly be an excellent method for use with very targeted audiences (for example, in intranet design).

User Interface Engineering (*www.uie.com*), whose staff specialize in usability testing, has successfully used a paper mock-up process to do pre-design testing. In this process, rough pen and ink sketches are

Usability resources

Use It (Jakob Nielsen's usability site)
www.useit.com

User Interface Engineering
www.uie.com

UsableWeb
www.usableweb.com

made of the site's intended pages. Each sheet of paper functions as a screen. The test leaders then present the user with the main "screen" from which they can select by touching an area on the paper. The leaders present each new page as it's selected. This method doesn't precisely imitate the Web, but it can be a low-cost and effective way to get some initial ideas about navigation.

Beta-testing a working prototype is still the best way to get feedback about your site. There's no better way to tell whether the site is apt to crash from multimedia overload, whether users understand the visual icons and hierarchies you've established, or whether they click out to an external site and never come back.

The prototype you test with should be as close to completion as possible while still allowing time for any revisions that are needed. Using storyboards or comping images for testing will tell you little about how users actually move around the site. Demonstrations tend to be even less useful, since whoever is demonstrating is likely to move fluidly and descriptively through the site, making it seem painless and easy.

Periodic testing of your site can help you make sure you're still on track as the site evolves. There is no ideal time frame for these checkups. Some people plan a major site evaluation annually, while others do small pockets of user testing as new pieces are added to the site. There's no need to be overzealous about running user tests, since they can sometimes be anxious times for designers and developers.

When you are approaching a redesign, user testing becomes an essential tool for defining what goes and what stays. It is an integral part of a redesign, perhaps more so than with an original design. Redesigns mean there are problems that need solutions, and user tests are a terrific way to help identify the trouble spots.

A final word about when to test: if you won't be able to incorporate the results of the test, or aren't willing to change your site or product, then there is really no point in spending the time and money on testing. Never go into a test looking for validation or compliments. If you're not open to correcting mistakes that might be unearthed, you're probably better off remaining in the dark.

Who should participate?

Selecting the users who will participate can be a daunting task. Ideally, you want members of your intended audience (or audiences) to participate. Email or postal mailing lists can often be a good start. Targeting possible organizations where people in your audience might come together is another technique. For example, if your site is about karate, you might consider approaching a local karate school for possible candidates.

Other web developers, or even other media developers, can often be a valuable source of advice and opinions. A common practice on web design mailing lists is for developers to post a site for critique. This is a bargain method, but it's one good option. Another is to contact a local web developers group (if there is one near you) and request a live critique.

Though it may sound odd, sometimes the most insightful comments come from people who are quite removed from your site or even from the Web. Rope in visitors, the mail carrier, your landlady or babysitter. Put Jehovah's Witnesses and door-to-door salesmen to work for you. You may not really be crazy enough to invite random solicitors into your office or home, but there are still many trustworthy people to be found. Sometimes, their comments can be surprisingly relevant.

Whoever does the testing, you might want to consider whether they will be compensated for their time. Some people will agree to participate just for the chance to see a hot new site or because they like your organization or purpose. Most people want to know what's in it for them. Often, that means cash rewards, but it can take the form of giveaways of products or services. For example, an online bookstore might offer gift certificates, or a health club could offer free memberships.

Who should do the testing?

Running a user test of your own site may seem uncomplicated until you're in the thick of it. Because you're the site's creator, the impulse to suggest, guide, and otherwise skew the results in your favor will be strong. If the test is to be of any use, it needs an objective leader. That can be you, if you can detach yourself from the vortex of your own design process to listen to what others think of your baby.

Navigation really must be tested by someone other than the person who designed it, which is why user testing is essential in the first place. This also takes the pressure off designers, who can rely on user tests to understand how people other than themselves will behave while visiting the site. Once you've accepted that you cannot be omniscient, it's a lot easier to be objective.

Another option is to have outside facilitators or usability consultants conduct the tests. Experienced consultants are by far the best option since they will offer knowledge and objectivity, though often at a steep price. They have conducted tests before, and they are aware of

The 80/20 rule

There's a down side to all of this user-centered design. It's possible to study, test, interview, model, re-test, rebuild, and generally really stress yourself out without ever launching your site. In the real world of site design, projects have deadlines. At some point, you've got to say enough is enough and let it all hang out there, come what may. After all, as the saying goes, on the Web everything is under construction—always.

So before you expire of a nervous condition, there's an old rule that will allow you to let go of your web baby: you simply can't please all of the people all of the time. If you've pleased about 80% of your chosen audience, you should feel proud. (Less than that, and your job is really not done.) Shoot for 80%, and you may live to design another day. It's a better average than we get in most of life.

the goals of user testing and of how the Web works. If budget is an issue, you might consider hiring an outside consultant to train staff members in how to test.

How should you test?

In addition to the paper mock-up and "blank slate" dummies mentioned above, there are several other approaches to user testing. User tests can be casual (such as informal and unplanned discussions) or formal (such as task assessment or questionnaires). Both are valid, and both may yield somewhat different results. One should not replace the other.

Whether casual or formal, one-on-one sessions remain the best source of feedback. These sessions allow you to focus on the exact behavior of one user, watching as he or she chooses a path through the site. Jakob Nielsen's method of asking users to "talk out loud" as they proceed is a good method for gathering information about individual reactions and rationale. You might also ask users to complete a questionnaire or interview once they have finished with the site. Ask them what they liked or disliked, whether they have suggestions, and so on.

Small groups can also be useful, providing they remain small. There is no point in assembling more than 10–15 people at a time, since it will be impossible to observe them all in any sort of meaningful detail. Because observation is the key to user testing of navigation systems (as well as any other media interaction), user-to-leader ratios should be kept small. Outnumbering users causes tension for your participants, and bringing in too large a group of testers makes it impossible for you to observe everyone. One-to-one is the best ratio.

In observing the actions of users, try to pick up clues about where they pause for guidance, whether they need to use the browser's Back button, how they approach search boxes or site maps, whether they leave your site by a link and whether they return, if they understand menu options and labels, and so on. You might also assign them tasks and see how they approach completing them.

If possible, conduct the test or interview in the user's setting. This may not always be feasible (for example, home users are not likely to invite you into their private sanctum), but do it whenever you can. A casual on-site visit with a member of your target audience is often as (or more) useful than a formal user test. (Find out more about these "ethnographic" methods in Chapter 6, *Looking at Process*.)

Another tool in your arsenal is the online user survey. These can be a source of some helpful information, but only if they're done right.

Forcing your users to fill out online surveys before they enter a site, for example, is almost certain to cause trouble. Users often give deliberately misleading information when pressured in this way, as one GVU User Survey found. Make the survey optional, and better yet, select regular users from email lists or site logs. Provide these online users with the same incentives you'd offer in person, and you're more likely to get reliable results. User surveys are most useful when combined with user tests and interviews. They shouldn't be used as a catch-all solution.

What sort of equipment will you need?

This depends entirely on how you decide to test. Not everyone has a two-way mirror installed in their office, complete with a computer lab and video camera. I'd say it's actually pretty rare. Luckily, the best user testing environments are the simplest. You can conduct a simple and perfectly effective user test with only a computer (with a browser and Internet connection) and pen and paper for note-taking.

Adding a tape recorder can ease the job somewhat, but people respond differently when they know they're being taped, and taping often causes interruptions for cassette changes or equipment checks. Video might seem to solve all your problems, if it weren't for the fact that it can make people terribly uncomfortable. If you do go with one of these methods despite these disadvantages, make sure you tell participants beforehand that you plan to tape them. It's also a good idea to have them sign a permission form for your records.

Try to avoid screen capture software, which records the activity on the screen, unless you have tested it beforehand and feel very comfortable using it. It's intriguing, but won't tell you much about your users' motives. Also, this type of program can only be used in relatively brief segments of several minutes at a time before file sizes become unmanageable, making it more of an interruption than an aid. Again, simple is best.

If you decide to tape, video record, or screen capture, take notes just in case. Murphy's Law of user testing says you're sure to put the tape in backward, crash the software, run out of ink or paper, and experience connection problems. Do your best to make sure all equipment is in good working order, or annoyed participants may use your site as a scapegoat, skewing the results.

How should you evaluate the testing?

It would be impossible to implement every suggestion made by a user during testing. Some comments will be contradictory, unrealistic, or unsuitable for your goals or the majority of your audience.

User testing resources

Guerrilla HCI: Using Discount Usability Engineering to Penetrate the Intimidation Barrier
http://www.useit.com/papers/guerrilla_hci.html

Using Paper Prototypes to Manage Risk
http://world.std.com/~uieweb/paper.htm

User Test Your Web Site
http://www.webreview.com/97/04/25/usability/index.html

Testing and Quality Assurance
http://www.pantos.org/atw/testing.html

The Use and Misuse of Focus Groups
http://www.useit.com/papers/focusgroups.html

Getting the Most from Paired User Testing
http://www.acm.org/interactions/vol2no3/columns/mandt/methtool.htm

Find out more

Cooper, Alan. *About Face: The Essentials of User Interface Design.* IDG, 1995.

Nielsen, Jakob. *Usability Engineering.* AP Professional, 1994.

Nielsen, Jakob, and Robert L. Mack. *Usability Inspection Methods.* Wiley, 1994.

Rubin, Jeffrey. *Handbook of Usability Testing: How to Plan, Design, and Conduct Effective Tests.* Wiley, 1994.

Schuler, D., and Aki Namioka. *Participatory Design: Principles and Practices.* Erlbaum, 1993.

Waters, Crystal. *Universal Web Design: Hands-On Instruction of Design Alternatives.* New Riders, 1997.

Web Site Usability: A Designer's Guide. User Interface Engineering (self-published), 1997.

Combining suggestions without a sorting process can actually make your site a less usable place than before. Finding patterns in the responses—areas that are consistently repeated across groups or interviews—is a much more effective way of focusing your evaluations.

This is especially true of qualitative comments, which are hard to measure or compare. Noting that most of your users disliked a certain feature is more important than remembering how they phrased their disdain.

More easily measured results—but not necessarily more meaningful ones—can be gathered by evaluating questionnaires or by assessing whether users were able to complete tasks. Some consultants time users with a stopwatch or clock as they try to find a certain feature of the site. Others record the number of clicks needed to arrive at a destination. These measures have yielded results for some consultants. However, keep in mind that you may not need *data* as much as you need *insight.* Narratives are by far the best way to get that.

Combining user testing with casual interviews, online surveys, on-site observation, and other research can help you understand the full scope of your task. Interviews and focus groups often suggest new avenues you might not have considered. User testing can ferret out problems you may not have noticed. Online surveys are useful for polling for opinions or attitudes. No one approach is a panacea. Together, though, they can offer remarkable and unexpected results.

Recap

Understanding users might seem like a daunting and time-consuming task. It is, to some degree. What makes it worth it is that it's often a lot of fun, and it may even save your site from obsolescence. The people who use your site are still the best experts you can find to assess its value. They are neither your friends nor your enemies. They won't stick around if things get bad simply to do you a personal favor, and they probably won't abandon you out of hand if you're doing your best to serve them. Give them what they need and want, and they are likely to return the favor in sales, hits, or participation.

## CHAPTER FOUR

SITE ARCHITECTURE

*To find a form that
accommodates the mess,
that is the task of the artist now.*
—Samuel Beckett

In this chapter

- The quest for order

- Organization defines content

- Building your infrastructure

- A closer look at process

- Recap

I used to work as a children's librarian in a large public library. Weird questions were part of what made the job fun. For example, a four-year-old girl once walked up to my desk and asked, "Do you have my favorite pink book?"

Miraculously, we found the book, but it shouldn't have happened that way. No library I know of organizes books by their color, never mind by how much one child liked them. But why not? Unfortunately for my four-year-old friend, it's not the norm. If every child asked for books by color, texture, or size, that would be a different matter. There would almost certainly be a section for pink books, and life would be good.

The quest for order

A good librarian will tell you that the reason for organizing information is so that people can get to it. It's the same on the Web. Grouping things—whether on the Web, in a library, or in the supermarket—is about providing paths to information by showing relationships: the mozzarella is in the cheese section, which is in the dairy department, which is in the grocery store. *The Lord of the Rings* is in the fantasy section, which is in the fiction department, which is in the bookstore. If things are where you expect them, they're easy to find.

The problem with knowledge is that it's not made up of simple linear relationships. It's a messy interrelated thing. The mozzarella might not

"The problem with knowledge is that it's not made up of simple linear relationships. It's a messy interrelated thing."

be in the dairy section—it might be in the deli section. *The Lord of the Rings* might not be in the fantasy section, but in with the classics. Heck, it might even be shelved with the pink books. Who's to judge which of these relationships is more important?

Relationships are subjective

Remember this old riddle?

> *Brothers and sisters*
> *I have none*
> *But this man's father*
> *is my father's son.*

Who is "this man?" He is the son of the riddle's teller. This tricky riddle plays with the idea that a man can be many things: father, son, brother, and so on. He is all of those things at once, but whether he identifies himself as a father, a son, or a brother depends on his context.

We have to struggle with the relativity of relationships on the Web as well. Concepts have ties to many other concepts, both larger and smaller. Try this exercise: Take the following list of items and ask five different people to organize them. Don't tell them anything more, regardless of how much they beg.

> refrigerator
> socks
> bureau
> living room
> dictionary
> kitchen
> milk
> bookshelf
> bedroom

The simplest way to organize these might be in an alphabetical list:

> bedroom
> bookshelf
> bureau
> dictionary
> kitchen
> living room
> milk
> refrigerator
> socks

But other ways of organizing those nine words also exist:

By size:

Large
kitchen
bedroom
living room

Medium
bookshelf
refrigerator
bureau

Small
socks
dictionary
milk

By room:

Stuff that goes in a kitchen
refrigerator
milk

Stuff that goes in a living room
dictionary
bookshelf

Stuff that goes in a bedroom
bureau
socks

By exact location:

kitchen: refrigerator: milk
living room: bookshelf: dictionary
bedroom: bureau: socks

Organization without standards

So what does this prove? When you asked five people you may have seen five completely different results, or at least a few different approaches. Organizing information is a subjective task, because relationships are subjective. People will approach it in very different ways, often based on their own context, knowledge, and experience.

Even in libraries, where organizing information is probably as standardized as it gets, there is a great deal of variation. Some libraries offer a shelf for new books, while others separate out all material that is larger than a certain size. In some cases, genres may be pulled out, or popular titles set aside, and so on. Some U.S. libraries organize

"How we organize information is a balance between how information 'wants' to be organized and how users want to find it."

books using the Library of Congress classification letters, while others still use the numeric Dewey Decimal scheme. If we can't get the pros to agree 100%, there's not much hope for standardized organization schemes on the Web.

And that's part of the problem. There's no shared understanding about how content should be organized on web sites, and we can't just fall back on generic solutions from other media. Consequently, two sites with similar content might organize them in completely different ways, a difference that might mean the success of one site and the utter failure of the other.

A standardized organization scheme for the Web is problematic, but there is a right—and a wrong—approach. It's right to take the time to structure information in ways that are meaningful to your audience. It's wrong to simply shovel things up onto the Web without a plan. The first approach brings order out of chaos. The second *is* chaos.

Organization defines content

How we organize information, whether it's on the Web or in a library, is a balance between how information "wants" to be organized and how users want to find it. Finding that balance requires equal parts experience, skill, trial and error, and common sense.

Nathan Shedroff, an interaction designer and the creative director of vivid studios (*www.vivid.com*), uses the design of the Vietnam Veterans' Memorial ("The Wall," shown in Figure 4-1) as a powerful example of this balance between information and users:

> When the monument design by Maya Lin was chosen by the committee, the first thing they did, of course, was decide that they were going to change it. They liked the ambiguity and the subtlety of the Memorial, but they decided that it would be impossible for someone to find their loved one if it wasn't organized alphabetically. So they decreed that the names would still be on the face of the granite, only that they would organize them alphabetically. This would have just destroyed the whole meaning and essence of the design because it would turn it into a huge granite white pages of dead people. You'd lose all of the connection and relationship that was inherent in the organization before, and you end up with a list with seven John Smiths. Which one is yours? You don't know.

> Fortunately, they went back to the chronological arrangement. When you enter, you're at ground level and the wall is starting below you. As you walk down into it, it grows really high until it overwhelms you. You get the reverse experience as you walk

Figure 4-1. *At The Wall's full height, the volume of names is overwhelming.*
(photograph by Deanna Gail Shlee)

out. This experience of submersion is because of the chrono-
logical arrangement: that's how the death toll mounted. You're
starting small, then at the height of the Vietnam War, it's overwhelming. You're covered with names of dead service people,
and then it trickles off again.

The nice thing about it is that you find people's names in relationship to other people who died with them. They're set into a different kind of context and they solve the problem of finding your loved one by having some books available on the pathways that are in alphabetical order that tell you the grid and panel where you could find their names. This is a nice way to supplement it. But here's an example where the design, organization, and presentation of the information—strictly information design—can create this powerful emotional experience that you don't really equate with yellow pages, directories, and other more mundane products.

How do you achieve this balance in site architecture? Start by considering the information itself, then explore how users want to find it.

Take a look at how you organize your computer's files and folders. There may not be a very well developed organization scheme there, but you may be more orderly than you suspect. You may have folders set aside for different projects you're working on. You may organize things alphabetically, add subfolders to keep the mess under control, and so on.

The material itself (in this case, the information in your files and folders) helps to drive its organization. In organizing information, we usually start with broad subjects represented in the information itself. But that's not the end of the story. If you've focused only on the organization schemes suggested by the information itself, you've failed to understand the other half of the equation: people. People are wonderfully unpredictable and full of unreasonable and selfish demands. To test this, go sit at someone else's computer and try to find something in their file system (see Figure 4-2). Tricky, isn't it?

The reason it's so tough to find your way through someone else's file system (or through their site, for that matter) is that the material itself is not the only organizational force at work. There are three major factors in most personal organization schemes that are not well understood in web site architecture: time, frequency of use, and pure randomness.

For example, in your computer's file system, you've probably found some way of grouping "hot" or urgent items. You may have a special folder or way of organizing frequently used items. And you might occasionally just stuff a folder full of random interesting things to sort out later. All of these behaviors occur on the Web. They simply aren't reflected often enough in site architecture plans.

On the Web, where we have a lot of fiercely independent Web homesteaders, we spend more time than we'd like essentially surfing

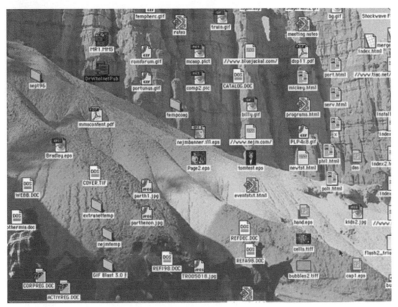

Figure 4-2. *Try to find something on someone else's computer. Tricky, isn't it?*

"There are a lot of wonderfully unpredictable folks out there creating wonderfully unpredictable sites that work just fine for them. The problem is they don't work for anyone else."

through someone else's file system. There are a lot of wonderfully unpredictable folks out there creating wonderfully unpredictable sites that are based on personal whims, not balanced and thoughtful presentation. Their sites (like their desktop file systems) work just fine for them. The problem is they don't work for anyone else. The context is often weak. Relationships between information objects are unclear. Most visitors end up feeling as if they've been asked to solve some devilish riddle, when all they came to do was find a piece of information.

When you're organizing the information on a professional site (i.e., one that you hope will gain you repeat visitors, sponsors, or accolades), keep in mind your own biases toward the information, your expertise in how the content wants to be organized, and the expectations of your visitors. Where will they expect things to be? What do you know to be accurate? Addressing these questions will help you find the right balance, and will help users pick the right path.

Building your infrastructure

Once you've thought about the relationships between your site's content pieces and the expectations of your site's users, you can begin to map out your site's terrain. You'll need to spend some time thinking about how many choices you want to present on the main screen, what terms you will use, and whether you will need short cuts or other extra help. When you're done, you should have a blue-print of your site's infrastructure—a map of the routes through your site.

Take a look at the following example.

Jabberwocky, Inc., a company that produces materials to help people learn a foreign language, wants to get on the Web. The web archi-tect meets several times with representatives of the company to discuss their mission and goals, help them target the audience, and determine what content should go on the site. The following basic guidelines are agreed to:

Goals

- To use the site to sell audiotapes, videotapes, CD-ROMs, and other products for learning a language.

- To provide customer support in using products.

- To model an online language course and possibly begin provid-ing regular Web-based language courses.

- To provide information about upcoming products.

- To conduct user research.

Audience Groups

- Business travelers (primary audience) concerned about learning quickly, speed of shipping, portable formats.

- Tourists (secondary audience) concerned with buying online, getting supplemental information about culture and customs.

- College and continuing education students (tertiary audience) interested in cheap alternatives to courses, casual learning at a personal pace, ease of use.

When the time comes to talk about content, the Jabberwocky team hands over various documents, including an org chart showing the corporation's internal divisions. Some team members suggest that these divisions be used as content categories on the web site. What will happen if these divisions are used? Figure 4-3 shows what this front door might look like

Not very scintillating ... and not very clear. If this approach is used, there will be no easy way of telling that materials are actually for sale, which was Jabberwocky's primary goal in getting on the Web. Things will need to be adapted for the Web. The web architect,

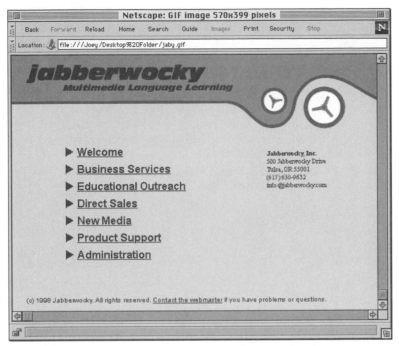

Figure 4-3. *Using the org chart as the interface is boring and unclear.*

working with the team, comes up with the following list of content areas that will be included:

- Searchable catalog of products, including sections for various media and languages

- Support documents and FAQs

- Information about the company

- Experimental web-based course(s)

- Related web resources on culture, geography, or travel booking

- Area for user feedback and product survey

Rather than turning this list into another poorly presented set of options, the web architect first looks at what kind of information is now being organized and what sort of relationships might be present. The architect also considers the tone of the site: travel is active, and language learning is often very task-oriented. Knowing this, the architect suggests to the team that they base their content categories on tasks, as shown in Figure 4-4.

This initial structure will be honed after talking with some of the site's intended users and looking in more detail at the content. Additional subcategories might be added, for example, or categories may be

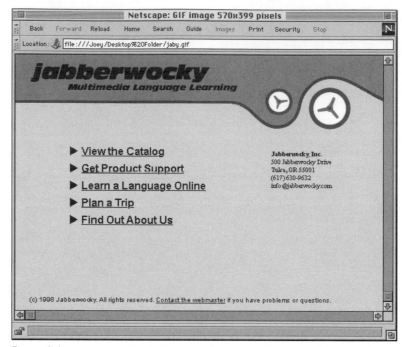

Figure 4-4. *Organizing the site by user tasks engages the user and suggests the nature of the content.*

extended another level down. Others may be removed. Labels may be made more descriptive. But the basic template for the site is in place, and it's a more cohesive and user-centered approach than the org chart was.

The Jabberwocky site, even when the content is extended to the next layer of subcategories, will be a good balance between *breadth* and *depth*. Its five simple categories on the main screen keep things from getting cluttered and reduce the chance that users will be overwhelmed with choices. Its controlled levels of information, which will probably end up at about three categories deep, means that users don't need to follow a path too far into the site in order to find what they need.

Depending on the site's purpose and content, there may be cases in which a somewhat broader site structure is called for—what web architect Lou Rosenfeld calls a *shallow site structure*. A shallow site structure, illustrated in Figure 4-5, usually means more choices on the front door, and fewer category levels to graze through.

A *deep* site, on the other hand, has few choices on the front door but a high number of category levels to navigate through. Figure 4-6 illustrates a deep site structure. The classic example of a deep structure is

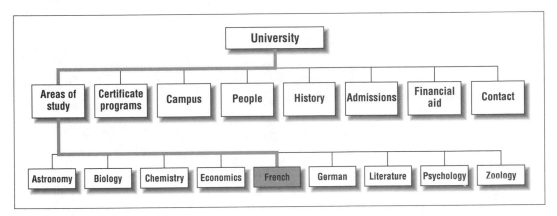

Figure 4-5. *A shallow site structure.*

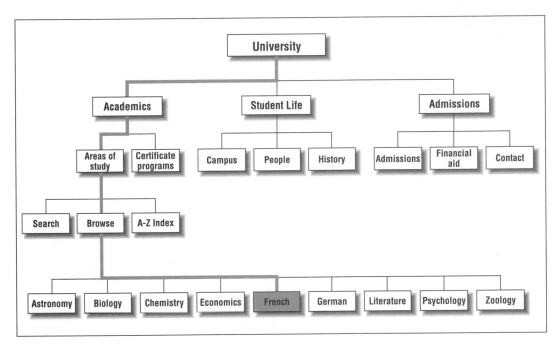

Figure 4-6. *A deep site structure.*

Yahoo! (*www.yahoo.com*), where it's not uncommon to go six or eight levels deep before getting to the content links.

Users are as frustrated by having to move through multiple levels as they are by having to wade through lengthy menus. Though a shallow or deep site structure might be the best way to order content on a particular site, it's best to seek a more balanced architecture

Lou Rosenfeld: "Design an integrated system"

Lou Rosenfeld is president of Argus Associates, a consulting firm specializing in web architecture. He's worked with clients such as AT&T, Border's Books, and the Annenberb/CPB Projects. Lou shares some ideas on the challenges of designing navigation.

"The Web is one of a host of new information technologies that democratize the world. They put incredible powers of presentation and dissemination in the hands of just about anyone. Not surprisingly, there are many more inexperienced designers of information systems out there on the Web than anywhere else. And these designers don't know enough to listen to users or investigate what other designers have found successful."

Lou explains that this results in numerous "designer-centered" sites that don't anticipate the different needs of the many audiences that might use a site. He adds, "Because we don't really know much about measuring the success of a navigation system (and don't usually have a tangible incentive to improve our site's navigation), sites aren't getting better very quickly. All of these issues result in poor navigation both within web sites and between web sites."

Offering words of advice about navigation design, Lou says, "Keep in mind that labeling systems are integrated with navigation systems, and are equally important. What you call that link is as important as having the link in the first place. Labeling should be as systematic as navigation. The same could be said for graphic design systems, which also need to be integrated with navigation."

In designing images for navigation, Lou warns of relying on undescriptive icons. "Almost any icon-based system is rife with clichés. They use many of the same icons to convey a message (for example, a house for a home page). But that would be OK if there were a universal or conventional language of icons. Instead, everyone uses them just differently enough to be confusing, and therefore meaningless."

Lou also points out the problems of inconsistent navigation. "I hate seeing a navigation system started but not finished. By this I mean seeing the system on some pages but not on others, or seeing it change slightly from page to page. When I use a navigation system, I don't want to have to think about it or even notice it. I just want it there and I want it to work the same way throughout the site."

Lou is co-author (with Peter Morville) of *Information Architecture for the World Wide Web* (O'Reilly, 1998). Visit Argus Associates on the Web at *argus-inc.com*.

The need for shortcuts

One navigation problem that is especially closely linked to architecture is the need for shortcuts. If I've planned a site with a deep architecture, and users need to navigate through many screens to reach a destination, the need for shortcuts becomes acute. This is especially true of large, complex web sites, where the sheer amount of information makes it very difficult to avoid going deep and broad.

There are several excellent methods available for creating shortcuts, including these typical approaches:

- *Searchability.* The keyword search box has become a staple on large information sites, but this doesn't necessarily mean the feature is always worthwhile. There are obvious benefits to having a well indexed database of terms and categories, one that has been carefully constructed to drop you where you need to go. However, many search features lack the care and regular cleanup needed to be of real use. If you're thinking about adding this powerful feature, read up on how to hone it carefully so that it will be a true asset.

- *Table of contents.* A table of contents (TOC) shows the structure of your site textually, usually by providing an expanded, clickable list of categories and their subsections. This is an excellent approach that is both quick and accessible, and has the added benefit of making your site structure clear to users.

Lou Rosenfeld, Argus Associates

- *Index.* A site index is much like a traditional book index. Usually, they are A to Z lists of content areas on your site. For many users, this all-purpose listing is comfortable and familiar. For some users, this concrete and selective index is also more manageable than a search box, which can seem dauntingly limitless.

  The downside to an A to Z index is that differences in terminology can frustrate users. You may be looking under I for "information architecture," but the index's creator may have listed it under S for "site architecture." To get around this, some sites feature a thesaurus of terms (though most commonly a thesaurus is used in conjunction with a keyword search box, which faces many of these same terminology problems). A thesaurus can be used to specify related terms for any given word or phrase. It's a time-intensive solution, but it can be effective in the long term.

- *Site map.* Site maps are graphical representations of your site's structure. They're wonderful for visually oriented people who want an overall picture of the terrain. Like their cousins, tables of contents, they can provide an excellent overview while also allowing quick leaps between structurally distant site areas. The downside of many site maps is that their graphical nature makes them slow to download, never a good trait in a shortcut. There are ways to slim down graphics used in site maps, which can help make them more rapidly accessible. (See Appendix A, *Technical Tips*, for a technical tip on optimizing graphics.)

- *Pull-down menu.* A pull-down menu is a hidden menu that expands when clicked on. Pull-downs make excellent shortcuts, but they have their drawbacks as well. For example, some users

Search engines: how, when, why

Lou Rosenfeld of Argus Associates offers more advice on search engines in the *Web Review* article "Using Search Engines with Your Web Site," which can be found at *http://webreview.com/96/11/22/arch/index.html*

don't understand that there is a hidden menu that can be revealed. Pull-down menus are often used as an afterthought, a place to dump a long list of choices that have little connection to each other. It's essential to carefully plan and architect your pull-downs just as you would a more traditional navigation menu. Users confronted with too many choices can be easily overwhelmed.

One important thing to understand about shortcuts is that they don't work very well by themselves, generally. They make excellent added tools, but often lack the flexibility to serve as standalone navigation systems that work for a variety of users. But in a complex and information-rich site, they're helpful additions.

A closer look at process

To get a better sense of how site architecture works, we need an understanding of process. Site architecture is much more than the creation of blueprints and flowcharts. It's also closely linked to content, strategy, and resources.

Argus Associates is one of the leading site architecture firms, and looking at their process offers both broad insights and practical techniques. Argus separates the architecture process into three main stages: research, conceptual design, and production/operations. Each of these stages has an important role to play in building an infrastructure that works.

Phase 1: Research

In the research stage of Argus's process, the focus is on information-gathering. Key techniques used during this phase include the following:

- *Face-to-face meetings* are held to help clarify client goals, ask difficult questions, and make discoveries about content and resources.

- *Site critiques* are used to find out about hidden preferences and to get the client talking about concrete issues and features. As Argus Associates' Lou Rosenfeld explains, one benefit of these critiques is that "it is much easier to express gut-level likes and dislikes about particular sites than to talk abstractly about aesthetic and functional preferences. It's also a lot more fun." Argus avoids critiquing existing internal sites, since often it can cause bad feeling—particularly if someone on the team was responsible for designing it.

- *Wish lists and content inventory forms* help the team gather and assess all content that is to be included on the site. Wish lists involve having the client brainstorm the content that should ideally be on the site, whether it exists or not. Content inventory forms assess whether this content exists already, who has created it, what format it is in, and who might be responsible for updating it. The focus here, according to Lou, is "to help the client develop a process that results in the efficient and effective collection of all content (and information about content) that you will need to design and build the site."

- *Index cards* are used to begin organizing content into groups. Argus calls this "content chunking." (Some firms also use sticky notes during this stage.) To do content chunking with index cards, Argus follows these steps:

    1. Invite the team to generate a content wish-list for the web site on a set of index cards.

    2. Instruct them to write down one content item per card.

    3. Ask each member of the group or the group as a whole to organize the cards into piles of related content items and assign labels to each pile.

    4. Record the results of each and move on to the next.

    5. Repeat this exercise with representative members of the organization and intended audiences.

    6. Compare and contrast the results of each.

    7. Use analysis of the results to inform the information architecture of the web site.

Phase 2: Conceptual Design

The conceptual design stage is probably the most exciting stage of a project. In this stage, idea generation is the focus of Argus's work. They use a variety of techniques to encourage group creativity and record the ideas that follow.

- *White boards* are excellent tools for group brainstorming. During group meetings in the conceptual design stage, Argus uses white boards to experiment with various architectures and approaches. Because things can be easily erased, team members usually can brainstorm freely. Recording the results of your white board sessions can be a challenge, but Lou also suggests that this can be a hidden benefit. It can often allow the team to focus on the end result instead of on the debates and struggles involved in getting there.

- *Flip charts* can also be used for group brainstorming. They are portable and make recording ideas as simple as tearing off the relevant pages when the work is done. Argus has found, however, that this recording component causes "a higher fear of error and greater resistance to change" in the team members. Flip charts are useful tools for an architect's arsenal, but white boards are the best choice when they are available.

- *Metaphor exploration* is an important part of the conceptual design stage. Argus makes time to explore any possible use of metaphor on the site, since they have found it helpful in communicating complex ideas. However, metaphor can also be restrictive. Argus is careful to ensure that any use of metaphor is "empowering and not limiting."

- *Scenarios* are used to help the client understand how users will experience the site. Often, using this situation-oriented approach can generate new ideas about navigation, architecture, or features.

- *High-level architecture blueprints*, shown in Figure 4-7, are used in the conceptual design stage to begin to transform chaos into order. These high-level blueprints are not finished plans. Instead, Argus uses them to stimulate discussions about where the site is headed, and what seems to be taking shape. These blueprints are then refined in later stages. "These high-level blueprints leave out quite a bit of information," Argus explains. "They focus on the major areas of the site, ignoring navigation elements and page-level details. These omissions are by design, not by accident. Shaping the information architecture of a complex Web site is a challenging intellectual exercise. You and your colleagues must be able to focus on the big picture issues at hand. For these blueprints, as with the web sites you design, remember the rule of thumb that less is more. Detailed page-level blueprints come later in the process."

- *Architectural page mock-ups* help clients envision the contents of any particular page. They don't show graphic design, but instead focus on what elements need to be on a page. Graphic designers can then use these mockups as a guide. Argus typically uses a word processing program such as Microsoft Word to create these mockups, but suggests that quick-and-dirty HTML mockups can also be used.

- *Design sketches* are used to begin to shape the interface. Argus approaches design sketches in a very collaborative way, encouraging various members of the team to have input. As they explain it, "It is much cheaper and easier for the group to work with the designer on these rough sketches than to begin with actual HTML page layouts and graphics. These sketches allow rapid iteration and intense collaboration."

- *Web-based prototypes* show how the site will look and function. "Once your architecture and navigation system are embodied in actual web pages," Argus explains, "it becomes much easier for you and your client to see whether they are working or not."

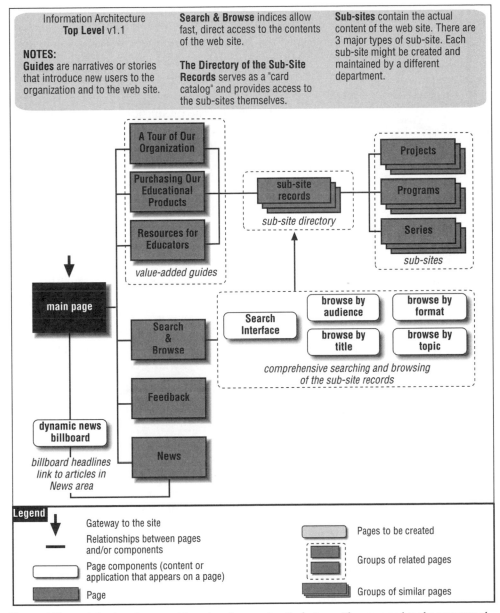

Figure 4-7. *High-level architecture blueprints show major site features. They are used in the conceptual design stage. (figure from Information Architecture for the World Wide Web, O'Reilly & Associates, 1998)*

Find out more

Brand, Stewart. *How Buildings Learn: What Happens After They're Built.* Penguin, 1995.

Lakoff, George, and Mark Johnson. *Metaphors We Live By.* University of Chicago Press, 1983.

Rosenfeld, Lou, and Peter Morville. *Information Architecture for the World Wide Web.* O'Reilly, 1998.

Sano, Darrell. *Designing Large-Scale Web Sites: A Visual Design Methodology.* Wiley, 1996.

Sullivan, Louis H. *Kindergarten Chats and Other Writings.* Dover, 1980.

Wurman, Richard Saul. *Information Architects.* Graphis, 1996.

Phase 3: Production and Operations

In the production and operations stage, the site goes into production. Issues such as maintenance and consistency are the focus of this stage.

- *Detailed architectural blueprints* are used to map out the site. These blueprints will serve as a guide for the production team throughout the production cycle. They typically include a high degree of detail, from broad structure to specific pages, and should clearly show labeling and navigation.

- *Content mapping* documents where content is coming from and where it belongs on the site. The production team shouldn't be expected to guess at where content belongs. Argus provides content maps to ensure that their careful plans are carried through the production stage.

- *Point-of-production architecture* consists of all the small decisions that need to be made during production. There may be a layout problem that comes up, or a question about content. Argus stresses that these should be small decisions, not large ones. The large decisions and plans should already have been handled during the previous stages, not in the production stage, since "discovery of a major flaw in the architecture at this point is an information architect's nightmare."

- *Architecture style guides* document how the site is organized, as well as the reasoning behind this structure. Style guides also explain how the architecture should grow over time, and how new content should be added. They are essential to maintaining a consistent and cohesive approach.

Recap

Planning your site's infrastructure is essential to navigation design, just as a building's structure is the base upon which everything else is built. Combined with the important visual messages of interface design, a well planned architecture can create an environment that supports user behaviors and allows freedom of movement. There may not be one "right" architecture for all sites, but following a goal-oriented process can lead you to the solution that will work for your site.

## CHAPTER FIVE

INTERFACE AND INTERACTION DESIGN

Focus on designing the action.
—Brenda Laurel
Computers as Theatre

In this chapter

- Visual messages
- Show and tell
- The psychology of design
- Recap

I f you've organized your site's content in a meaningful, logical way, you've built a solid infrastructure to support active users. You've laid down roadways through your site. Your job shouldn't stop here, though, any more than a traditional architect would consider blueprints the final step.

For a successful navigation design, it's important to consider the interface as well. The interface is the intermediary between users and content, an interpreter and guide to the complexities of a site. In the graphical environment of the Web, interface design has to do with constructing visual meaning. The happy marriage of architecture and interface—of logical structure and visual meaning—creates a cohesive user experience. This marriage is crucial to helping users get around on the Web.

Visual messages

Look at the example of a subway system. The Boston subway system has several routes that bisect the city, reaching a large part of the population. The subway's infrastructure is generally well planned, well labeled, consistent, and predictable. No small feat for the nation's oldest subway system, which (like many web sites) grew over time.

To make the subway as easy as possible to use, its designers used color to help differentiate routes. There is a Red Line, a Green Line, a Blue Line, and so on. Cars are painted in the color of their route, to

"The interface is the intermediary between users and content, an interpreter and guide to the complexities of a site."

help riders make connections. Subway maps showing the various routes and their colors are prominently displayed in station stops. Walls, signs, and stairwells are also appropriately colored.

While the Boston subway system has its quirks, it's relatively easy to figure out where you need to go. Architecture (the system's logical structure) and interface (visual cues and guidance) work together to help the subway's riders make decisions and plan routes.

If the subway provided visual cues that were at odds with its architecture—for example, if Red Line trains were occasionally used to service the Green Line—there would be confusion. Many web sites do the equivalent of running Red Line trains on the Green Line, though. These sites construct environments in which logical structure is not supported by visual cues. Instead, these two important ways of organizing information contradict each other, and there is confusion.

How can this be? Some people will tell you that a solid site architecture will stand on its own. I don't believe it can. Even in an "undesigned" site (which is hard to imagine, since virtually all sites have some level of design), there must be a relationship between visual messages and logical structure. How large are headers? Are some items indented? How are fonts and styles used? What content appears first? How we present information—unintentionally or by design—sends messages about its relationships and context.

Hierarchies can be visual

If you read the previous chapter, you may have a growing sense of the importance of information hierarchies, the careful organization of information into clear, logical categories. Hierarchies can also be visual.

Visual hierarchies show relationships between elements on a page. This is done by paying attention to factors such as:

- The relative size of elements on a page
- Their placement or position
- Color and contrast
- Movement

Relative size can communicate information about the importance of one item over another. Large items will generally draw attention first and will be seen as the more important elements on screen. Headers, for example, are almost always larger than text, which communicates that they have weight and importance. When these clues are not available, sorting through information can be an overwhelming experience for users.

Placement or position of elements can also communicate their relative importance or the sequence in which we are meant to digest them. In English, we're accustomed to reading and writing from left to right and from top to bottom. The way we approach the screen is the same. Items to the left and top of center tend to be noticed first, and are usually considered more important than other items. The famous left-hand navigation panel took off partially because of its natural, comfortable location. Grouping or placing elements in proximity also provides information about their logical relationships.

Color and contrast also show relationships between items, establish importance, and most importantly draw attention. A highlight color on a page, such as yellow or red, draws the eye because of its difference from the other elements. A high-contrast black element used on a light-colored page has a similar effect. Color is also an excellent way to show a continuing path, since we can interpret color information rapidly and with a high degree of precision (yellow brick roads are as useful in life as in film). Using the full rainbow of colors without meaning or association—a common occurence on the Web— makes for poor visual hierarchies.

Movement draws our attention, an unfortunate instinctive reaction for anyone faced with a page full of eye-popping animated ads. If everything on screen is vying for attention in a Las Vegas-style glitter of color and lights, it becomes difficult to make decisions about information paths or judge relationships among content elements. Used judiciously and with purpose, animation can be an exciting and effective way to communicate information.

Rather than being seen as a solution to some of the Web's usability problems, graphic design is often regarded as their source. While they are central figures in print communication, designers are not yet playing a serious role in this medium.

Clement Mok of Studio Archetype explains, "We're playing catch-up. Generally, designers are not driving the agenda. The agenda is driven, nine times out of ten, by the tool makers and the manufacturers, but designers can play a very significant role in determining how layout and design can provide a new language and structure on the Web.

"This role is slow in coming," he says, jokingly adding that, "when you come in with Photoshop files and say, 'This is the new way of dealing with this problem,' engineers and developers look at designers as fuddy duddies. As much as we believe it's true, there has not been a precedent set that we are credible in this category. Unless we prove that, it's still going to be questioned."

Good communication design has little to do with decoration, though it can be a thing of beauty. It's as important to a site's success as

"Good communication design has little to do with decoration, though it can be a thing of beauty."

Nathan Shedroff: "It's about what people can do"

Nathan Shedroff, vivid studios' Creative Director, has written a great deal about interaction and information design for the Web, and has plenty of insight into the process behind the results.

"When we start any project," Nathan explains, "we begin by asking our clients what their goals are for the site, which will determine how the site's success will be measured. We also ask who their audience is, and what their messages are to that audience. This is where everything important happens. The answers to these questions affect every other question down the road."

Early on, vivid looks at the amount and type of content a client has and experiments with organizing and presenting it in different ways. "We try to bring fresh eyes to their materials, and approach it as their audience would rather than from the perspective of how the company itself views or values the content—and certainly not how the company is organized internally. Most clients tend to approach their information from their own inside perspective because that's what they deal with every day. It's hard for them to see anything new."

Nathan points out that most companies are still approaching the Web with the idea that they can post a lot of marketing materials and be done with it. He says this approach results in "Phase 1 sites," and adds that "most companies find out that while there is some value to this, they need to think about other concerns, especially branding, identity, and navigation. So they redo their sites (Phase 2 sites). They find out that while the site may look better, be more appropriate to their company, and be easier to navigate, it doesn't do much more for them and certainly wasn't the hotbed of activity they once thought.

"So they go off in search of more," Nathan continues. "If they figure out that branding is really about experience rather than identity, then they are often led to the idea of interactivity being an enhancement for their products, services, support, and so on (Phase 3 sites). If not, they usually get duped into believing that cool new technologies are the answer and add lots of VRML, JavaScript, and Shockwave online tchotchkes that cost a lot and do even less for them."

Because the word "interactive" has become a buzzword, confusion is understandable. "Every client is different," Nathan explains, "but we need to teach clients about what 'interactivity' is most often. They usually think it has something to do with Shockwave or Java."

Offering words of wisdom for new web developers, Nathan stresses that "Web developers need to understand 'interactivity' just as much as clients. Interactivity isn't about non-linear navigation or moving animations on the screen. It's about what people can do on the site, what they can participate in, what the site does to address their needs, interests, goals, and abilities."

"Developers also need to learn to build what their clients need instead of what they want to build because they think it's 'cool' or fun for them. Too many sites don't reflect what a company's business is all about. They're out of character for the company. This is often a fault of the client too, but it's up to us to inform our clients of the potential mistakes they may be making. That's the value and responsibility we bring to the relationship."

The vivid studios site can be found at *www.vivid.com*. They've outlined their creative process in detail at *www.vivid.com/form/*. Nathan also provides diagrams, writings, and other information on his personal site at *www.nathan.com/thoughts/*.

quality content, architecture planning, technical wizardry, and usability testing. When these areas come together, each presenting solutions in a unified way, each understanding the strengths of the others, the result is a well-crafted user experience

Meaning through metaphor

If you read much writing on design, you'll soon discover that there are many approaches to communication design. Visual hierarchies are the basic building blocks, but there are other tools available for our use. Metaphor is one of the most powerful—and most misused—of these.

In the literary world, authors use metaphor to explain a concept by associating it in the reader's mind with another, more familiar concept. For example, *traffic slowed to a crawl* explains that traffic was moving very slowly. The cars weren't actually crawling, but they may as well have been.

Nathan Shedroff, vivid studios

If you use a familiar device to help guide shoppers (such as FAO Schwarz's shopping bag, a clever device for the storage of purchases), you're using metaphor. If you use the image of a highway to explain the Internet (the "information superhighway" of Al Gore's famous speech), you're using metaphor.

Take the example of PhotoDisc (*www.photodisc.com*), a well-known source of digital stock photography. In their search engine, an excellent feature allows artists to collect possible images for a project and keep them in a "lightbox" to look at later, as shown in Figure 5-1. You can name your lightbox and send your colleagues there later to look over your selections. You can even leave notes about images, or read notes left by colleagues. It's an amazingly helpful feature.

In planning this new feature, Photodisc had to give some thought to how designers would relate to it. How could it be explained to this audience in the best possible way? They could have gone with a literal explanation, such as, "We'll be using cookies to maintain state for seven days," or even, "We'll store your user profile and relevant thumbnail images in a database and allow multiple users to access it." Snooze.

The metaphor of a lightbox conjures up images of designers clustered around one of the "old-fashioned" devices of that name, viewing and selecting slides for a project. This communal decision-making process is what PhotoDisc's lightboxes are all about, and this is how it was best explained. By choosing the concept of lightboxes to help explain this new digital tool, PhotoDisc associated a potentially scary technology (cookies, or a database) with a familiar and comfortable design process. It's a metaphor that's as effective as the product itself.

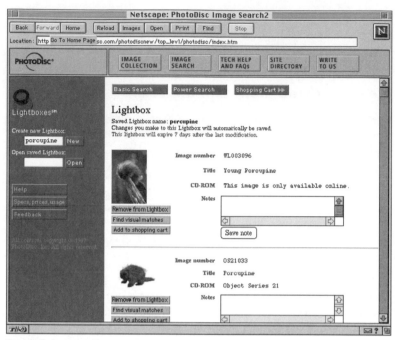

Figure 5-1. *Photodisc's "lightboxes" work well as a metaphor, conjuring up images of designers clustered around a traditional device of that name.*

Metaphor can be as restrictive as it is helpful, however. Selecting the wrong metaphor for a concept, failing to carry it through, or even taking it too far can result in awkwardness or confusion (not to mention "cute-ification").

For example, Yahoo-style lists of subject categories are often called "channels." This began around the time that so-called push media exploded on the scene, but these channels have nothing to do with broadcasting. They don't relate to TV either. They're misleading and misnamed, and despite having useful content, are likely to be overlooked by some visitors.

Show and tell

News flash: readability is coming back into vogue. Even understanding the current controversy over design approaches, this strikes me as unbelievably bizarre. It's a bit topsy-turvy that we work in a communication-oriented field that perversely considers the clarity of written communication to be optional.

How has this happened? Design is a broad and varied field, encompassing aspects of art, business, and psychology. Because of its frequent association with sales, design has had a longstanding affair with getting attention. But lately, it seems this has led to an interest in pure shock value: bright colors, chaotic layouts, hostile typography, convention turned on its head.

Much of this has been done in the name of innovation. That's a shame, since it's a fallacy that innovation means breaking all the rules. Sometimes it means understanding them better than anyone else—getting at the core of why rules exist, and extracting nuggets of truth about communication that have never been explored before.

Clarity versus chaos

On the Web, it can be especially troublesome to play with chaos in design. For many users, the Web already represents chaos. Adding a veneer of confusion is sometimes the last straw. If scripts and animation are battling for attention, adding unreadable type and bad color contrast is probably not going to help.

What's fun and different in an MTV video or cutting-edge print magazine does not automatically translate well to the Web. If you're designing a band site or a grungy e-zine, you'll certainly have more flexibility than if you're designing a medical information site, since purpose and audience will affect the approach. But even MTV buffs deserve a structured layout. Even the nattiest hipster deserves readable text in an e-zine. Without these basic design values, you're creating art (which is about individual expression), not practicing design (which is fundamentally about communication). It's a crucial difference—especially to your users, and especially on the Web.

Things have gotten so out of hand that it's become a bit of a joke in the field (one that would be funnier if there weren't still a raging controversy over it). One site, jodi.org, uses a deliberately chaotic interface to satirize the current trend. It's purposefully confusing and makes no claims to guidance or instruction. Essentially, it's the Web's first real piece of performance art, letting visitors experience what chaos in interface design feels like.

In navigation design, it's cruel and unusual punishment to offer chaos instead of guidance, self-expression instead of shared communication. Interface design, like many areas of design, is service-oriented— it's in service to the message, the client, the users, and the medium. That makes the work of an interface designer a serious challenge, since it is much harder to understand others' needs than it is to know your own tastes. There may not always be glory in it, but service is the hallmark of good design.

Visual explanations

Could better design have prevented the space shuttle Challenger's disastrous explosion? Edward Tufte thinks so, and he's not even talking about the shuttle's design.

" 'Form follows function' has been widely misinterpreted to mean form versus function, a battle of opposing forces. In fact, form and function go hand in hand."

In *Visual Explanations* (Graphics, 1997), Tufte explains that shuttle engineers knew the night before the launch that there was the possibility for disaster. A critical part, a seal called an O-ring, was not expected to work correctly in the extreme cold forecast for the morning of the launch. The engineers put together multiple charts to explain the danger, none of which convinced the decision-makers to halt the launch. The shuttle was launched the next morning in 29-degree cold. Less than two minutes after launch, it burst into flames.

What went wrong? The direct cause was that the O-rings were not designed to withstand extreme cold. But Tufte shows a more tragic design flaw: the sadly unpersuasive charts used to explain the O-ring problem.

Tufte argues that the charts failed to display the data causally, or in a way that would clearly show cause and effect. It was clear to the engineers that low temperature caused O-ring damage. They simply failed to *show* that it did.

Navigating the Web could hardly be called a matter of life and death (though cases of fatal misinformation exist). But if misinterpreting information could cause a group of intelligent people to proceed with a doomed launch, imagine how it could confuse and mislead web users! We should be as concerned with how we show connections within a site as Tufte is with showing relationships within data. Visual displays, whether charts, books, or interfaces, have the power to be expository—a power far beyond decoration.

Form is function

Periodically on mailing lists and at conferences, a small brush fire is ignited when someone brings up the old debate over "form follows function." This debate is based on a common misunderstanding, one that becomes clear if we look at the work of Tufte and other great designers. "Form follows function" has been widely misinterpreted to mean form versus function, a battle of opposing forces, and so designers and technologists seem doomed to duke it out.

But form and function, as the architect Louis Sullivan meant when he originally coined the phrase, go hand in hand. In Sullivan's view, "The architect who combines in his being the powers of vision, of imagination, of intellect, of sympathy with human need and the power to interpret them in a language vernacular and true—is he who shall create poems in stone."

Good architects tend to understand what this is all about, and some of our finest public buildings and corporate workspaces are the tangible results. Information architects understand that this same concept can be applied to information spaces. Design is not a battle between form and function, emotion and reason, decoration and purpose. In your users' eyes, these elements are intertwined, for better or for worse.

The psychology of design

It's virtually impossible to separate the design process from end users, readers, or visitors. They're the reason we bother with visual messages in the first place. Without these users, you may as well be broadcasting into deep space. Understanding human quirks is as much a part of a designer's toolbox as high-end graphics software or a good set of drawing tools. If anything, it's more important.

On the Web, where we're shaping new and sometimes experimental interactive spaces, these issues are thrown into high relief. It's essential that we try to understand how people are likely to react to problems, why they sometimes fear the screen, and how they learn new things. Without understanding some of these areas, predicting the active process of navigation becomes little more than guesswork. Without understanding some of these areas, we'll never get past our reputation as an unfriendly and butt-ugly medium.

Designing for action

If you accept that a web site is a space, then it's natural to assume that there are objects in it—things we can pick up, manipulate, press, or otherwise interact with. There may be control panels with buttons to press, or drop-down menus to scroll through, or objects that change when you roll your mouse over them. All of this may end up sounding a lot like building a transistor radio—and in a way, it is.

There are lessons from industrial design that we can borrow for use in web design, many of which are based on solid cognitive science. They help explain how we think, react, interpret, and learn. They explain why we sometimes push handles that are meant to be pulled, and why a large segment of the population doesn't have a clue how to program a VCR.

The psychologist we have to thank for most of this research and writing on user-centered industrial design is Donald Norman. Norman's most famous book, *The Design of Everyday Things,* sheds some light on how design can be brought more into line with human needs. It's an appealing thought—a world in which we don't struggle to understand objects; instead, they are designed to "understand" us.

Norman's survey of poorly designed objects can be damn funny. He tells stories of people walking into glass doors, rigging up cabinets with string, and standing helpless before bathroom faucets whose use was a mystery. Other stories—of "human error" at a nuclear power plant or "pilot error" related to a crash—are less humorous, and make the importance of human-centered design very clear.

In studying how people use tools and complete processes, one of the things Norman looked at was actions. He highlighted seven stages of completing a task:

1. Forming the goal

2. Forming the intention

3. Specifying an action

4. Executing the action

5. Perceiving the state of the world

6. Interpreting the state of the world

7. Evaluating the outcome

In order to support each stage of this process, Norman suggested using these seven stages of action to ask design questions, described in Table 5-1.

Table 5-1. *Seven stages of action and relevant design questions for each*

Seven stages of action	Relevant design questions
Forming the goal	How easily can one determine the function of the device?
Forming the intention	How easily can one tell what actions are possible?
Specifying an action	How easily can one determine mapping from intention to physical movement?
Executing the action	How easily can one perform the action?
Perceiving the state of the world	How easily can one tell if the system is in desired state?
Interpreting the state of the world	How easily can one determine mapping from system state to interpretation?
Evaluating the outcome	How easily can one tell what state the system is in?

Source: *The Design of Everyday Things* (Doubleday, 1990)

These specific design questions can be boiled down into broader principles, based on cognitive processes. These are Norman's "principles of good design":

• *Visibility.* By looking, the user can tell the state of the device and the alternatives for action.

- *A good conceptual model.* The designer provides a good conceptual model for the user, with consistency in the presentation of operations and results and coherent, consistent system image.

- *Good mappings.* It is possible to determine the relationships between actions and results, between the controls and their effects, and between the system state and what is visible.

- *Feedback.* The user receives full and continuous feedback about the results of actions.

Paying attention to these user-centered design principles—visibility, conceptual models, mapping, and feedback—is not just for designing phones and transistor radios. Think of how many times you've clicked on something believing it to be a link, or gone to a page that offered no feedback about location. These are important design principles, whether it's industrial design or navigation design. Keeping them in mind could save your users a lot of trouble since, as Norman puts it, "If an error is possible, someone will make it."

Designing for interaction

We talk a lot about "interactive media," but what does this really mean? Interactivity has become a bit of a buzzword. Is it synonymous with "responsive technical feature" or is it synonymous with "good conversation?" I'd argue that it's more of the second, though it can also be the first, when things have been done well.

Interaction, in a nutshell, is two or more people having an exchange—of ideas, of emotions, of physical objects, of words. On the computer, interaction is still two or more people having an exchange, with the exception that the interaction is mediated by technology. Interactions on the computer are often as complex as interactions off the computer, and it's helpful to understand both.

For example, what makes an interaction positive instead of negative? Politeness is one essential ingredient of a positive interaction. We know this is true in daily life, but surprisingly, it seems to be true in computing situations as well. In *The Media Equation: How People Treat Computers, Television, and New Media Like Real People and Places* (Columbia University Press, 1996), Byron Reeves and Clifford Nass present some interesting findings about people and technology.

It turns out that, if Reeves and Nass are right, we had all better brush up on our Emily Post. Netiquette doesn't begin to cover what we'll need to know. Reeves and Nass found that "individuals' interactions with computers, television, and new media are fundamentally social and natural, just like interactions in real life." One of the more interesting things they found is that, odd as it sounds, we are actually polite to computers (or in computing situations).

"Interaction is two or more people having an exchange. On the computer, interaction is still two or more people having an exchange, except that the interaction is mediated by technology."

Find out more

Albers, Josef. *Interaction of Color.* Yale, 1963.

Gelernter, David. *Machine Beauty: Elegance and the Heart of Technology.* Basic Books, 1998.

Johnson, Steven. *Interface Culture: How New Technology Transforms the Way We Create and Communicate.* HarperCollins, 1997.

Mullet, Kevin, and Darrell Sano. *Designing Visual Interfaces: Communication Oriented Techniques.* Prentice Hall, 1995.

Norman, Donald. *The Design of Everyday Things.* Doubleday, 1990.

Reeves, Byron, and Clifford Nass. *The Media Equation: How People Treat Computers, Television, and New Media Like Real People and Places.* Cambridge University Press, 1996.

Spiekermann, Erik, and E.M. Ginger. *Stop Stealing Sheep & Find Out How Type Works.* Hayden Books, 1993.

Tufte, Edward. *Visual Explanations.* Graphics, 1997.

From these findings, Reeves and Nass extrapolated that, on the principle that reciprocity often drives interactions, we expect computers to return the favor. We expect that they will be as polite to us as we are to them. As the authors explain it:

> When media violate social norms, such as by being impolite, the media are not viewed as technologically deficient, a problem to be resolved with a better central processing unit. Rather, when a technology (or a person) violates a politeness rule, the violation is viewed as social incompetence and it is offensive. This is why we think that the most important implication of the politeness studies is that media themselves need to be polite. It's not just a matter of being nice; it's a matter of social survival.

How are we supposed to create "polite" computers? It's an interesting question. The authors of *The Media Equation* suggest starting with Grice's Maxims, a set of politeness principles (mainly for conversation) that were set down by philosopher and psychologist H. Paul Grice. According to Grice, these principles are:

- Quality (saying true things)
- Quantity (saying neither too much nor too little)
- Relevance (saying things that relate to the topic at hand)
- Clarity (saying things clearly and well)

Quality. Quantity. Relevance. Clarity. These politeness maxims sound an awful lot like what we're striving for in web design these days. They may be less tangible than "responsive technical components," but they're probably more essential to understanding what people want from our mediated interactive spaces.

Recap

Our understanding of the interface and how to design for it is constantly evolving, but there are some things we have already discovered. The importance of social interactions in our dealings with computers is increasingly clear. The concept of continuity in space is also becoming more accepted in computer-based design. Design principles such as visual hierarchies and metaphor remain an important part of how we process information, on screen or off. These elements help sculpt environments for real humans, based on social morés and messages. While trends in interface design may change (for the better or for the worse), there is one design principle that hopefully will not: what we do for the screen is for and about people. They must drive our efforts.

## CHAPTER SIX

LOOKING AT PROCESS

If I see an ending, I can work backwards.
—Arthur Miller

In this chapter

- Process: A six-phase approach

- Phase 1: Information gathering

- Phase 2: Strategy

- Phase 3: Prototyping

- Phase 4: Implementation

- Phase 5: Launch

- Phase 6: Maintenance & growth

- Recap

Many companies are now spending less time contemplating products and more time developing *processes*. This often comes from a real desire to find out why a project succeeds or fails, or what happens when people work together in teams. For many organizations, it arises out of a need to better understand creativity and innovation.

Understanding the creation process—from idea generation to finished product—offers a competitive edge. It means that knowledge can more easily be transferred from project to project. On the Web, having a definable process is as important as having a client roster. Without it, the quality of your "product" becomes unpredictable. If the creation process can happen in a thousand different ways, how can you prove to clients that it will work? If all aspects of that process are changeable, then your results may be, too.

This focus on process doesn't mean that rigidity rules over creativity. It does mean that innovation is only partly based on serendipity. The other ingredient is careful planning.

Process: A six-phase approach

Your approach to the process of web development is part of what separates you from the competition, part of what makes your firm unique among web firms. Some firms specialize in a particular broad stage of the process, such as Argus Associates' specialty in site architecture. Others bring a particular set of methods to bear on the

"Innovation is only partly based on serendipity. The other ingredient is careful planning."

problem, such as Digital Knowledge Assets' (*www.dkaweb.com*) use of ethnographic methods for researching user goals.

Your process will also differ depending on your setting. If you're working as part of a corporate web team, you may tend to view process as an ongoing and organic thing, liberally sprinkled with political hurdles. If you're working for a daily Web publication, you may tend to see process as a very focused daily event, one that is mightily concerned with standards and workflow. A freelancer may see the development process as something with a discrete beginning and ending, with client relations making up the bulk of the middle.

All of these perspectives are valid, and no one is more important than any other. Yet firm to firm, web-wide, there is more that is shared than not. It's still early in the life of this medium, but a consistent vision of the Web development process has begun to emerge. Though it might be spread across months or compressed into hours, this process tends to encompass six phases (shown in Figure 6-1), described below.

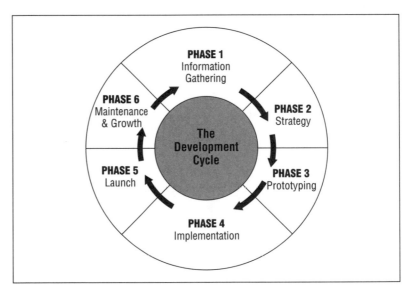

Figure 6-1. *An overview of the web development process.*

Phase 1: Information gathering

Phase 1 focuses on collecting the background information you need before you begin. What do you need to know about the project goals and mission? Who is the target audience and what do they want? What sort of resources do you have?

Phase 2: Strategy

In Phase 2, the focus is on defining your approach. How should you identify problems? What solutions are possible, and how do you discover them? This phase focuses on brainstorming and problem solving.

Phase 3: Prototyping

In the prototyping phase, you create a rough plan for how the site will work. What can you do to predict how people might move through the information? What assumptions have you made so far, and how can they be tested? Both the strategy and prototyping phases are crucial for navigation design.

Phase 4: Implementation

Using the results from Phase 3 as a guide, you'll build the site in Phase 4. What content issues present themselves in this phase? How can design, back-end systems, and content be smoothly integrated? How should you address new problems that might surface in this phase?

Phase 5: Launch

Launch covers the period just before and after the site's premiere. In this phase, you should plan on extensive testing. What testing needs to happen to ensure consistency, compatibility, and stability? When will you know you're ready to launch? Once the site is live, how can you help people find it?

Phase 6: Maintenance & growth

Web development is a cyclical process, not a linear one. Ideally, you don't just publish and move on. You publish and check, update, revise, reinvent. How can you maintain consistency without hampering growth? What else should you do to keep the site in good condition? When is it time to redesign?

Before I get ahead of myself, let me offer a brief disclaimer. Breaking the overall development process into phases tends to communicate that it is tidy and controlled, easily understood in tasks and check-lists, and strictly linear. It's not. What follows is a bird's-eye view of the development process when it works, when it's whole, and when the right resources and staff are present. You may spot this mythical beast in the wild, but it's more likely that you'll see its distant cousins.

Phase 1: Information gathering

If there is a hallmark of the information-gathering phase, it might be that it's often pitifully brief. And yet information gathering is the best way to make sure you have all the facts you need to begin a project. Is there time or budgetary pressure that will affect the scope of the project? Has someone conducted user testing in the past? What's the competition up to? You'll want to find all this out, especially if you're an outside consultant. There's a lot in this phase that can affect navigation design—and several areas that can make or break the development process itself.

Major tasks to be completed in the information-gathering phase are:

1. Understand project mission, goals, and history.

2. Define the audience.

3. Define standards for success.

4. Take stock of project resources.

5. Research the climate and competition.

6. Determine user goals and expectations.

7. Put communication methods in place.

Understand project mission, goals, and history

The first thing you need to understand going into a project is what the goal is. If you're working for a client, what is that client's agenda? What do they really want? It might not be easy to determine at first, either because they aren't allowed to tell you everything that's going on or because it's so obvious to them that they forget to mention it. You won't get answers in a 15-minute conversation. You'll need to spend some more time trying to ferret things out, and to do that you'll need to ask some pointed questions.

It's essential that you find out what these goals are, since they will color all your dealings with the client or organization. More importantly, they will drive what the client asks for and how the site is shaped, which affects the site's visitors as well. One company I know, for example, has a web site that's like an old house: its owners just keep adding to it over time, and it's steadily losing any character it once had. This company had no driving goal when they started their web project, nothing to keep them from becoming a sprawling, unfocused maze. Users are hard-pressed to understand what (if anything) is being communicated.

Another part of making sure you've understood the client's perspective (or, if you're in-house, the organization's perspective) is understanding the history of the project. In a few cases, you'll be the originator of a project, it will be in-house, it will be the very first web project ever undertaken there, and you'll have no outside client to fuss with. More commonly, there's some history you'll need to know. If you're a freelancer or outside consultant, there's generally quite a lot you'll need to find out. Did the client experiment with a service or product, only to have it flop? Do they have an existing site, and if so, is there feedback you should know about? Gems of knowledge are frequently mined from clients, not just from users.

How to do it: Directed conversation, ideally with several people who are closely involved with the project, is the best way to get at these gems of information. One-on-one conversation is by far the best, since people will say things individually that they would not say in a group. If the client seems reluctant to answer these questions, let them know that this is an important step in the process, that it helps you to serve them better, and that it may ultimately save them money and time. Treat clients as a respected part of your team—not as adversaries—and they're more likely to share what they know. You may also need to sign a non-disclosure agreement (NDA), an agreement that assures your confidentiality and helps to gain your client's trust.

Some web firms use a worksheet with clients, or require "homework" assignments such as surfing the Web for sites that are appealing. David Siegel at Studio Verso uses what he calls a "project profiler." Seigel's profiler includes questions designed to ferret out important information on company goals, history, and needs. His profiler is available on the Web at *www.secretsites.com*.

Define the audience

Who do you want to serve? What do you know about them? Defining the audience is one of the earliest steps in the development process. You may know the proposed content relates to medicine or sports or history, but the approach will differ radically if the site is intended for children instead of adults. Almost everything you do from here on in will depend on a clear understanding of who you're interacting with. It's worth the time you'll spend on it, and then some.

How to do it: The client (or, if you're in-house, the decision-maker) will drive the selection of the audience, but you'll very likely need to help them refine their ideas. It's not enough, for example, to say "we want to serve kids." That's pretty generic. "Kids" could be anywhere between 1 and 17 years old (and anyone who's tried to foist Barney off on a teen will know the danger in this). "Adults" doesn't help much either, and neither does "shoppers." What subdivisions of a broad audience exist, and which ones are important to the client? What traits does the client believe (or wish) his or her audience possesses, and how can that help you narrow the field? Read more about defining your audience in Chapter 3, *Designing for Users*.

Define standards for success

As the client's goals and intended audience begin to take shape, you'll need to talk about how they will measure success. If you're working in-house, you may have a very specific directive, such as "increase sales by 10%." That's one measure of success, though not a very interesting one. Other ways of "measuring" success, or determining a site's value to a client, might be less precise. Succeeding in gaining new customers, building a technology-savvy reputation, raising awareness of an issue or cause: these are other possible expressions of the potential value of a site to a client.

Asking the client how they will measure success also ensures that they aren't hoping for something unrealistic. The words, "I'd like to make a million dollars on the Internet" bursting forth from a client's mouth are your first clue that trouble's brewing. Better to find that out *before* you build that overpriced brochureware.

Another key part of this scenario is finding out what sort of business model, if any, applies. If you're working for a client that ultimately wants to make money directly from the site (and the savvier ones do), you need to talk seriously about the options. Will you try to support the site with advertising, and will the market support it? Your business model will affect many other decisions down the line; for example, how you integrate ads into the design, what back-end tools need to be in place, or what client resources need to be available. Talking about these issues up-front can save you from getting burned down the line.

How to do it: Conversation with the client or decision-makers is essential. Find out how they evaluate the success of other projects, and how that might be the same or different with a web project. You will almost certainly need to educate them about the feasibility of web business models, especially banner advertising (which is cloaked in hype and misleading information, and is not the lucrative income source it's sometimes made out to be).

Take stock of project resources

One of the last sensitive areas of information gathering (or one of the first, depending on how you handle it) is understanding what resources you have available. In-house developers often run up against problems relating to budget and staff shortages, both of which can undermine a project. Outside consultants and web firms need to be able to offer sound advice based on a practical assessment of resources. It's a key step.

Above all, the budget and timeline affect how you will proceed. Given enough time and a large enough budget, you can hire a squad of crack developers and turn out first-rate content. Given a tight timeline but a flexible budget (or vice versa), you'll have more serious constraints. As a developer, part of your job is helping the client understand what's possible with what they have. And to do that, you'll need to understand it, too.

Misjudging the time it takes to complete a project means you won't be able to test properly, or will need to make do with imperfect solutions. Misjudging the skills of available staff or the amount of content that needs to be created will have the same results, or worse. All of this will affect the final product and the quality of the user experience.

During this assessment period, you'll need to do a content inventory. With the client's rough goals in mind, review the content they have available and what large areas of content might need to be created. Don't get too bogged down in details; you're just looking at broad strokes in this phase. What sort of content exists, if any, and how might it be used? Your estimates about resources will rely on your understanding of existing content.

How to do it: At the beginning of a project, you'll need to create a timeline outlining major phases of development and the resources (staff, budget, content) needed to complete tasks. If the project concept changes later in the game, you'll need to reevaluate this document. Many web firms sign on for a strategy phase in order to determine the scope of a project before attempting a timeline or resources assessment. If the client is willing, this is by far the safest way to begin.

Research the climate and competition

Every week, Bill Gross reads 2,000 pages of news and information on a variety of topics. He does this not because he's a glutton for punishment, but because he's testing the waters. Gross is the founder and chairman of idealab! (*www.idealab.com*) and the impetus behind sites such as CitySearch, CareerLink, and GoTo.com. His company funds and supports promising web projects, and Bill Gross's understanding of the climate and competition has meant an impressive record of success.

Bill Gross, idealab

You may not have the time or patience to read 2,000 pages every week and methodically track patterns, but you'll still need a sense of the web climate. You'll need to know what users are excited about, who's just come out with a service or product that will change everything, and what events or trends will affect the way you do business.

If you're a consultant or outside web firm, part of your responsibility to the client is making sure they don't blow half a million dollars on something that makes no sense for users. If there are already a dozen really good web bookstores, does it make sense to create another? If there are a dozen web music stores but all of them are understocked and maze-like, maybe it makes sense to fill that gap. Users operate within a social and economic climate, not in isolation. The more you understand that climate, the better off your project will be.

How to do it: To research the current climate, reading industry news and views is a good start. You can also spend time lurking on mailing lists and newsgroups related to your development topic, or read related magazines and books. There is always something to be learned from what your competition is up to, as well. If they're doing something right, find out why it works. If they're doing something wrong, learn from it. Don't fall into the trap of just reacting to their moves, but do find out where they're heading.

Determine user goals and expectations

Before you go any further into the development process, you have to understand what users want and need. It's a key part of any successful product: a responsiveness to users. After all, they're the ones who will be using it.

How to do it: There are a variety of ways to determine user goals and expectations, many of which are discussed in Chapter 3, *Designing for Users*. You can use focus groups, interviews, and other research. You can create user profiles and scenarios based on known traits and behaviors. You can even involve users in the design process. Some of the most intriguing methods are being used by Digital Knowledge Assets (dka). dka uses ethnographic methods to find out about the needs and wants of users. These methods include contextual interviews, shadowing, and disposable camera studies.

* *Contextual interviews/storytelling*. Contextual interviews are conducted in the user's setting. For their research on information sharing, dka sits with people in their own workspace, not in a generic conference room. Marc Rettig, dka's vice president of design, explains, "We avoid asking leading questions ('Would you like it if you got less email?') or hopelessly general ones ('What do you need?'). Instead, we ask for stories."

To get at these stories, dka asks questions like: "Tell me a story about a satisfying experience—a time when you really needed a piece of information, and it was right there for you." Or, "Tell me about a time when you were frustrated because you just couldn't find the information you needed." Marc reports that stories work well for "discovering the daily activities and resources that are so common they've faded into the invisibility of everyone's mental background."

Marc stresses the importance of conducting interviews in the actual work setting, largely because of these "invisible details." He explains that "a person might casually gesture to the right and say, '...then I get the sales report....' We'll ask, 'What were you pointing at when you referred to the sales report?' We might find out about a book full of reports that are distributed manually. Or we might find out that Rita down the hall has all the sales reports, and people walk down the hall to talk to her."

- *Shadowing.* When they can get permission, dka "shadows" people as they go about their daily business. "The idea is simply to follow people around, keep quiet, keep out of the way, and watch what happens," Marc explains. "If you ask people to tell you what they do all day, you'll get one thing. If you watch them and take notes, you find something very different." dka uses shadowing to "discover tacit needs, patterns of work, and patterns of interpersonal interaction."

- *Disposable camera studies.* Sometimes shadowing is not feasible, so dka turns to another method: disposable camera studies. In these studies, users are given disposable cameras and asked to record what happens in their own work environment. When dka uses disposable camera studies, they do the following:

  — Give a number of people (possibly 6–12) a disposable camera and a small notebook.

  — Tell them to take photos of whatever activity you're interested in studying (shopping, information sharing, etc.). Make sure they "shoot up the roll."

  — Ask them to write an entry in the notebook after they take each photo. The entry should describe what was shot and why.

"Wonderful real-life data can come out of a disposable camera study," Marc reports. "It's a way to send eyes into places you could never reach by shadowing."

"The quality of the communication and collaboration methods you put into place will affect the quality of the product you end up with."

Put communication methods in place

One of the final things you need to make sure you do in the information-gathering stage is to set up opportunities for information exchange among team members, and between team members and the client or decisionmaker. When a company like dka collects information from users, how does it get distributed through the development team? You can bet dka gives as much thought to their internal information-sharing needs as they do to those of their clients.

The quality of the communication and collaboration methods you put into place will affect the quality of the product you end up with, since you can't achieve a creative vision if everyone has a different concept of what you're doing. What will you do about archiving discussions? How will you handle updating the information you collect? What about version control (making sure everyone is working with the most current version of a document)? If you're a solo developer, it might be enough to rely on email alone. If you're working with others, it can be extremely difficult to carry the required information through the completion of the project using email alone.

How to do it: Some people choose to build a project site (or project extranet) to help them cope with these information sharing needs. At present, there is no one tool I would call a good solution for web team communication. It's probably just around the corner...but until then, the project site is one useful approach. David Seigel covers project sites in depth in *Secrets of Successful Web Sites: Project Management for the Web* (Macmillan, 1997).

Phase 2: Strategy

I believe that the strategy phase is the most important phase of a project. I may be biased, since it's also the phase I enjoy most. The Web being what it is, though, I don't think I'm wrong about this. This is a fast-moving medium. Cutting out strategy and planning may save you a month of development time, but it may cost you the ballgame. Isn't it worth the extra time needed to create a winning site, one that is based on what users want and need to do?

This is the phase in which you determine how to best address the goals and expectations of your users. It's also the phase in which you define the scope of the project and experiment with possible solutions. Throughout this phase, clients or decision-makers should be closely involved (or at the very least frequently updated). Tasks for this phase include the following:

1. Identify problems.
2. Explore real-world models.

3. Look at other media.

4. Brainstorm possible solutions.

5. Define the concept and scope.

6. Organize content.

7. Explore design and technical alternatives.

Identify problems

Identifying problems is the first step in determining your approach. It's no small task. Identifying problems can be as difficult as identifying solutions—sometimes more so. Our brains tend to work fast, and it's easy to come to the table with quick answers already in hand. Often, they skew the presentation of the real problem. For example, the following "problems" might be presented:

- We need more color.

- We need to switch to a database.

- We need to redesign.

- We need frames.

- We need to do e-commerce.

And the biggie, the one we've all heard at some point or other:

- We need a web site.

IBM had a hilarious TV commercial a while back. In it, a businessman looks up from the newspaper he's been reading and says to his co-worker, "We need to get on the Web." His co-worker dutifully asks, "Why?" There's a moment of puzzled silence as the businessman scans the newspaper, then replies, "Doesn't say."

It's easy to lose sight of the problems, especially with hype and deadlines causing a headlong rush toward finding solutions. Whatever the specific reason, someone brings the wrong problem to the table. Your job, then, is to get at the real problem, the one that will lead toward solutions that work. For example:

- The stated problem: "We need more color."

  The real problem: "We're worried that we're coming across as stodgy. We'd like to be seen as fun and upbeat."

- The stated problem: "We need to switch to a database."

  The real problem: "We can't keep up with all this hand-coding. We need better and faster ways to store and present information."

"Letting technology drive solutions is a natural experimentation process for a new medium, but it's time we moved away from it."

- The stated problem: "We need a web site."

  The real problem: "Our biggest competitor has been eating our lunch. Now they just got on the Web. If we don't get on there too, and do it better, we're doomed."

Now these are problems you can sink your teeth into. Starting with these problems allows you to conceptualize freely, and may lead you toward some fascinating results. This is especially crucial in navigation design, since our current tools and models are pretty underdeveloped. Rather than saying, "I need a sidebar" or "I need frames," you'll have better luck with statements like, "People will want to shop/learn/play/talk/etc. What's the best way to make that happen?"

Living in the fast lane of a new medium, it's easy to let technology drive solutions. It's a natural experimentation process for a new medium, but it's time we moved away from it. Instead of letting a desire to experiment with technologies drive solutions (or, in other words, letting solutions drive solutions), the really exciting developments will come when we let people and problems drive solutions. Particularly in navigation design, understanding the scope of the problem is essential to getting at solutions that work.

How to do it: Using the information you gathered from users in Phase 1, look for patterns in their comments. Interview people who have been involved in the project so far, such as staff members. What do they think the problems are? Again, look for patterns. When you have a list of potential problems, cross off anything that reads like a proposed solution ("Need to use more Java" gets scratched, for example). Next to the remaining items, write in what you think might have caused the problem. Trace these possible causes as far back as you can, and always look for patterns.

Explore real-world models

Once you've identified the problems at hand, you can begin exploring possible solutions. One of the best ways to start is to look at life. There's a wealth of insight to be had from observing what goes on around us. There are whole fields with long and rich histories that we can borrow from. What can storytellers teach us about audience interaction, for example? What can museum exhibit design teach us about traffic flow? What can architecture teach us about constructing spaces?

The possibilities seem endless, once you begin to look at life as an ongoing experiment in design. Is that chair you're sitting in comfortable? How are highways constructed? Why do you hear tones when you dial the phone? Who thought up the drive-through restaurant?

The wonder is that we rarely wonder about these things. We take many of them for granted—especially if they work.

If we study other fields, we'll usually find models we can learn from. If we watch people shop, work, study, and create away from the computer, we'll learn things we can apply to what happens on the computer. Find out how other people have solved problems similar to yours, regardless of the space or medium. Find out how things have been done up until now, and how the Web can improve services. Contrary to some pundits' predictions, the Web won't replace life as we know it. The Web will co-exist with it.

How to do it: Exploring real-world models requires at least some fieldwork. Think of it as a field trip, and make a day of it. If you're planning a web storefront, for example, go to a local mall or department store. Stop and think about who might have designed the environment. How wide are the aisles? Where are displays located? Did something draw you into the store when you hadn't planned to shop there? How did you find the checkout? A department store is as complex as a web site, usually more so. What real-world models might apply to your project?

Look at other media

Many intriguing approaches can also be found by looking at other media, and CD-ROM in particular offers a wealth of possibilities. For example, one award-winning CD-ROM, *Passage to Vietnam*, features a navigation device called a Quebe (pronounced "cube"). The Quebe (shown in Figure C-4) is, well, a cube. It sits quietly in the lower right-hand corner of the screen, and rotates when one of its sides is clicked on to reveal options. In the space of approximately one square inch, multiple options can be provided without visual clutter or screen-hogging menus. It's an ingenious device, and one that perfectly suits the CD-ROM's photographic content.

From CD-ROM, books, exhibit design, advertising, and many other media and professions, there are lessons that we can bring to web design. Finding these sources of inspiration is part of "thinking outside the box." They will often suggest solutions that are ideally suited to your purpose.

How to do it: There are two categories of this sort of media research: 1) what you do in an ongoing way to feed your brain, and 2) what you do for a specific project. Both are necessary. If you're lucky, you'll have a bit of a budget to play with. This sort of exploration of related media and approaches will come under the heading of "R&D." (Don't write a line into your budget called "Purchase of cool

"CD-ROMs, books, exhibit design, advertising, and many other media and professions provide lessons that we can bring to web design."

CD-ROMs" and expect the client to pay for it. It's damn hard to explain, though it's completely justified.)

Early in the project, before your ideas begin cementing themselves, pick up CD-ROM titles and video games, watch selected movies or television programs, or take an interactive course. Oh, and don't ignore print media such as books and magazines that are reputed to be "dead." (Hint: They're not.) What specific problems was the designer trying to solve in each of these media? How did the designer solve them, and how might you approach it differently on the Web?

Brainstorm possible solutions

During the brainstorming process, your team (or a group you assemble for the purpose) comes together to generate ideas. Your information gathering should be done by this point, and all team members should have access to the raw results. By the time you reach the brainstorming stage, you should already have looked at other information models and ways of addressing similar problems. Now you're ready to let the ideas flow.

It's tougher than you might think. Sitting at a table and tossing some ideas around isn't going to cut it. There's more to brainstorming than just random thinking, and the quality of the process improves dramatically the better you understand how to do it.

How to do it: The man credited with originating the term "brainstorming," an advertising executive named Alex Osborn, laid down four rules he felt were essential to effective brainstorming:

- *Suspend judgment.* People have trouble thinking creatively if they believe they will be judged.

- *Encourage wild ideas.* If anything goes, then team members can feel free to make connections they might not have considered before. This can yield surprisingly insightful results.

- *Encourage quantity of ideas.* Don't give people time to self-evaluate or to discard ideas before they are spoken. Again, anything goes.

- *Build on each others' ideas.* The whole group can be "smarter" than its individual members. Applying several brains to an idea can expand the concept in exciting ways.

Michael Schrage, author of *No More Teams! Mastering the Dynamics of Creative Collaboration* (Doubleday, 1995), adds to these guidelines by suggesting that there are discrete stages in a successful brainstorming session. These stages include:

- *Criteria.* Establish how the merit of ideas will ultimately be judged (i.e., cost, entertainment value, feasibility).

- *Collect.* Gather and record ideas from the group. Anything goes.

- *Connect.* Make connections among ideas. Create clusters and look for themes.

- *Correct.* Weigh the merits of ideas against the established criteria. Discuss and refine.

People entering into a brainstorming session will need to have relevant background information a few weeks before the session, if possible. Schedules often don't permit this sort of lead time, but for brainstorming it is an important part of the process. Allowing information and ideas to incubate is one of the stages in successful problem-solving. The tight schedules we face in Web production can hurt this process. How often have you had a brilliant new concept two weeks into production? It's probably happened to more than a few of us.

Define the concept and scope

If you're like me, you could stay forever in the brainstorming phase, happily considering possibilities and building magnificent sites out of caffeine and hot air. But eventually, even the most serious brainstorming junkies among us must come to earth. To keep the process moving, you'll need to define the scope of the project, distilling the breadth of possibilities into one central, feasible concept you can work with—the tighter and more focused, the better.

For example, in a recent web project involving a new community site, our brainstorming team came up with what seemed like all possible services the audience might expect. When it came time to define the concept, many of those almost-features had to be shelved (much to our disappointment). Our budget wasn't sufficient, and our timeline wouldn't support them. The concept we went with centered on an approach that was both exciting and manageable, and that related closely to goals and resources.

Digital Knowledge Assets (dka) uses sticky notes to document the team's common vision after a brainstorming session (shown in Figure 6-2). Sticky notes make it easy for the team to change the way they "chunk" their raw ideas.

How to do it: The best approach is to come up with criteria, as Michael Schrage advises. When you're ready to refine and weed, use your goals as a guide. Estimate the production time and resources needed to complete each particular proposed idea. Then assess the impact of each idea. Use these three factors—goals, resources, and impact—to arrive at a concept that works. If possible, bring in a few users as a reality check.

90   Chapter 6: Looking at Process

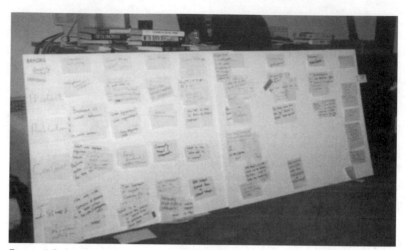

Figure 6-2. *Digital Knowledge Assets (dka) uses sticky notes to document the team's common vision after a group brainstorming session.*

Organize content

By this point, you should already have done a content inventory (during Phase 1). You should have a rough idea of what content is already available, and what focus it might suggest. In Phase 2, you're ready to begin organizing it. You'll need to come up with a draft architecture plan, a sort of blueprint for how your site might be structured. This is mainly a top-level plan; it shouldn't go very deep yet, but should consider how the site might grow.

How to do it: List broad content and features that you decided on in the "Define the concept" stage. How might these be organized? What relationships exist between different pieces of information? Are there some small features that could be pulled out and turned into rotating highlights, tips, a sidebar, etc.? Are there some content areas that are larger than others, and how will you handle breaking them into manageable chunks? You should end up with a list of content categories and some sub-categories as well. It's often useful to run this preliminary structure past some of the site's intended users to see if labels are understandable and if the structure makes sense. Read more about site architecture in Chapter 4, *Site Architecture*.

Explore design and technical alternatives

Once you have defined your approach and drafted your architecture and features, you'll need to consider design and technical alternatives carefully. Each decision you make in this stage directly affects the user experience. For example, it might make sense from a technical or design standpoint for you to use Shockwave to develop a particular feature. However, you might decide against it because of user preferences and behaviors.

How to do it: Each technical and design choice is made by weighing two major factors: 1) the best way to implement it from the developer's standpoint, and 2) the best choice from your users' standpoint. Your approach should consider both factors. A gorgeous, graphics-rich design approach that perfectly communicates your vision might fail to win over users because of downloading delays. A cutting-edge implementation of Java might be the most sophisticated way to address a technical problem, but it may alienate some users. One way to keep choices balanced is to check proposed solutions against hard facts about modem speeds, browser compatibility, and known preferences of your audience. Make yourself a checklist of development criteria that must be met, and stick to it.

Phase 3: Prototyping

For navigation design, prototyping is second only to strategy in importance. Yet because of time considerations, the prototyping stage is often left out of the web development process. Tight schedules and small budgets conspire to make prototyping difficult in most projects, and many web sites go directly from concept to premiere without feedback from clients or users.

Hopefully, as we better understand the process of creating user-centered spaces, more developers will write a prototyping phase into project proposals—and more clients will understand the value of it. Without the methods used in this phase (such as storyboarding and flowcharting), it's very difficult to understand how people will move through a site. If you're committed to navigation design, you'll need to plan for this phase of development. Expect to complete the following tasks in this important phase:

1. Map the site flow.
2. Do design comps.
3. Build and test a prototype.
4. Create final architecture plan.
5. Outline production specifications.

Map the site flow

One of the reasons the prototyping phase is so crucial to navigation design is its concern with mapping site flow. How will users move around your site? Will they want to move laterally (across topics or sections) as well as between sections and the front door? What do

Flowcharting software

Visio
www.visio.com

Inspiration
www.inspiration.com

you want them to experience upon entering the site? Upon leaving it? This is the stage in which you'll chart your site's territory, and build paths through it.

How to do it: I'm very partial to storyboards, but flowcharts are also invaluable for mapping actions. These two tools are not redundant. Each offers a different and important perspective on plotting movement.

Flowcharts are most useful when they're specific to a certain task. For example, instead of doing one broad flowchart mapping out all possible ways of moving through a site, which gets chaotic really fast, try doing flowcharts based on one feature at a time. Consider where someone might go from each step in your chart. You might, for example, map out what happens when someone does a search of your site or puts an item in their shopping cart (an example of a flowchart is shown in Figure 6-3). These specific charts are much more effective than broad, site-wide flow plans. For that sort of upper-level flow, you should rely on your architecture chart.

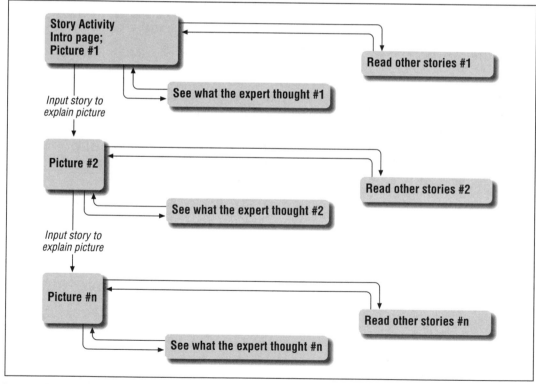

Figure 6-3. *A flowchart shows possible movement or actions.*

You can buy software to help you create flowcharts (Visio, Inspiration, etc.), which is useful if you need to show them to clients. However, using low-tech pencil and paper works just fine too, and has the benefit of being a lot faster (and more flexible) for most people.

Storyboards show something that flowcharts can't: what's happening on the level of the interface as the user moves through. Storyboards are common in movie production, advertising, and television. They show a flow of screens, illustrating how the story will play out or what the viewer will experience. The best storyboards are the ones that are really rough and sketchy, not beautifully illustrated in full color (though those are great for client presentations). The purpose of a storyboard is to experiment before production, and a very elaborate, polished storyboard discourages any further experimentation. As with flowcharts, storyboards can be used to great effect on concrete, specific tasks. They're also useful on a site-wide level, though. Figure 6-4 shows an example of a rough storyboard.

Do design comps

Design comps are useful once you've explored possible approaches and are ready to show the client some more concrete options. Usually, you will show one design approach in your comps, sometimes with an alternate. You can also use design comps to show different color schemes or font treatments for an approach (as shown in Figure C-5). This is an essential phase in client-designer relations. If you don't get signoff from the client on the design in this phase, it's very difficult to protect yourself if they ask you to redo it later on. Expect to do a couple of rounds of design comps with the client. It's well worth it if it saves you from redoing an entire, coded design.

How to do it: Many designers choose to "mock up" screens in an image editing program like Adobe Photoshop. Some (such as Studio Verso) also use page layout programs such as Adobe PageMaker or QuarkXPress. An illustration program such as Macromedia FreeHand or Adobe Illustrator can also be a great help, since it will allow you to move elements around easily (which Photoshop doesn't). For mock-ups, don't worry about content. You can "greek" it for now. Greeking involves pouring in nonsense text (usually starting with the pseudo-classical text, "lorem ipsum dolor") to show chunks of content.

Some web shops do design comps as part of the proposal-writing process. This is a sad fact of the business world, since you can occasionally lose clients if you don't submit comps with a design proposal (the other guy often does submit them, and the flashier proposal wins). That said, comping before you have done your research and

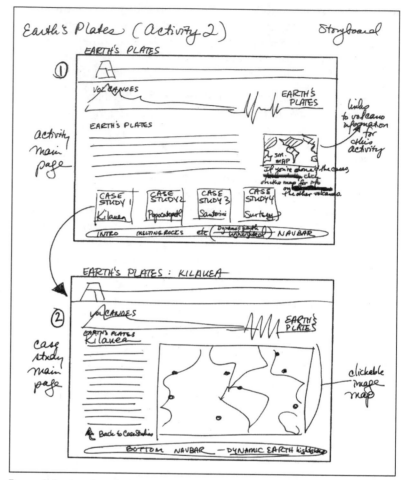

Figure 6-4. *Storyboards show what's happening on the level of the interface as the user moves through. They don't need to be pretty to work.*

strategizing is quite useless, and can even be grossly misleading. Try to navigate the proposal process without design comps, if you can. If you can't, be sure to explain to the client that further research and strategizing may suggest a different design approach.

Build and test a prototype

Prototypes are not easy to pin down, since they can be anything from a very rough, text-only walkthrough to a very refined demo. For the purposes of testing with users, it's important to be able to show information design and interface features. A text-only walkthrough is also very useful, but if there's time you should consider creating a more designed version.

How to do it: Create a functional version of your site, either as a text-only walkthrough or with interface design included. If there are obvious problems with how you've constructed the prototype (bad links, hard-to-read text), it won't be of much use to you in user testing situations. Users will get bogged down in the errors, and won't be able to focus on the site flow and approach. When a reasonably clean prototype has been constructed, bring in several users and ask them to use the demo. Give them specific tasks, if possible ("Look for and purchase an item"), but also watch how they react to the overall structure of the prototype. Use their reactions and comments to refine the prototype before taking it into production.

"Specs help ensure that the hard-won knowledge of earlier stages is not lost when the project goes into production."

Create final architecture plan

When you've tested your approach with users, either as a text-only walkthrough or a more refined prototype, you should have a good sense of whether your architecture is working. If it's not, you'll need

---

Interface lift: Tips for redesigns

While there are no hard-and-fast redesign rules (other than that you should never underestimate the time involved in doing one), there are some guidelines that can help smooth the process for the development team and for users:

- Remember that your users don't see the site as much or as thoroughly as you do, so be cautious about doing substantial redesigns too frequently. Users like some degree of stability, and won't want to relearn tools every few months.

- Try not to "save up" minor maintenance changes for big designs. Maintenance is maintenance, and it shouldn't be grouped in with big revisions. Keep your old site clean until your new one premieres.

- Plan a redesign that's right for your site and your resources. A total overhaul might not be feasible for you, but several smaller evolutions may be. As long as your purpose and plan are clear, you can still achieve solid results.

- Offer help screens and tutorials to the new site, and let users know where their favorite parts are. If you've deleted something, tell them that too. You might even point them to something else on the Web that's similar to what you no longer offer.

- Create a 3-month plan for the site during the redesign. What might change? What might be added? Trying to predict these things will help you design a scalable site that will remain effective as you grow.

- Get advice and opinions from people who haven't been involved in the design. This should certainly include the site's intended users, but it might also involve consultants, fellow designers, or (if it's an organization) other employees.

to make some adjustments before going into production. This might necessitate running corrections past some users for a reality check, if time allows. Once you've constructed what you can be reasonably sure is a workable architecture, you'll need to record it in a final blueprint: the architecture plan.

The architecture plan is used throughout the production phase to ensure that content components are placed where they belong, not simply tacked on somewhere. Argus Associates, a firm specializing in web site architecture, creates an architectural style guide and implementation notes to accompany the blueprints they create. In Argus's case, they work closely with clients to ensure that content is placed according to the blueprints. This helps avoid stragglers—afterthoughts or add-ons that don't fit into the existing architecture.

How to do it: Revise your draft architecture plan from Phase 2. If there were any labels that users were confused about, make sure those are clarified. If you have content that appears in a rotating feature, make sure that is noted as well. You can use a program like Visio to create your architecture plan. Make sure your plan is distributed to everyone involved in production. There are more tips and examples of site architecture in Chapter 4.

Outline production specifications

Specifications, better known as "specs," document specific design and technical requirements that you've identified during the strategy and prototyping phases. They serve as directions for the production team on how to build the site, and ensure that the hard-won knowledge of earlier stages is not lost when the project goes into production.

How to do it: Create a brief list of items that represent important design and technical considerations. For example, "keep animation under 40K" might be a part of the specs for a GIF animation used somewhere in the site. List items should be clear, direct, and brief, since a lengthy specs document is much less likely to be used. Specs are most successful if used for concrete components (especially technical ones), such as a search function, animation, or shopping cart.

Phase 4: Implementation

Once you've tested and revised your proposed solution, you're ready to build the site. Before you move on to this production phase, you'll need to make sure the client or decision-maker has signed off on the approach. Ideally, that person has been involved throughout the strategy and prototyping phases. If not, you may be facing some difficult times.

In the implementation phase, your major tasks are:

1. Prepare and edit content.
2. Complete the interface design.
3. Develop the back end.
4. Troubleshoot new problems.

Prepare and edit content

Early in the production stage, someone needs to collect and track the development of all content. This might mean writing content from scratch, or chasing down materials the client has. It will almost certainly mean adapting content for webspace, converting it into usable formats, and editing for structure and style.

The Web hasn't exactly been a place where good editing reigns, but hopefully that will change. Editing is part of usability. It's also related to architecture, labeling, even perceptions about identity. The way text is structured and presented can be an important part of how we experience a site. Are there sub-headings to make the document more easily scanned? Are there typos that will confuse meaning or reflect poorly on the site's creators? Has someone structured the content for the way people read in webspace (which is much more like the way we read a newspaper than the way we read a book)? All of these things will need to be done by a web editor (or content developer) in the production stage.

How to do it: If you have no writing or editing experience, you'll need to hire someone who has experience in web content development. There are freelance editors and writers who can help you on a per-project basis. Whether you're doing content development in-house or hiring a freelancer, you'll need to make very sure you're thinking about version control. With version control, you set up a system so that all team members understand what the most current version of content is. This may be a system based on dates, in which the most recent version of the content is the one with the most recent date. It's possible to lose a really stunning amount of time simply by using the wrong version of content in production (yes, I've done it).

Complete the interface design

Working from the approved design comps, you'll need to finish the design work in the production phase. One of the first things you'll need to complete are page templates. Page templates are HTML shells that do not have content poured in yet. Your content team will need these shells in order to shape the text. Your technology team

"Editing is part of usability. The way text is structured and presented can be an important part of how we experience a site."

"Unless your back end infrastructure is as good as your content and design, you're not out of the woods."

will need them if you plan to generate pages from a database. They should be one of your first priorities in production.

How to do it: You need to have a reasonable sense of the content that will be poured in, otherwise your page templates may have to change later (for example, if you find that an article you thought was 300 words was actually 3,000). Once you know what you're working with, create all graphics. Create your HTML files without content, but don't greek them. Leave them blank. Test your code and you're ready to send the templates along.

Develop the back end

There are a lot of back-end considerations that affect navigation. For example, if your site is slow to load because of a tired server or thin connection, users will tend to blame you for designing with fat graphics. It doesn't matter if you've run every single one of them through Equilibrium Debabelizer or some other image-slimming software. Unless your back-end infrastructure is as good as your content and design, you're not out of the woods.

You will also need to make sure that the measures you put into place in the production phase are stable. One client of mine reported using a server that was so unstable, it would crash every half hour. Needless to say, this makes for a less-than-perfect user experience. (And needless to say, that server company lost his business when he switched to another product.)

Another factor you'll need to consider is the number of users you expect the site will get. It's tough to be sure. If you realistically expect a large number of visitors, you'll need to give some thought to your infrastructure and the way you choose applications and databases. How many consecutive users can you support? How scalable is the system if content grows, or if activity increases? These will directly affect the way users experience the site.

How to do it: If you're not sure how to judge whether your infrastructure is stable and scalable, there are very highly priced technology consultants you can hire to evaluate your setup. You can also contact product developers directly, who should be able to provide information on how their product will perform (though not necessarily in all settings). If you're using an ISP, make sure to ask them about their equipment and setup.

Troubleshoot new problems

When you put it all together—design, back end, content—new problems sometimes crop up that you'll need to troubleshoot. Content may be more extensive than originally planned, and you'll need to either cut back or alter the design. A back-end tool may not support a minor feature you wanted to offer, and you'll have to consider whether to keep it or drop it. One of the worst things that can happen is that you'll discover the site you built can't live on a client's server (this is rare), or that a client or decision-maker throws a whole new content area at you just as you're finishing. You'll need to be able to make quick, last-minute decisions.

How to do it: Use your project knowledge so far—particularly the architecture plan and strategy decisions—as a guide when solving these last-minute problems. For example, if the client hands you new content that doesn't jibe with the defined audience, think twice about just including it. Instead, suggest other possibilities for that content. (If you're an outside firm, clients should not be handing you new content this late in the game anyway, though it does happen.) Keeping a tight focus until the end is easier if you keep project plans at hand.

Phase 5: Launch

The site is built, and you're almost done—or if you're taking on regular production, you're just beginning. In the launch phase, which focuses on the period just before and after the site premieres, you should plan on doing a lot of testing. Scripts may be buggy, design may not be compatible with a certain platform or browser, and there could be other unforeseen problems you need to deal with. During this phase, you can also do a final usability test to ensure you've thought everything through. Finally, you'll need to market your site and submit it to search engines to help people find you.

In this phase, important tasks include:

1. Do quality assurance testing.
2. Market the service.

Do quality assurance testing

Before you launch, you'll need to test your site to see that everything is in good working order. In this final stage, you'll need to test for:

- Usability
- Consistency and accuracy
- Compatibility and degradability

vivid studios takes this testing stage so seriously, they do three separate kinds of testing before they launch. vivid's three types of tests are *functional testing*, which includes stress and browser/platform

"The development process (whether it's in the software industry, in print publishing, or on the Web) is a cyclical thing."

"Periodic testing can point out major problems, or tell you that things you thought were major problems really aren't."

compatibility testing; *content testing*, which includes HTML verification, proofreading, and usability testing; and a final phase called *iteration and bug fixes* for checking any last-minute problems.

How to do it: For some testing, you'll need to find someone who has not been involved directly in the site production, yet is familiar with the project. Someone with a little distance from the actual production should be the one to do the quality assurance (QA) testing. In QA testing, you're looking for broken links, inconsistencies, typos in headers or titles, and other snafus. These are hopefully easily corrected.

In compatibility testing, the developer tests the site on relevant browsers and platforms. You don't need to test on every web browser ever made, or on every conceivable computer/monitor combination. You do need to test on a reasonable sample that represents the middle ground of what your intended audience will be using. If home users (parents, children, older people) are part of your intended audience, you'll have to test on America Online, on monitors with only 256 colors, and over a modem. If tech-savvy users are part of your intended audience, you'll need to test on upper browser versions, which can be a bit quirky. Your site doesn't have to look the same in all situations, but it should degrade well (i.e., be navigable and readable) for your primary audience.

In usability testing, you'll want to either find an experienced usability consultant or read up on proper methods. There's quite a lot you can do to bias testers, if you're not careful. To make your tests as effective as possible, make sure you don't ask leading questions like "Does that navigation bar bother you?" There are some excellent "talk out loud" methods you can use to get people to talk about what they're doing. Your role is primarily as an observer in usability tests, not as a tour guide. If the testing highlights any problems at this stage, you can either take the extra time to correct them or plan to correct them in another version of your site. For more on how to do user testing, see Chapter 3, *Designing for Users*, or pick up a copy of *Usability Inspection Methods* (Wiley, 1994) by Jakob Nielsen and Robert Mack.

This is it. You're down to the wire. When this testing is done, you're ready to launch.

Market the service

At last! The site you've worked so hard on is finally live. So where is everyone? What happened to the big splash you were going to make? If you haven't marketed your site, people may have some trouble finding you.

How to do it: There are two types of marketing that can help you here: traditional and web marketing. Your web marketing tasks begin with submitting your site to search engines and directories. Make sure that you have used META tags within your files to provide information about the site (such as relevant keywords and a description). Not all search engines support META tags, but they're useful for the ones that do. Get as many links as you can from other sites—without compromising your mission or your integrity, of course. Being linked to from other destinations is possibly the most effective way to get visitors.

Traditional marketing measures can help, too. How many commercials, billboards, and brochures have you seen recently that sported a URL? I've stopped counting, it's become so common. Sending a press release to technology magazines or to periodicals related to your subject area is a good start. You might also want to try sending out direct mail, doing a prize drawing, buying or bartering advertising space (online or off), and printing the URL on stationery and business cards. All of these help bring people to your site. In a way, it's the first form of navigation they'll do: arrive.

Phase 6: Maintenance & growth

When your site finally premieres, you'll probably want to plan an extended vacation—and by this point, you'll need one. But unless you're a web firm that avoids maintenance (and some do), your work is only beginning. The development process (whether it's in the software industry, in print publishing, or on the Web) is a cyclical thing.

The maintenance and growth phase can be a difficult one for some sites. You may discover that you haven't considered a major piece of content that suddenly needs to be included, or you may find that you need to scramble to keep up with a competitor. A new business alliance or sponsorship might require you to make changes to your site. New back end or production tools might require you to adapt your approach. These unforeseen factors can sometimes make the maintenance and growth phase as demanding as anything that's come before.

In the maintenance and growth phase, you should expect to:

1. Manage new content or features.

2. Interpret server logs.

3. Check links.

4. Conduct periodic testing.

Creating a style guide

According to "Creating Your Site's Style Guide," a Web Review article by Brenda Kienan and Daniel A. Tauber, a style guide should include information about the format and structure of the site; conventions for HTML and page layout; specifications for using graphics and multimedia; standards of editorial style and usage; policies regarding linking and crosslinking; guidelines for using the company logo, copyright notices, trademarks, and other legalese; and procedures for reviewing and approving content before it is posted.

Read more at *webreview.com/wr/pub/98/02/06/webmaster/index.html*

Redesign resources

Design for Change: Looking Beyond Opening Day
www.webreview.com/96/04/12/webarch/index.html

ZD Internet Magazine's Website Makeovers
www8.zdnet.com/zdimag/makeover/

Swack on Design
webreview.com/97/01/10/feature/index2.html

Manage new content or features

Because growth is often not only inevitable but desirable, you'll need to plan for it. One of the best ways to ensure consistency of approach (especially when more than 2 or 3 people are working on a site) is to use a style guide. A style guide lays down the specifics of your approach to typography, layout, color, linking, tone, and whatever else might come up in regular production.

What about other new content that might be outside of the scope of your architecture or site plan? Review ideas on a case-by-case basis. If they have merit, plan for an "upgrade" of your site from version 1.0 to version 1.1. If it's extreme and might merit a redesign, you'll upgrade to 2.0—and go back to square one of the process.

How to do it: To create a style guide, you may first want to see examples from other organizations. A style guide should be detailed but not too dense, or it won't get used on a regular basis. Instead, it will sit on a shelf somewhere. An online style guide, placed on an intranet or extranet, can be an excellent solution, since it's easy to update and takes up no space on workers' desks.

Interpret server logs

If you've done your marketing, you've probably got some traffic by now. Tracking and analyzing your visitor logs can reveal some interesting patterns. For example, you can tell from your logs what files or pages are most frequently requested, which can tell you what features people are clicking on most. You can also tell what things people are clicking on least, which may help you ferret out labeling problems or weed out content that is not important to your users. It's always a good idea to support server log analysis with user tests if you're going to use them to make design decisions. Real humans will often tell you clearly what a hit log can only vaguely imply.

How to do it: There are numerous decent site analysis packages you can buy, though the quality and scope differs. Determine what you want to try to track, and then try to find a package that suits your needs. If you're using an ISP, you won't have much choice but to go with what they're using. Sometimes, you can get your "raw" hit logs, however, and run your own site analysis on them. Ask your ISP for more information if you're in this situation.

Check links

If I had a penny for every dead link I've come across on the Web, I'd be living on a yacht floating somewhere in the Mediterranean. Dead links are as ubiquitous as you can get in this medium, as commonplace as cracks in a sidewalk. For users, however, that does nothing to dull the fact that they are really, really annoying. No, you don't have to check links daily. The situation is not that far gone. But you do need to check them about once every month or two, just to be on the safe side.

How to do it: You can check links the painful, manual way if you have a small site. Simply go through every link on every page, methodically, until you know they're all working. Don't try this if you have more than ten screens, or more than about 30 external links. For anything larger than this, you'll want to invest in link checking software. You can also visit an online site checker such as Web Site Garage (*www.websitegarage.com*), which will "inspect" the links on your site.

Conduct periodic testing

Every so often, you should plan on checking in with your users to see if you're still meeting their needs. Has the climate changed since you first launched? Is a competitor going one better? Has your site's growth made it awkward and hard to use? Users are the only ones who can really tell you this. Don't pay much attention to comments you get from feedback forms, though they're sometime interesting. They tend to lean toward the very positive or very negative, instead of representing the reasoned middle ground.

Part of understanding where your site stands is knowing when to redesign. Periodic testing can point out major problems, or tell you that things you thought were major problems really aren't. Because growth and maintenance is an ongoing thing, and because the Web is still moving faster than other media, you'll have to stay on top of things.

How to do it: Regular testing can be conducted in much the same way as the usability testing you do near launch. You may want to add an occasional focus group or some of the user interviewing methods employed in Phase 1. These will help you make sure your site still serves users, and isn't just taking up webspace.

Recap

Process can be widely different depending on your setting and project. Small development firms and sole developers may find that they can't handle all stages with equal competence. If you're in this predicament, don't feel bad; it's common. Even among large firms, partnering with organizations that offer services you can't is an effective strategy.

Find out more

Adams, James L. *Conceptual Blockbusting: A Guide to Better Ideas*. Addison-Wesley, 1986.

James, Geoffrey. *Success Secrets from Silicon Valley: How to Make Your Teams More Effective (No Matter What Business You're In)*. Times, 1996.

Mok, Clement. *Designing Business: Multiple Media, Multiple Disciplines*. Macmillan, 1996.

Moody, Fred. *I Sing the Body Electronic: A Year With Microsoft on the Multimedia Frontier*. Viking, 1995.

Schrage, Michael. *No More Teams! Mastering the Dynamics of Creative Collaboration*. Doubleday, 1989.

Sellers, Don. *Getting Hits: The Definitive Guide to Promoting Your Website*. Peachpit, 1997.

Siegel, David. *Secrets of Successful Web Sites: Project Management on the World Wide Web*. Macmillan, 1997.

There's a marked trend toward alliance-building and team development that puts the sole developer at risk—and rightly so. Today's sites are increasingly complex and require the skills and experience of a group of web developers. Call me crazy, but I think the days of the sole webmaster are dead. Long live the web team.

## CHAPTER SEVEN

NAVIGATION DESIGN FOR SHOPPING SITES

No clever arrangement of bad eggs
ever made a good omelet.
—C.S. Lewis

In this chapter

- Laying the groundwork

- Outlining specific goals

- Who's doing it right: Amazon.com

- Who's doing it right: Garden Escape

- Who's doing it right: FAO Schwarz

- Recap

Why does Nordstrom's, a retail chain, consistently win customer service awards? What makes Amazon.com one of the Web's shopping success stories? Luck and timing may have something to do with it, but not much. Responding to customer demands in better, faster, and more creative ways is what really drives these successes.

What these and other successful stores show, whether they're online or off, is a concern with the whole process, as well as with the "whole" customer (not simply their credit card number). What will users expect to do or find at various stages? What requirements need to be met before, for example, customers will give any credit card information? Understanding the process of shopping—the entire experience, from start to finish—helps these stores successfully guide users through it.

Think about the last time you went to a mall or department store, and what that experience was like. What store did you shop in, and why did you choose it over others? Did you go with a specific item in mind? Did you need to ask the sales staff any questions? Were you able to try items before you bought them? If you used a credit card, how did you know whether the store accepted Visa or American Express?

Most importantly, if something went wrong at any of these points, was it enough to make you walk away? For most shoppers, frustration is a powerful deterrent.

"Successful stores, whether they're online or off, show a concern for the whole process."

Laying the groundwork

Thinking over questions like the ones above can help you become more attuned to shopping behaviors we take for granted in daily life. For shopping sites, whether you're selling pork rinds or music CDs, there are some shared concerns that can help form a checklist for navigation design. After "first-tier" user expectations such as understanding one's current location, shoppers tend to have the "second tier" expectations shown in Table 7-1.

Table 7-1. *User goals and expectations: Shopping*

First Tier (general navigation questions)	Where am I? Where can I go? How will I get there? How can I get back to where I once was?
Second Tier (purpose-oriented questions)	How do I know my financial information is secure? How can I protect my privacy? How can I find the item I want? What if I'm not sure exactly what I'm looking for? How can I preview products to see if they're right for me? What if I have problems or returns?

How do I know my financial information is secure?

For most shoppers, feeling secure about entering financial information is the most important consideration in shopping online. In the 8th GVU User Survey (*www.cc.gatech.edu/gvu/user_surveys/survey-1997-10/*) conducted in the fall of 1997, shoppers overwhelmingly listed security as a concern. The issue of security is also bound up with issues of trust, and even with misconceptions about Internet commerce. You may know that e-commerce can be safe and secure, but your average user may have heard rumors and reports to the contrary.

But why be concerned about security in the context of navigation? Failing to handle security issues can create a serious obstacle for your users, as surely as if you hung a sign warning "Keep Out!" Solving these issues by incorporating security measures (and also advertising them to users) communicates just the opposite. It tells shoppers that you have thought about and handled their most important concerns—so that they don't have to.

If you can create a shopping environment in which you both ease shoppers' immediate security concerns and gain their trust, you've gone a long way toward success. FAO Schwarz does this skillfully within the space of one page, shown in Figure 7-1, sending the soothing message that "shopping at FAO is easy and secure." By promoting their familiar brand and promoting the ease and security of their store, FAO Schwarz has become one of the success stories of online shopping.

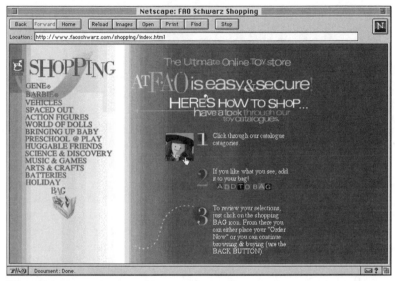

Figure 7-1. *FAO Schwarz sends a reassuring message to shoppers: "Shopping at FAO is easy and secure."*

How can I protect my privacy?

Privacy is second only to security in most shoppers' minds, according to the 8th GVU User Survey. Like security, it can be an obstacle or an incentive to users, depending on how it is handled. Advertising a policy that supports the privacy of shoppers' data and preferences helps to create a safe and welcoming environment.

Reassurances about privacy can be useful regardless of what you're selling, but are essential for some types of merchandise. Anyone selling porn on the Net has probably already discovered this, but booksellers, stores selling products for children, merchants selling services instead of products, and many other commercial ventures can also benefit from creating a "privacy-friendly" environment. Would you want a record of all of your purchases to be available over a network, or sold to other companies? Probably not.

One large shopping site offers an example of putting privacy-related obstacles in the paths of shoppers. In an effort to find out more about its visitors, the store forces shoppers to fill out a market

"Directed shoppers know exactly what they want. They don't need advice or a sales pitch. They just want to find a product as quickly and simply as possible."

research questionnaire before they can purchase products. The use of a survey as a barrier is pretty common on the Web (and despite good intentions on the part of the site developers, it does act as a really effective wall), but this has to rank as one of the most unfortunate places to put a survey. Why block shoppers on the way to the checkout line? If there has to be a survey, it's better to place it after the checkout.

How can I find the item I want?

Some shoppers will come to your site knowing exactly what they want. If you sell computer equipment and supplies, you may get a customer who wants to find a specific part number for his printer. Another customer may want to purchase a particular piece of software for a particular platform. These are directed shoppers. They probably don't need encouragement, advice, or a sales pitch. They just need to get the product they want as quickly and simply as possible.

How do you build for directed shoppers? The ability to do a quick search of a product database is an essential feature for these shoppers. A product index can also be crucial. You may find that a very high volume of requests have been made for a certain item, and decide to put a shortcut to the most popular products on your site's front door. These methods can't replace a clear and descriptive architecture, but they can help build in fast routes for these focused users.

What if I'm not sure exactly what I'm looking for?

Another segment of your audience will be people who are shopping for gifts, doing the online equivalent of window shopping, and browsing in large categories. These casual shoppers often enter your store with little or no idea of what they're looking for. They might know that they are looking for a new couch, but haven't decided on a color or style. They might be shopping for new clothes, and are interested in what your site has to offer. They may need to buy a holiday gift for a video game junkie, but don't have a clue where to begin.

Serving these users is a little more complicated than serving a focused shopper. Often, they need guidance or advice on purchases. They may want to ask the opinion of a knowledgeable sales clerk, or even find out what other people are buying. Amazon.com, a Web-based bookstore, features a Recommendation Center that is perfectly tailored for these casual shoppers (Figure 7-2). If you visit their Recommendation Center—even when you're not in the mood to buy—hold onto your wallet. Getting recommendations is so easy, you'll forget you weren't even looking for any.

Figure 7-2. *Amazon.com's Recommendation Center is perfect for casual shoppers.*

Building a store that welcomes casual shoppers may involve offering store or product tours, tailored gift recommendations, easily browsed categories and departments, and possibly even access to a real live human being. If you can't hire someone to answer questions and give advice, consider building a discussion forum where customers can talk to each other. These shoppers may take a much longer and more circuitous route to get to the checkout line, but if you offer them the help they need, they could become your most loyal customers.

How can I preview products to see if they're right for me?

Would you buy a car sight unseen, without a test drive or even a glossy brochure? Probably not. Most people want to "try before they buy." Providing this important feature removes a common navigation obstacle from your shopping site.

What people need to preview depends a lot on the product. A car is one of the most complex items that could potentially be previewed on the Web, but someone's creative mind came up with 360-degree "surround video" to help solve that dilemma. Previewing a book is

Design tip

Use natural language. Putting choices in the everyday language of your audience helps avoid confusion. Terms should be descriptive enough so that users know what their options are, which may require using a brief phrase rather than one clever catch word.

relatively easy, and would probably involve a cover shot, some vital statistics, and maybe a brief selection. Clothing is also not terribly complex, requiring mainly that people can view all color options, sizes, and other specifications, and possibly get a sense of the fabric.

Some sites now offer novel and exciting ways to preview products, ways that surpass even what we can do in person. Being able to rapidly "configure" outfits is a growing feature on clothing sites. Try this in your local mall, and it'll take you the better part of a day (and probably cause the salespeople angst).

Not every product is made to sell on the Web, so not all products can be previewed with the same degree of success. For example, Wal-Mart offers roasted chicken for sale on its web site. How would you preview taste on the Web? We're not there—yet.

What if I have problems or returns?

Before people will put their hard-earned money down, they need to know a few things about what they're buying. They also need to know about store policies, especially returns. The ability to predict what will happen if something goes wrong is part of the shopping process, and in today's climate of telecommunications scams, it's also part of being a savvy consumer.

Web shoppers need these customer service functions as much as or more than they do when they're shopping at the local market. Even experienced Web users will have questions about potential problems. What if they need to stop in the middle? What if they decide they don't like the purchase? What if their browser crashes, or their credit card doesn't work, or they enter the wrong shipping information? Knowing in advance that the store can offer help if things go wrong allows people to be much freer in purchasing.

As with security or privacy, the best way to remove navigation barriers associated with customer service functions is to advertise policies openly. It doesn't mean you need to place the full text of the policies in the path of your users, or make them read lengthy legal documentation. A simple and obvious statement encouraging people to "find out about our return policy" or follow a clear link to customer service is usually enough.

Outlining specific goals

If we organize these common shopping goals into our goals and expectations chart, it will look like Table 7-1. But there is still another layer, or tier, we need to add to this chart in order to complete a navigation design. This third tier will outline questions and expectations that are specific to a particular type of product and audience.

For example, if you run a Web-based bookstore, you'll quickly discover that book lovers have many shared demands. If you are in the business of selling real estate on the Web, you'll find that home buyers have a particular set of goals and needs. Each audience and approach will introduce a third tier of goals into the mix. Table 7-2 shows how you might map out typical user goals for a bookstore.

"Casual shoppers often enter your store with little or no idea of what they're looking for. Often, they need guidance or shopper's advisory."

Table 7-2. *User goals and expectations: Shopping: Books*

First Tier (general navigation questions)	Where am I? Where can I go? How will I get there? How can I get back to where I once was?
Second Tier (purpose-oriented questions)	How do I know my financial information is secure? How can I protect my privacy? How can I find the item I want? What if I'm not sure exactly what I'm looking for? How can I preview products to see if they're right for me? What if I have problems or returns?
Third Tier (product- or audience-oriented questions)	How can I find books by a particular author? How can I find books that are similar to books I like? How do I know what the reading level of a book is? Where can I get reviews or recommendations? How do I find out about new releases and awards?

Discovering user goals

Finding out what these specific third-tier goals are may seem like guesswork, but it's actually relatively straightforward: ask people. By conducting focus groups, user tests, and other research, you can get a staggering amount of information about what people want and expect. Often, these research results contain the seeds of ideas that can put you head and shoulders above the competition.

To find out more about shopping behavior and shoppers' goals, you might try some of the following methods:

- Spend some time in a local mall, observing what draws people into stores. What other shopping behaviors seem to repeat themselves?

- To find out more about selling a particular type of product, such as fishing equipment, arrange to talk with a local retailer. Ask them what their most frequently asked questions are, and what visitors seem to be looking for. Then talk to someone (or several

"Successful stores know that keeping customers happy is part of winning sales."

people) who might buy that type of equipment, and ask them similar questions.

- Keep a pocket notepad with you. The next time you go to the grocery store, go gift shopping, or need to purchase a piece of software, observe the process from start to finish. At what points, if any, did you need to ask for help? At what points, if any, were you ready to abandon the sale if something went wrong?

- Research books and articles on shopping behavior and store design. You can find a good deal of material in architectural publications. There may even be a local course you can take on the topic. The issues involved in retail architectural design may not be exactly parallel to our issues, but there are certainly shared concerns. Understanding how architects handle guiding people in a retail space can offer some interesting insights.

- Browse books and articles on consumer advice and tips. What are consumers asking? What advice are they being given? How can you incorporate these findings into your site?

- Arrange some user tests and interviews. With one user at a time, have the tester look at a variety of shopping sites, including yours if you have one. Ask them to talk you through what they are doing, and to talk about their reactions as they navigate through these sites. Avoid giving them any guidance or tips along the way. When they've had a chance to use several different sites, ask them to explain what they liked about each site, and what they didn't like. Finally, ask them what they'd like to see these sites offer, if they could have anything their hearts desired.

In looking at all of these methods, search for patterns in what you find. Do shoppers consistently ask for a particular feature or function? Is there a question that continues to come up? These patterns can help you not only isolate problems, but identify potential solutions.

What about merchants' goals?

With all of this focus on what shoppers want, what about the needs of the merchant? Merchants need to make money, or the store will eventually go under. Luckily, pleasing customers is not a matter of giving products away or suffering impossible discounts (though a bargain is always nice). Shoppers routinely pay full price for products, both on the Web and off, because of loyalty to a merchant or because of convenience. Price is a factor, but ease, support, selection, and trust are the real indicators of success.

Most successful stores know that keeping customers happy is part of winning sales. It's fairly simple math. Building in features that support

Figure C-1. *An @tlas feature on illustration puts links where people will need them and labels them clearly.*

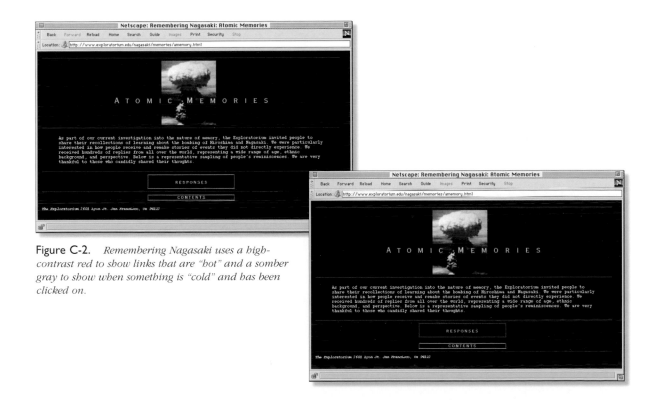

Figure C-2. *Remembering Nagasaki uses a high-contrast red to show links that are "hot" and a somber gray to show when something is "cold" and has been clicked on.*

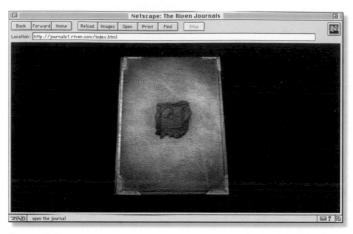

Figure C-3. *The navigation used in the Riven Journals fits the entertainment purpose perfectly.*

Figure C-4. *The "Quebe" at Passage to Vietnam reveals multiple navigation options within the space of about one square inch.*

Figure C-5. *Two design comps show experimentation with typography.*

Figure C-6. *Garden Escape's designers took the time to understand gardeners' habits.*

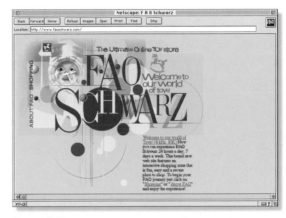

Figure C-7. *FAO Schwarz is one of the most intuitive and entertaining shopping sites on the Web.*

Figure C-8. *Firefly was one of the Web's first community spaces, and it continues to attract a large and active pool of members.*

Figure C-9. *Café Utne is the most active online community in North America.*

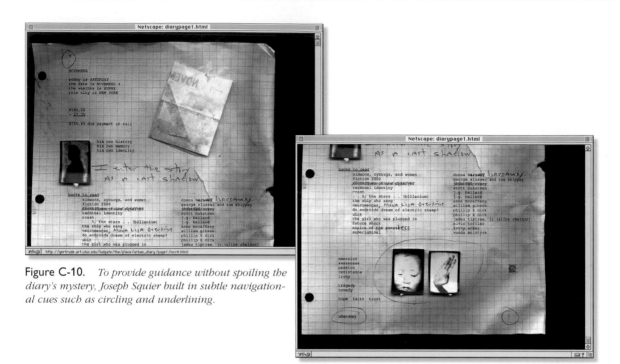

Figure C-10. *To provide guidance without spoiling the diary's mystery, Joseph Squier built in subtle navigational cues such as circling and underlining.*

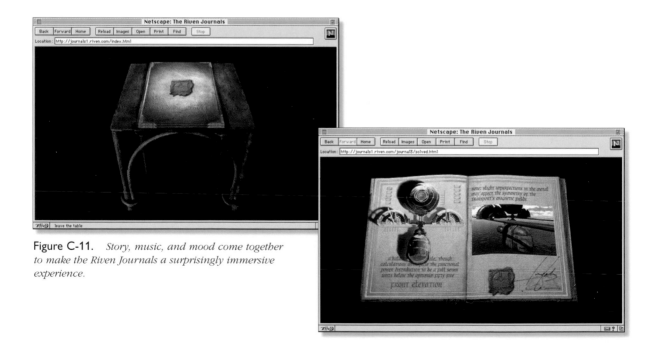

Figure C-11. *Story, music, and mood come together to make the Riven Journals a surprisingly immersive experience.*

Figure C-12. *When a frame in the Crimson Empire comic has finished animating, a gray border appears around it, signaling that you can move on to the next frame.*

Figure C-13. *Razorfish's corporate site skillfully balances guidance and flexibility, cutting-edge technology and accessible browsing.*

Figure C-14. *Razorfish uses rollovers to provide additional cues to the site's content.*

Figure C-15. *IBM's corporate site is an information-rich destination, not a skimpy marketing pamphlet.*

Figure C-16. *Powazek.com is Derek Powazek's showcase for his personal and professional projects.*

Figure C-17. *Derek Powazek links to previous versions of his personal site, encouraging people to explore its ongoing evolution.*

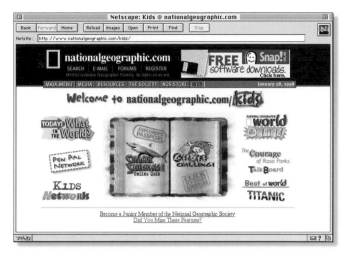

Figure C-18. *National Geographic has consistently been ranked one of the Web's best learning sites. Shown here is its "Kids" section.*

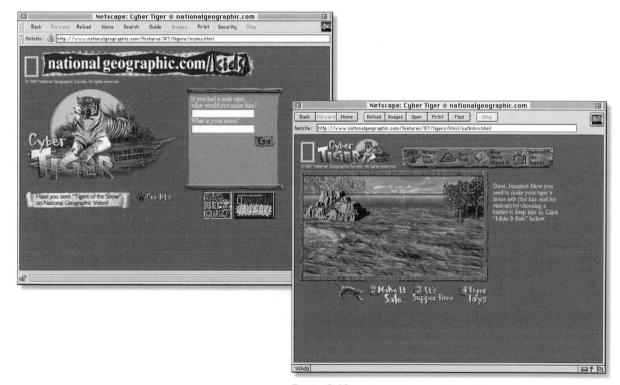

Figure C-19. *National Geographic's Cyber Tiger module is a good example of how guidance can make learning fun.*

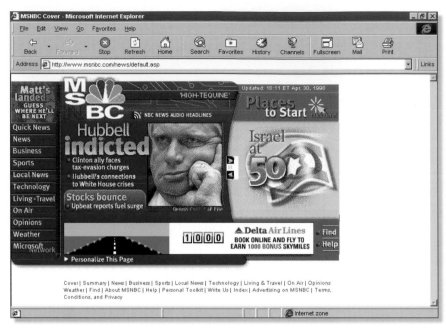

Figure C-20.   *MSNBC's site manages the complexity of a daily news site.*

Figure C-21.   *Computers.com builds in features designed to increase the speed and effectiveness of your equipment quest.*

typical shopper goals and expectations is part of investing in the store's future, not just the customer's success. On the Web, e-commerce is a proven technology, but only a handful of companies are doing it right. In this current climate, merchants who understand how to serve shoppers on the Web face little real competition.

Amazon.com

www.amazon.com

Who's doing it right: Amazon.com

Many shopping sites are "born" from someone's existing database. It's a common but uninspired beginning, since the experience of shopping bears little resemblance to entering keywords into a search box. The Web's best shopping sites are already pushing past their roots as search boxes, developing into flexible spaces with support for many different shopping behaviors—from searching and browsing to more personalized, guided shopping.

Amazon.com, founded by Jeff Bezos in 1995, is the undisputed leader when it comes to a personalized, user-centered shopping experience, as shown in Figure 7-3. Though it once consisted of little more than a search prompt on top of a vast database of titles, the site is now one of the best online destinations for book lovers—and one of the most lucrative ventures in the brief history of e-commerce.

Figure 7-3. *Amazon.com offers a personalized, user-centered shopping experience.*

What's behind Amazon.com's success? Timing probably had something to do with it, but service is what it's really about. Give customers more selection, easier access, better previewing, simpler purchasing, more content. As Kay Dangaard, Amazon.com's director of media relations, explains, "The changes we've made, the innovations we've introduced, have been in response to real customer needs and desires." With the frequent addition of new ways of revisiting this vast collection of titles, every road seems to lead to the checkout.

Amazon.com's strengths lie in its speed, accessibility, flexibility, feedback, and customization. Combined with an exhaustive database of titles and a responsive staff, it's a formula that's hard to beat.

Speed

Amazon.com is a directed shopper's dream store. It's possible to blaze in with a particular title in mind and blaze out again three minutes later having ordered it. Amazon.com has been constantly improving the search and purchasing features of their site, making it a haven for impulse buyers and the book obsessed. They've streamlined their regular shopping cart as much as possible. A simple keyword search box is available on every page. More importantly, they've added "1-Click[SM]" ordering, shown in Figure 7-4.

1-Click is possibly the fastest way to buy a book, online or off. At the moment of purchase, no credit cards change hands, no addresses are exchanged, no one asks for shipping information. You simply press a button and it's done. (You do need to enter all that personal information in order to register for 1-Click Ordering, but you need only enter it once.) Ordering is literally as easy as clicking a button.

1-Click is so rapid and easy that the store actually felt they needed to build in some safeguards. As Kay explained, "We combine 1-Click orders in reasonable ways to save shipping charges for customers. We also make it simple (and obvious) to cancel a 1-Click order if someone places an order by accident, or if they simply change their mind."

Accessibility

I first came across Amazon.com when I was working in a library. Librarians were some of the first to latch onto the site, since not only did it offer something closely resembling *Books in Print* on the Web, but it was also accessible on the text-based web browsers most libraries had (and many still have).

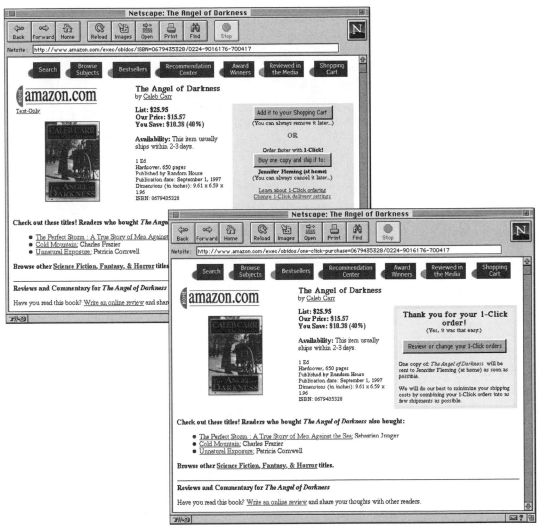

Figure 7-4. *1-Click ordering on Amazon.com is possibly the fastest way to buy a book, online or off.*

Amazon.com continues to be accessible to a very wide audience of web users, from underfunded public libraries using Lynx or archaic versions of Netscape to corporate users with all the latest equipment. A text-only version is available from every page—no small feat for a site that is updated daily, handles traffic in the millions, and has an expanding number of content areas. Even with help from a database, it's a daunting job.

Their commitment to the widest possible audience has served them well, as it turns out. And it makes a lot of sense. Why not spend the extra time to make a site accessible, if it means you'll win a larger pool of potential customers?

Jeff Bezos, Amazon.com

Flexibility

In its early days, Amazon.com offered three or four different ways of searching their database of titles, and that wasn't bad. Now, however, there are more ways of accessing book information than even the neighborhood library offers.

Kay points out that "different people want to navigate in different ways. Even a single individual may have different navigation needs at different times." Directed shoppers can search by a variety of fields, including author, title, subject, or keyword. Casual shoppers can browse through the virtual aisles, looking at recommended books in a variety of subject categories. Building in this flexibility means that most customers find what they want—even if they weren't quite sure what they wanted.

Feedback

There's a lot of jargon in the world of e-commerce, and some sites do a better job than others of diffusing it. Amazon.com, especially in its shopping cart, offers everyday language and labels and a high level of feedback about actions.

How do you know your order has gone through, for example? How do you know what to do if you've made an error? In both the 1-Click Ordering and the standard shopping cart, the site tells you clearly what you've ordered, whether you were successful, and what you should expect now, as shown in Figure 7-5.

Amazon.com has also improved feedback about location within the site. A small colored dot marks the section you are in, helping to establish a sense of where you are within the space.

Customization

The site has also been adding sophisticated options for customizing your experience. From a navigation perspective, customization can be an excellent way to build in highly tailored shortcuts for users, often saving them the time of having to enter repeat information or preferences.

One of the best examples of customization is their recommendation center, which (among other things) features personal recommendations for registered visitors. When you visit the site, a personalized welcome message offers you the latest crop of recommendations based on your buying history. This personal touch is sure to bring users back to the site to get the next batch of book tips.

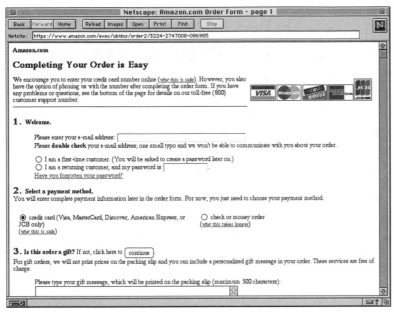

Figure 7-5. *Amazon.com's shopping cart uses everyday language to avoid confusion.*

Design tip
Keep navigational choices to a minimum. More is not necessarily better when it comes to navigation options, and many users will feel overwhelmed.

To extend this personal focus and, as Kay explains it, "leverage the knowledge and opinions of other customers—a million or so of them," Amazon.com also offers BookMatcherSM, part of the recommendation center. By first rating a number of titles you've already read, you can have BookMatcher generate additional titles you might like, as shown in Figure 7-6. BookMatcher uses NetPerception's Group Lens technology to generate these recommendations.

On every title screen, the site also lists other books purchased by people who bought the current title. It's almost as good as getting someone's hand-picked booklist, or being able to snoop through their bookshelves. Often, the database being what it is (vast), this is the only way you might come across a title, and it's an excellent way to build in shortcuts.

Amazon.com is topping the investment charts despite increasing competition from large chains. What's kept this bookstore prospering in changeable times? More than anything, they have a clear mission and a proven strategy. It's tempting to think their success is based on some impossibly clever technology, but in reality it seems to be more centered around people—around understanding customers better than anyone else does.

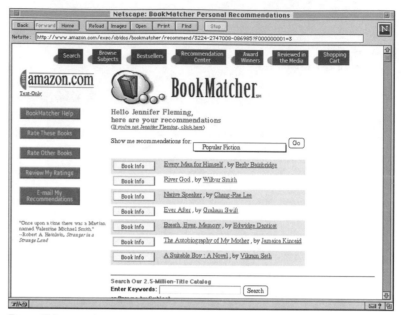

Figure 7-6. *Based on the books you like, Amazon.com's BookMatcher can suggest others.*

"Stay focused on serving your customers," Kay advises developers who are getting into e-commerce. "The technology is a means to that end. It should never be an end in itself."

Who's doing it right: Garden Escape

Coming from a gardening family, I know that gardeners can be a tough lot to cater to on the Web. It's not because of any cranky disposition or lack of technology skills. It's just that if they have spare time they'd usually rather spend it in the garden, not at the computer. To really succeed with this audience, then, it takes a close study of what they need, what would bring them out of the garden and onto the Web. Garden Escape, shown in Figure C-6, has done this foot-work, and the result is one of the Web's most compelling gardening destinations.

Spend a little time with gardeners and you'll notice that they usually horde plant and seed catalogs, and spend most of the winter months planning purchases and nursing seedlings. Most gardeners also have some sort of special interest, such as peonies or roses or pumpkins, and will want to not only purchase specimens but find out about plant history and cultivation techniques. Some gardeners are nearly religious about tools, collecting the latest trowels, stools, gloves, or machines. And most importantly, nearly every gardener starts out with a garden that's already been planted with something. "Mix and match" takes on new meaning when you're trying to coordinate growing things.

Garden Escape offers a spectrum of products and services carefully designed to draw gardeners in by understanding their habits. Throughout the site, Garden Escape balances a wealth of information with a down-to-earth presentation (pardon the pun), using clear and friendly language to help establish a welcoming tone.

Garden Escape's strengths are in the areas of community, support, and previewing. Their focus on community means they don't easily fit into simple categories. Is it a shop? A magazine? A forum for discussion? The site is all of those, because gardeners want all of those, ideally in one place.

| **Garden Escape** |
| *www.garden.com* |

Community

Gardeners frequently come together to talk about techniques, exchange cuttings, and brood over pests or the weather. There is a river of underground information passed from gardener to gardener along with cuttings and seeds. This makes it an entirely natural idea to build community features into a gardening store. It not only serves shoppers and provides them with ways to increase their knowledge, it's an excellent way to encourage people to linger at your site.

Getting a good definition for community is a tough proposition, but the most crucial component is allowing participation among visitors, not simply between visitors and the site. In the section called "Let's Talk Dirt," Garden Escape builds in simple and easily used discussion forums (both Java- and HTML-based, for maximum access), shown in Figure 7-7. Guests can pick a username or log in as a guest (in which case they assume the name and image of a flower species). User needs about privacy are calmed by the ability to be anonymous.

Being able to talk with others about whether a certain plant is a good choice or what product might control their pest problem is an excellent method for promoting products "second hand." If a user discovers the organic pest control method they've been looking for, they're likely to buy it from Garden Escape. The site provides navigation icons for its main sections—including shopping—on every page, so that a trip from the forum to the shop is a mere click away.

Support

The site very strongly communicates that they are there to help. Remember the second-tier shopper concern with what happens if

Design tip

Provide return users with shortcuts to important sections and ways to skip over information they've already seen. Keep a balance between the availability of shortcuts and a clear, simple interface in order to avoid clutter.

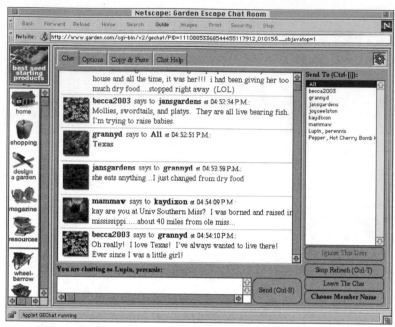

Figure 7-7. *Garden Escape offers Java and HTML versions of their chat area, "Let's Talk Dirt."*

there are problems? Garden Escape seems to go one step further, offering a proactive approach that offers support from the front door to the checkout and beyond.

Simple language helps. In the shopping cart (called the Wheelbarrow), shown in Figure 7-8, customers can click on "What's going to happen when I click the order button?" to find out what they're getting themselves into. Alternatives are offered for many of the site's potentially browser-specific features, such as the discussion forums, graphical navigation icons, and even ordering.

A wide array of resources provide the majority of information a gardener might need to make shopping decisions, significantly lowering the chance that a shopper will need to leave the site during the shopping process. A magazine offers articles and commentary. A zone map provides climate information for your area. A garden planner means you don't even need to get pen and paper to sketch layouts. And a glossary provides explanations for potentially confusing terms, which are linked where they appear. Each of these sections also maintains a consistent navigation scheme, making it easy to jump among areas of the site.

An additional support feature helps to increase the likelihood of purchases. A "notebook" allows customers to store the name and

Figure 7-8. *For a gardening site, a wheelbarrow works well as a shopping cart metaphor.*

description of items they might be interested in, offering a sort of layaway or very long-term shopping basket. The site features a large selection of products, and this is an excellent way to help shoppers keep track of ideas as they move through.

Garden Escape also excels at cross-selling, which not only provides a support feature but is a smart business practice. At the end of most plant descriptions, the site includes related books, companion plants, and tools and accessories. For gardeners, this is an excellent service. For the store, this is a brilliant way to introduce other items the shopper might have missed, and potentially increase sales.

Previewing

Garden Escape's Garden Planner, shown in Figure 7-9, is a powerful feature that helps solve one of a gardener's main problems: layout. Planning a garden sometimes seems like an exercise in guesswork. How tall will that plant grow? When does it flower? What color is it? How much room do I need between plants? How many plants will I need? Allowing gardeners to experiment with layouts on the Web is an excellent way to support product previewing.

The Garden Planner, which is a Java application, looks a lot like the common CD-ROM gardening software with a similar purpose. Gardeners can open an existing garden plan, such as a Butterfly

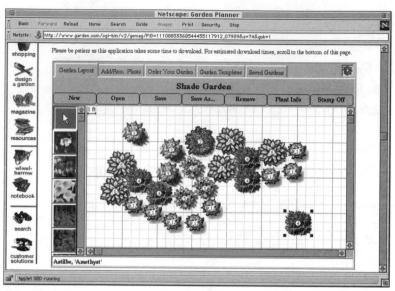

Figure 7-9. *Garden Escape's Garden Planner lets you try before you buy. You can order your garden right from the planner.*

Garden or Shade Garden, and make changes. Braver souls can start a new plan from scratch, adding plants from a picture glossary on the left-hand side. An underlying grid provides information on how much space a plant will take up.

What makes this feature particularly strong is that you can "Order Your Garden" directly from the planner. Like Amazon.com's 1-Click Ordering, this feature takes advantage of the fact that speed and simplicity support sales. A less maze-like ordering process means a higher success rate, since fewer customers drop out from frustration or boredom.

Garden Escape is one of the finest examples of a service-oriented site on the Web. With their wealth of resources, community features, and excellent shopping process, gardeners are treated to a one-stop shopping experience, with both site and visitors reaping the benefits.

Who's doing it right: FAO Schwarz

FAO Schwarz is one of the most intuitive, entertaining shopping sites on the Web. Anyone who has ever been inside their well-known toy stores will recognize the trademark look and feel, but may be surprised to find that shopping at their web site is as easy as shopping in the store.

Avalanche Solutions developed the FAO Schwarz web site, shown in Figure C-7. Peter Seidler, Avalanche's creative director, explains their approach. "The strategy was to develop an FAO Schwarz-branded interactive toy box that recreates the store's whimsical atmosphere, engaging site visitors to easily purchase merchandise online," he explained.

The site's strength is its ease of use. For most web shoppers, ease of use is a rare and wonderful find, a fact that helps to explain FAO Schwarz's success in the web market so far.

Ease of use

A number of factors combine to make FAO Schwarz's site easy to use. Text is edited down to a minimum, and presented in small, digestible chunks. Navigation options are limited to avoid confusing visitors (the main screen, for example, has only two possible paths: About FAO and Shopping). Everyday language is used to give directions ("Add to Bag" or "Put Back"). Bright colors are used to visually separate the navigation frame from product information, and also help set the playful and upbeat tone important for a toy store.

Peter Seidler, Avalanche Solutions

The main screen of the shopping section features simple instructions on how to shop. "Shopping at FAO is easy and secure," the screen reads. "Here's how to shop..." Visitors are offered three simple steps, an easily digested (and easily remembered) shopping process:

1. Look through our catalogues. Click on a toy to get a closer look.

2. If you like what you see, add it to your bag!

3. To view your selections, just click on the shopping BAG icon. From there you can place your order.

This screen resulted from internal testing and is an extension of the site's overall friendly approach. "Users have expressed appreciation about the ease of use of the whole system," Peter says of some of the feedback they've received.

To extend this ease of use throughout the shopping process, Avalanche also created a custom commerce application to allow for secure online transactions, shown in Figure 7-10. "The shopping cart technology that we programmed overcomes the awkwardness ordinarily associated with shopping on the Internet," Peter said.

"The forms that are required to capture the user's information for transactions are generally boring to look at and are largely determined by operating system software constraints. We modified aspects of the layout to create a smooth flowing experience that carries the user through the process and maintains a sense of fun."

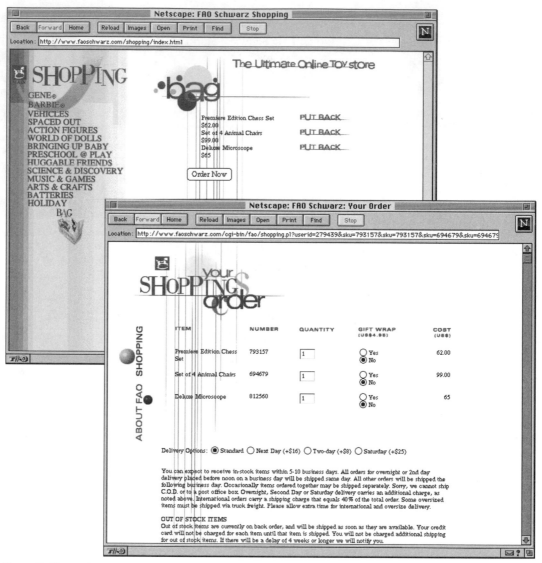

Figure 7-10. *Avalanche created a custom commerce application, designed for ease of use (something most shopping carts don't offer).*

The site uses borderless frames for navigation, keeping a shopping menu on the left side of the screen and product information on the right, shown in Figure 7-11. It's a simple and well-planned approach, which helps it avoid becoming a tangled mess of frames that would defy usability.

"We wanted the experience to be as simple to understand and to use as possible," Peter says of their decision, "and we felt that frames enabled us to do that. We used frames in the simplest possible way and avoided multiple frames. Throughout the site there are really only two fields of experience."

Using borderless frames also helps create a seamless experience for most shoppers. "The user is given a visually streamlined environment that encourages them to move through the information easily."

Find out more

Brand, Stewart. *How Buildings Learn: What Happens After They're Built.* Penguin, 1995.

Lakoff, George, and Mark Johnson. *Metaphors We Live By.* University of Chicago Press, 1983.

Rosenfeld, Lou, and Peter Morville. *Information Architecture for the World Wide Web.* O'Reilly, 1998.

Sano, Darrell. *Designing Large-Scale Web Sites: A Visual Design Methodology.* Wiley, 1996.

Sullivan, Louis H. *Kindergarten Chats and Other Writings.* Dover, 1980.

Wurman, Richard Saul. *Information Architects.* Graphis, 1996.

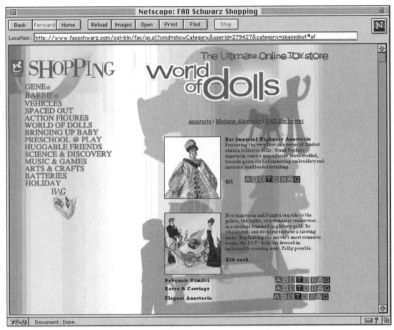

Figure 7-11. *FAO Schwarz's simple approach uses borderless frames for navigation, with the shopping menu on the left and product information on the right.*

Offering advice for other designers wanting to create more navigable sites, Peter outlines Avalache's approach. "We always operate at the intersection of design, technology, and strategy. Each of these vectors is always changing. As a result, the intersection that is perfect for a specific client and project needs to be considered each time."

Recap

These successful shopping sites show a concern with the whole process, from how to bring shoppers into the store to how to guide them safely through the checkout line. On the Web, shoppers are easily put off if the process seems too difficult or if the store has not given them assurances about security. Taking the time to understand the shopping experience, from start to finish, can help you remove frustrating barriers—and gain loyal customers in the process.

## CHAPTER EIGHT

NAVIGATION DESIGN FOR COMMUNITY SITES

To make an apple pie from scratch,
you must first invent the universe.

—Carl Sagan

In this chapter

- Laying the groundwork

- Outlining specific goals

- Who's doing it right: sceneServer

- Who's doing it right: Firefly

- Who's doing it right: Café Utne

- Recap

What communities do you belong to? You might be a member of several communities, all with different goals and mores. I'm a Bostonian (a regional community) and a web developer (a professional community). I'm part of a family, a circle of friends, a political group, a neighborhood, and so on.

What makes all of these community affiliations so interesting is that my involvement in them differs in complex and subtle ways. And that's one of the things we're missing in developing Web-based communities. We've traded all these rich, complex affiliations for generic solutions, and it's just not the same.

To begin to develop this sort of richness on the Web, we need to balance the encouragement of progress in supportive technologies (chat, information sharing, etc.) with equal progress in "soft and mushy" social attributes. Amy Jo Kim, whose company, Naima (*www.naima.com*), specializes in creating online environments, suggests that these qualities, what she calls "social scaffolding," are needed for web communities to grow and thrive. She outlines nine principles for building communities:

1. Define the purpose.

2. Create distinct member-extensible gathering places.

3. Create member profiles that evolve over time.

4. Promote effective leadership and hosting.

5. Define a clear yet flexible code of conduct.

"Community sites should integrate users into development, making them informal partners and co-creators."

6. Accomodate a range of roles.

7. Facilitate member-created subgroups.

8. Organize and promote cyclic events.

9. Integrate with the real world.

This "social scaffolding" should drive your entire solution, from the technology you choose to the way you handle navigation. For community sites, which are often a confusing blend of software and society, this scaffolding becomes the starting point for staging interactions.

Laying the groundwork

Like other sites, planning begins with user goals. More than most other sites, though, community-oriented sites need to integrate users into development, making them informal partners and co-creators. Without this added measure of participation, you're not really fostering community. You're publishing—a noble pursuit, but not quite the same.

Because of this high level of user involvement, community sites often end up looking like (or even consisting of) software. This is not necessarily a bad thing, depending on how it's done, but it does introduce the need for a higher degree of software-style usability testing. Some of the more recent community endeavors show a trend away from the software interface, but for the moment it remains a by-product of this type of site.

Second-tier expectations for community sites include this desire for participation, as well as the others listed in Table 8-1.

Table 8-1. *User goals and expectations: Community*

First Tier (general navigation questions)	Where am I? Where can I go? How will I get there? How can I get back to where I once was?
Second Tier (purpose-oriented questions)	How can I participate? What are the rules? Can I keep my identity private? When will I get feedback? Should I trust what people tell me? What can I learn about the people in this community? Where do I turn for help?

Jim Bumgardner: "People are content"

Jim Bumgardner is the creative and technical mind behind The Palace, a popular tool for interacting in virtual communities. With years of experience in community building, Jim has valuable advice to offer other developers.

The greatest challenges for designers creating community spaces on the Web are not just technical ones, he explains. "They're the same social issues that face us in real life."

"There are two principal challenges as I see it. One, how do you get a community started in the first place? That is, how do you convince a group of people to hang out together? The typical method used is to create some compelling content to attract the people. The basic problem with this method is that people are much more attracted to other people than to content. To put it another way, in a virtual community, the people form the principal content. This is the central Catch-22 for virtual communities that are trying to get started."

The second challenge for community builders has to do with growth. "Once a community has formed, how do you keep it healthy? As in real life, when you put a large group of people in one location, things happen. Disagreements. Romance. Politics. Civil unrest. Banal chatter. Genuine connections. Maintaining healthy communities is a real challenge, and one which probably can't be accomplished through good planning (or 'social engineering') alone.

"Ultimately, the community itself has a major stake in its future. Ideally, designers should try to create channels to take advantage of the energy of the community, to allow it to grow and thrive in an organic way. This includes making sure there are sufficiently numerous and diverse channels of communication, appropriate means of self-empowerment and self-expression, and sufficient controls to prevent widespread social abuse."

From a creator's point of view, there are other navigation issues in community building. "One of the biggest design problems, interface-wise, is that as these environments get more complex, more like real life, the number of things you can do in the environment grows, and it gets harder to simplify the interface enough so that people can learn to use it. For example, in The Palace, you can move around, you can pick up things, drag them around, you can paint on the screen, you can play sounds, and so on. Interpreting what someone wants to do from something as basic as a mouse click can be a challenge."

Jim believes that people are the single most important criterion for web navigation. "These other things—games, chat rooms, virtual spaces, databases—they are all just the excuse for people to commune with each other," he says.

"Ultimately," Jim continues, "I believe the focus of the Internet should be about communing. It should be about making connections with people in deep and meaningful ways, rather than browsing, which is ultimately a casual and soulless activity."

How can I participate?

If there's one essential ingredient of web communities, it's the ability to participate in the creation of a space. As a developer, then, your

Jim Bumgardner, The Palace

initial efforts should go toward developing meaningful and inter-esting ways for people to participate, and making sure that visitors know about these features. It's no good creating a revolutionary way to exchange ideas if users don't have any inkling that you did it.

Deciding what level of participation you'll allow is mainly a question of trust. You have to trust community members in order to foster participation. The best community sites show a high level of trust—letting members create their own subspaces or niches, encouraging their involvement in the site's growth, giving them a stake in the community's future.

This raises an interesting development issue, one that might go against the grain of ideas about central site control. The community model you create will need to be scalable (have the ability to grow over time) and flexible, because once users take over, growth becomes organic, not dictated.

What happens to your carefully planned architecture and navigation when users claim the space? You'll need to be open to altering or expanding in user-driven directions, which will mean you'll need to be watchful of how your site is changing. You might also want to brainstorm methods that encourage consistency without sacrificing self-expression.

Firefly was one of the first sites to take on this challenge. They offer members the ability to manage their own pages, but require that they include certain consistent elements (certain navigationals, the Firefly brand, and so on). Someone exploring Firefly's network of sites can expect to find a high degree of interest and diversity, but will always be able to quickly return to Firefly's hub. It's an impressive balance of freedom and control. See "Who's doing it right: Firefly" later in this chapter.

What are the rules?

It's important for people to understand not only what is expected of them, but what they should expect in a community space. Under-standing these social rules helps ease feelings of fear and distrust that can keep people away from forums. It also lets people focus less on mechanics and more on interaction.

Having and advertising these social guidelines is what separates successful communities from those that are mired in arguments, irrel-evance, and abuse. Think about a "real world" community or forum, such as Alcoholics Anonymous. You're expected to play by their rules during meetings, for the benefit of the group. Everyone knows the rules and agrees to play by them, making it possible to relax and focus on understanding the problem at hand.

In your navigation design, then, placing community guidelines so that they are obvious to users will mean they are available when there are problems, that new users understand them upon entering, and that they reinforce the idea of a monitored community.

Can I keep my identity private?

For many people, having to reveal their identity among strangers is truly off-putting. Imagine how awkward you'd feel if you had to go about your daily business emblazoned with a sticker that said, "Hello, My Name Is ___." Most people seem to prefer relative anonymity, and are especially protective of it on the Web.

This is at odds with the fact that community sites usually require logins—and for a good reason. The login process tends to make people take responsibility for their actions, a necessary step for joining a community. It can be a real turn-off for many people who were not intending to wreak havoc or stir up trouble, however.

To reach a balance between encouraging responsibility and easing privacy fears, some sites allow users to login as a guest, or create a false identity. These options can be explained in a simple FAQ or other help area. Café Utne provides an example in their FAQ in a section explaining "Why Register?":

> The Café is free and all that is required is registering. We won't provide any of the individual information from this form to anyone else. We ask for it in case we need to contact you, and also so that we have some idea of the mix of people in our community. Only your first and last name are required, along with your email address. We do send occasional email notices regarding your enrollment and Café events in your geographic area.

Digital Knowledge Assets shows a similar approach in "black background," a demo of their sceneServer technology. Visitors to "black background" can log in with a "false" username, but are still asked to provide a real name and email address. It's a nice balance between usability and responsibility.

When will I get feedback?

There are a lot of different options for encouraging community, including promoting discussion through live chat or threaded discussions. Developers and savvy users tend to understand the difference between these, but many new users don't.

When should they expect a response to a posting? Immediately? Next month? Will they need to check back, and if so, how will they find

---

Rules of conduct

Setting up guidelines for conduct in community spaces (and being prepared to enforce them) allows people to immerse themselves without distractions, such as spam, needless arguments, or off-topic posts.

"Advertising social guidelines is what separates successful communities from those that are mired in arguments, irrelevance, and abuse."

their question if other new questions are constantly added? If feedback is immediate, will they need to reload the page to view responses?

There are a lot of potential navigation problems within forums, especially when it comes to getting or posting feedback. You can't predict what people will do, and how quickly they will respond, but you can tell community members what they should expect from the technology. A FAQ, orientation, or more contextual approach could help communicate this information.

In their sceneServer technology, Digital Knowledge Assets uses an excellent contextual approach to communicating information about feedback, as shown in Figure 8-1. When someone contributes to a topic, sceneServer shows a sort of "freshness" indicator—a small dot next to the topic that changes color depending on whether it is new, recent, or old. This is a simple and elegant solution to the problem of communicating the timeliness (and volume) of feedback.

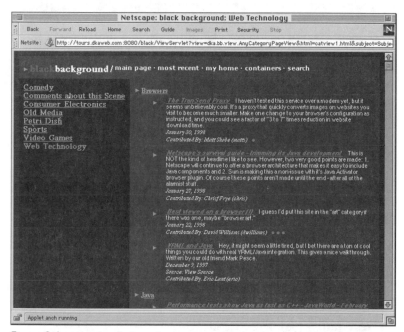

Figure 8-1. *sceneServer shows how active a topic has been recently by using a small, colored dot next to messages. Shown here is black background, a public web scene.*

Should I trust what people tell me?

Most people understand that there is a qualitative difference between the advice you get from a book or expert and that you get from the general population. Take the subject of AIDS. Medical experts have one view of how it can spread, while the public has tended to have another (more paranoid) view. If you're running a community around a sensitive topic, this potential for misinformation could become a problem for both you and your users. It's no reason to avoid communities, but it's important to think about how you'll handle this in advance.

As a developer, how should you address this potential for misinformation? This potential trust issue is part of being in a community, and there's not a lot you can (or should) do to police it. However, communicating to users that there are ways to check information and advice, and even providing pointers to sources, is one helpful way to support your community members. If your topic is very sensitive, you may also need to provide a disclaimer and an easy way to contact an expert with concerns.

What can I learn about the people in this community?

To really foster community, you want to encourage people to talk to each other, not just to you. It's part of encouraging the high degree of participation that is the mark of a successful community site. The best community sites allow members to become personalities and resources, not just meaningless login names.

For example, Firefly offers members the opportunity to create a profile that other members can see. When you first sign in, your profile consists of your username. As you get more involved and feel more comfortable, you can add to your profile, outlining your interests, background, or other information. These profiles become a resource for the whole community, since you can search on members' interests, as shown in Figure 8-2. It sure beats the telephone book for quality of information, and it's completely user-created so privacy concerns are kept to a minimum.

Where do I turn for help?

Because many community features closely resemble software, or require people to register, there's a pretty good chance that people will need help. When I teach computer classes, about one out of five students usually enters logins incorrectly. A much higher percentage miss some crucial step in whatever process is being introduced. The more complex things get, and the greater the number of steps involved in completing a task, the more likely that people will make mistakes.

"The best community sites allow members to become personalities and resources, not just meaningless login names."

Cross-platform software

If your site requires users to download special software, consider whether it can be available for both Macintosh and Windows. Offering it to one without the other cuts a large number of visitors off from your content.

Figure 8-2. *Firefly members can search other users' profiles for similar interests.*

In this regard, community sites are like shopping sites. Telling people where to go if they have problems will increase the chance that they successfully join your community. It also sends the message that you value community members enough to support them, and that they are not simply on their own when interacting in your space. The best web communities build in these support features to a high degree, and their traffic reflects the positive response they get from users.

Café Utne has excellent support features, including a FAQ and a forum devoted to new users. Their best feature is their "mentors," people who are available to give tours through the discussion space or answer questions about the site. This spectrum of help features sends the clear message that Café Utne is serious about supporting people, and helps remove potential barriers of mistrust and fear.

Outlining specific goals

Finding out about specific third-tier goals helps you design a site that works for your users, not just on the drawing board. For example, if you run a parenting site with a community focus, you'll find that parents have a specific set of needs and goals when it comes to interacting on the Web. Parents often have additional concerns about privacy and trust, or want to interact with other parents going through the "terrible twos" or some other specific stage.

Table 8-2 shows how the goals and expectations chart could be used to map out typical user goals for a parenting site.

Table 8-2. *User goals and expectations: Community: Parenting*

First Tier (general navigation questions)	Where am I? Where can I go? How will I get there? How can I get back to where I once was?
Second Tier (purpose-oriented questions)	How can I participate? What are the rules? Can I keep my identity private? When will I get feedback? Should I trust what people tell me? What can I learn about the people in this community? Where do I turn for help?
Third Tier (topic- or audience-oriented questions)	How can I talk about a specific problem (bedwetting, tantrums)? How can I talk about a specific age or developmental stage? Is my child's identity safe, as well as my own? Will chats and events take away from my family time, or are they offered when it's convenient for me?

To find out more about what people want from communities, you might try some of the following methods:

- Snoop and loiter in web communities, especially ones that relate to your area of development. What are people talking about in chat and discussion forums? Are social rules posted? What other factors (tone, approach, features, etc.) contribute to a sense of community?

- Look at as many examples of user participation as possible. Spend time on sites that allow people to customize content, or view the opinions of other visitors. Try out features that let people post content—whether resumes, drawings, opinions, or other material. What models exist for user participation? Could they be extended in new and exciting ways?

- Observe social rules and behavior the next time you go to a family gathering, the local pub, your church or temple, or other "real world" forums. How do people learn the rules? What cues are there to help them remember these guidelines?

- Research how psychologists and sociologists view community— or better yet, go talk to one of these professionals. Are there common "ingredients" in the way communities are described? What sorts of things are written about peer pressure, "group think," social controls, or friendship? How might these apply to the choices people make on the Web?

Uncovering history

Consider not only how people will participate in ongoing conversations, but also whether they will want to view previous discussions in an archive.

There's a lot of psychology in community building, so be prepared to "people watch" as much as possible. And don't ignore the problems of communities that aren't working well, since those social problems can provide insights that are as important as the ones you gain from successful communities.

What's in it for me?

You're about to spend a lot of time researching goals, developing and implementing technical solutions, writing up social codes, and generally setting the stage for other people's interactions. So what's in it for you (or the client)? If you're independently wealthy (or well funded), participating in a fascinating social experiment is reason enough. But what if you aren't either of those?

With a shopping site, your main interest is probably sales. A learning site might feature fee-based training. An information or entertainment site could sell subscriptions or accept ads. For a community site, the benefits may not be as obvious, but they are perhaps most important of all.

When you put the time and energy into developing (and maintaining) a community, your profits are in people. Visitors usually become loyal, active members if you give them a stake in the space. Anyone might be able to steal or duplicate your content (as disturbing as that might be), but stealing your community is a much tougher job. Need proof? Look at how long it's taken Barnes & Noble to gain a foothold in Amazon.com's loyal market. People are your most important assets, so it makes sense to keep them happy.

But community doesn't have to mean allowing random, meaningless chatter on your site just to keep people amused (though in many unmoderated forums this is common). Adding opportunities for people to interact around topics that relate to your site means you'll have an untapped source of knowledge at your fingertips.

You'll be able to eavesdrop (or better yet, interact) as people collectively analyze a product you developed, discuss a trend in your industry, or extemporize about some cool service they wish existed. A community can be a small gold mine of insight and experience, and excellent "fish food" for people who want to interact. (See the sidebar "Would you like fish food with that?" in Chapter 10, *Navigation Design for Identity Sites*.)

Planning for advertisements

Community sites are a new focus of advertiser attention, and we're likely to see more and more companies sponsoring these spaces. As a site developer, planning for advertisements ahead of time can help you avoid alienating users. Because navigation is an active process that requires us to make choices, visualize routes, interpret labels and feedback, and otherwise pay attention to the environment, badly placed ads can be frustrating and disruptive. Try these quick tips for effective ad design:

- Think about where you'll place ads, and how they'll be integrated into your *layout*. Will they simply be dumped somewhere at the top of the page, without concern for how they may interrupt the flow of information? Will they be relegated to the bottom, where users will never see them? If you know you'll be taking ads, plan your page design accordingly.

- Plan ad *animation* to avoid endless looping and reduce eyestrain. Animation has become a core part of banner advertising, and studies show it can increase clickthrough rates substantially. However, animation is not uniformly effective. It can work against an advertiser to create an ad that features painfully fast, bright, or repetitive animation. In some cases, rather than encouraging users to click, it forces them to leave the page.

- Be careful about using *sound* in ads. It's possible with Shockwave, and I've come across some ads that use it. It can be a truly disruptive experience, however, which helps neither the advertiser nor the hosting site. Blaring music or annoying noises don't usually act as effective incentives to users.

- Think twice before using *pop-up* ads. It may seem like a good way to expose people to products, but many people are seriously peeved by them. Geocities is a big offender when it comes to pop-up ads that interrupt users and litter the screen with new windows.

- Plan for interactivity. New levels of interactivity within ads promise higher clickthroughs, but can introduce the need for micronavigation. Casio has an interactive banner ad, for example, that offers users the chance to browse products and even purchase from within the Java-based ad. The more sophisticated ads become, the more likely it is that users will have trouble with them, so make sure to build in planning and testing time.

What's next for web advertising? People are endlessly creative. For example, Black Sun Interactive has created SpokesBot, an animated advertising critter that interacts with users in VRML worlds (until they tell it to scram). There are a wealth of possibilities. Not all will work for users, however. It pays to consider the effects on the audience. After all, they hold the checkbook.

For more information about web advertising, try these sites:

Microscope Weekly Ad Review
http://www.pscentral.com/

Internet Advertising Bureau
http://www.iab.net

CyberAtlas: The Reference Desk for Web Marketing
http://www.cyberatlas.com/

sceneServer

www.dkaweb.com/
sceneServer/

Who's doing it right: sceneServer

Imagine what your friendly neighborhood search engine would be like if you could read what other people thought of a particular site, contribute something you thought was missing, or get a constantly updated report on things you seemed to like. Most search engines do not offer all these features yet, but you can find them (and many others) in sceneServer.

sceneServer, shown in Figure 8-3, is a technology created by Digital Knowledge Assets to power community sites, whether on intranets or the Internet. It delivers rich, group-annotated content and powerful collaboration features to communities organized around a mutual information interest.

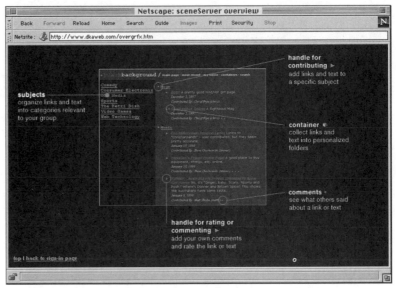

Figure 8-3. *sceneServer delivers rich, group-annotated content and powerful collaboration features.*

In a typical sceneServer session, a user logs on and views a list of topics available for browsing. Choosing a topic, the user can view resources that had been contributed for that topic, and can then contribute a new resource or comment on an existing one, as shown in Figure 8-4. The comments of other community members can be accessed by clicking on a small icon next to each resource, the color of which indicates whether comments have been added recently. Members can also collect favorite resources into "containers" and allow some or all community members access to them. All of these features are designed to dramatically extend the way people find and rate information.

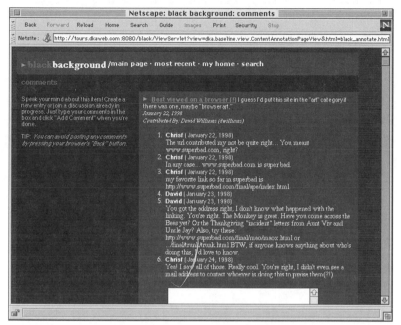

Figure 8-4. *sceneServer users can view other members' comments about a resource.*

"A big theme for us is the way community forms around content," explains Marc Rettig, dka's VP of design. "The underlying technology could be expressed as a number of different products, but sceneServer is aimed at communities of interest."

Marc defines "communities of interest" as "groups of people focused primarily on ideas and information." In doing research on communities, dka found three main types:

- Communities of interest: groups of people focused primarily on ideas and information

- Communities of practice: groups of people following a process or making something together

- Communities of transaction (markets): groups of people engaged in buying and selling

dka specializes in how people learn and share information in corporate settings, and sceneServer closely reflects that specialization. "The community of interest area seemed closest to what we had already

Marc Rettig, Digital Knowledge Assets

started to do in supporting groups of people who want to learn and 'stay current' by pooling their collective personal bandwidth."

Because it is organized around communities of interest, sceneServer offers many of the strengths of a well-planned information site in addition to its strong community focus. A public demo called "black background" demonstrates sceneServer's strengths in the areas of feedback and flexibility.

Feedback

With sceneServer, you can easily find out if someone's added a new resource, category, topic "container," or annotation. Icons next to resources indicate whether new content has been added and whether it's "hot" (very recent). You can also choose to display only the most recently added items, a nice way to make sure you're always up to date.

This sort of feedback can save a lot of time, particularly in a corporate setting (where sceneServer can be used to greatest effect). Being able to determine "freshness" means community members can skip postings that might no longer be relevant.

Another excellent feedback-related feature is the ability for members to exchange resources. You might miss a great article, but a co-worker could still find it and send it along to you. This mirrors what tends to happen in most office environments, where a great deal of information-sharing happens in this informal way. sceneServer allows you to get feedback not only from the system, but directly from peers—who are still the best source.

Flexibility

There are more ways to get and share information with sceneServer than there are in most web search sites, even in most libraries. To start, members can browse by subject, a traditional approach to the system. Unlike most traditional subject lists, though, you're not restricted to what you see listed. Don't see the topic you want? You can add one by creating your own "container," as shown in Figure 8-5.

Containers are brilliantly useful devices. They're also a lot of fun, offering participation at its highest, melded perfectly with a useful storage feature. A container you create can be used to store resources you like so you can easily return to them. You can comment on them and make them available to other members if you choose—one, some, or all, handpicked by name if you're particular about who accesses your container. It sure beats bookmarking.

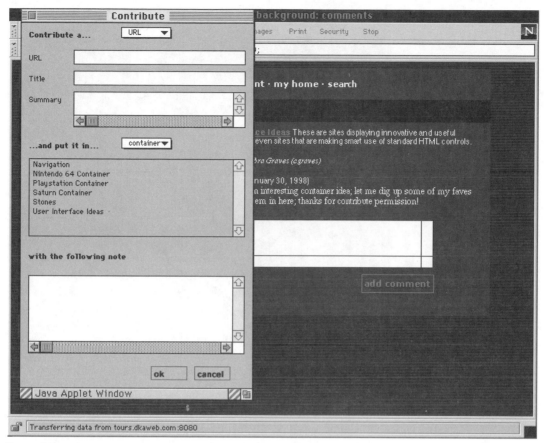

Figure 8-5. *Members participating in a scene at sceneServer can contribute a "container," a useful place to collect resources on a topic.*

An alternative to containers is a tour, shown in Figure 8-6. With containers, resources are listed and annotated on one page. With a tour, resources are presented one at a time, also with annotation and comments.

Marc describes tours as "a way to tell a story about content, to develop a narrative about a seqence of things. Think of a museum tour, in which the tour guide selects a few highlights from a huge collection and helps people understand each one in the context of the whole." Tours and containers each serve a slightly different purpose, but together they offer a high degree of flexibility to community members.

For corporate settings, a "neighbors view," shown in Figure 8-7, allows you to not only view resources that you have rated most highly, but to find out about other community members who have rated things in a similar way. It's an effective way to discover other

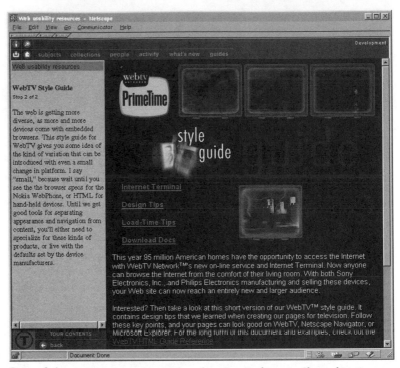

Figure 8-6. *sceneServer users can also take a "tour" of a topic. Shown here is a sceneServer tour in use in a corporate setting.*

people's interests within private webs. As Marc explains it, "This view is of great value in corporate settings, where it can be hard to find the 'like minds' across the org chart."

dka used Java servlets to create sceneServer, a decision explained by Steve Olechowski: "We could have used any number of server technologies to create sceneServer. We chose the Java servlet architecture for a number of reasons.

"First, Java is just a great object-oriented language," Steve points out. "Most of us on the team had a lot of experience with object-oriented programming languages, and Java seemed like it provided us with the best combination of features given the languages we had worked with previously. Java allows us to create 'objects' which interact to form the system that is sceneServer."

Java also offered the benefit of cross-platform accessibility. "Java servlets work across web servers and platforms," Steve says. "This means when we create our Java servlets, we can plug them into any web server that supports Java servlets without changing our code. If we had used C++, we would have had to create separate versions for both Netscape and Microsoft's web server on both Unix and Windows NT."

Figure 8-7. *For corporate settings, sceneServer's "neighbors view" allows people to find others who share their interests.*

Efficiency was another benefit offered by servlets. Steve explains that "every time a CGI program is called, it takes up more memory and processor time, so that n requests results in the usage of n times the memory. Java servlets are architected in such a way as to share resources so that n requests is only greater than 1 times the memory of the servlet."

Finally, Steve points out that using Java meant they could avoid troublesome plug-ins. "Java can run in the browser without downloading additional plug-ins. This means we can create more active applications for the user in which to navigate sceneServer. Many of the Java objects used in sceneServer servlets are also used in the client-side applets."

"There are probably a few other 'religious' reasons for choosing the Java servlet architecture," Steve concludes, "but all in all it has worked out very well for us, with no regrets."

sceneServer is sure to shine in corporate settings, especially on intranets, but its potential for adding strong community features to the public Web is also great. dka's technology definitely raises the bar for developers: plain vanilla discussion forums just aren't going to cut it anymore.

Who's doing it right: Firefly

Firefly, shown in Figure C-8, is probably the best known web community space. It was created in 1996 by MIT researchers, and it

Firefly

www.firefly.com

continues to offer insight into the evolution of web communities. Firefly was acquired by Microsoft in early 1998.

Firefly, like sceneServer, is a technology for powering community sites. The company has made their own site a showcase and laboratory for community interaction. Firefly's excellent features are reflected by a large and active pool of members, the best measure of success for a community space.

To become a Firefly member, a visitor selects a username and password to log in. Once logged in, members can create or alter a personal profile, search for other members with similar interests, or stop by one of Firefly's "Venues," user-created spaces organized by topic, shown in Figure 8-8. In addition to excellent communication and standardization, Firefly offers its members portable profiles and excellent search features—both unparalleled among community sites.

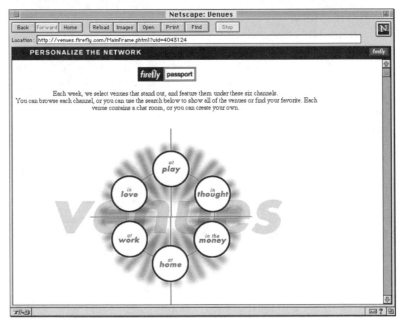

Figure 8-8. *Firefly's "Venues" are user-created spaces organized by topic.*

Portability

One of the best features Firefly offers is the potential to store your settings in a "passport," shown in Figure 8-9, and travel around the Web with it. The passport works only at selected sites using Firefly technology, but the promise is enormous.

At the moment, most web users have to register at each community they visit. Go to My Yahoo (*my.yahoo.com*) and you'll need to enter

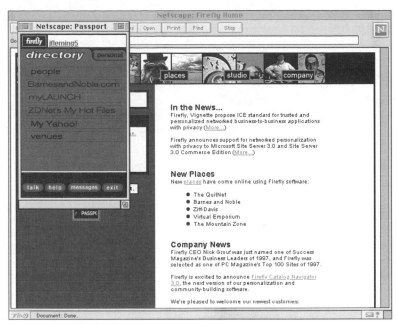

Figure 8-9. *Members can store settings in a Firefly "passport" that can be used on other participating sites.*

your information preferences. Go to Amazon.com and enter your shopping preferences. These repeated logins are time-consuming, and with community features on the rise, likely to become more so.

Within the web of sites powered by Firefly, members can simply carry around a sort of digital ID card, and their preferences travel with them. It's a powerful feature, and one that would be even more so if it were more of a standard.

Searchability

Firefly excels at the idea that people are resources, and that there should be meaningful ways to connect with other people. To facilitate this, Firefly offers the ability to search for people by member name or interest.

If you'd like to know whether anyone else is interested in photography, for example, you simply type "photography" in the search prompt (a JavaScript popup) to show a list of members with a similar interest. The results page shows the username of each matching member. You can read more about members who share your interest and then send them Firefly email if you like.

If you're looking for other ways to search for people, Firefly provides alternatives. You can view a list of all people online or find out if "your friends" (people you've chosen for this special privilege) are online. Firefly puts more effort into these people searches than many sites put into searching through content. In this case, people are content, and Firefly lets you navigate this content in flexible, interesting ways.

Firefly may be one of the oldest community spaces on the Web, but it's still one of the most exciting and promising. Barnes & Noble, Yahoo!, myLaunch, and Ziff-Davis are just a few of the sites that are taking advantage of Firefly's software to provide community features. Firefly remains a company to watch, especially as web community building evolves.

Who's doing it right: Café Utne

According to Forum One, a search engine for web forums, Café Utne, shown in Figure C-9, is the most active online community in North America, surpassing even Salon Magazine (*www.salonmag.com*). No small feat, considering Salon's devoted audience and the excellent reputation of their community forums. Café Utne accomplishes this in large part through rigorous support and monitoring.

The Café consists of little more than a software tool (Motet, shown in Figure 8-10), but don't let that fool you. The core of their service is conversation, or as the Café explains it: "In the 'saloning' tradition, this is a dynamic and evolving community where it is our goal to discuss ideas and issues in a thoughtful and respectful manner."

Café Utne's strengths are in the areas of mentoring and previewing, both of which suggest a supportive and watchful community leadership. With the wealth of support features, Café members can sit back and talk issues, not logistics.

Mentoring

In addition to clear communication about who hosts each forum, new users can get actual human assistance when they need it. As the Café's "SOS" explains: "A friendly and capable cadre of Mentors can assist you in getting acclimated to the Café, both technically and socially." One quick email, and you'll be assigned a mentor to help walk you through it all.

Mentoring is an excellent way to address a problem of community sites. Many community features are as complex and difficult to learn as desktop software. And yet most web users don't want to invest the time to learn web applications, though they may spend time learning their desktop software. It's a Catch-22. How do you provide the instant gratification and ease of use that web users want while also incorporating the tools you need to get the job done?

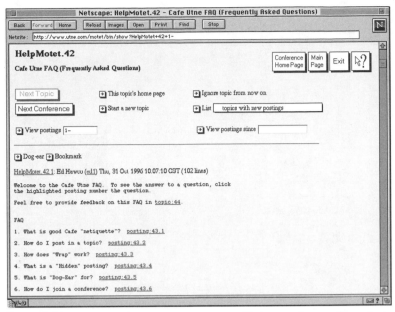

Figure 8-10. *The Café's discussion area consists of little more than a software tool, but don't let that fool you—it's a dynamic and evolving community.*

For Café Utne, which uses a complicated but very powerful software tool like Motet, this is a serious issue. By addressing it through the mentor program, they not only offer a user-centered solution, but one that fits perfectly with the community focus of the site.

Previewing

Another area in which the Café excels is previewing, the ability to predict what's coming up. Building in features that support previewing means that people can more easily make decisions about routes, about outcomes, even about whether they trust your site enough to go on.

The Café's best previewing feature is "Hear Say," shown in Figure 8-11, an opportunity to eavesdrop on what's happening in 28 of the most popular forums. For example, you might discover that in the conference called "Absurd," there is a thread going on about limericks. The only other way you could have discovered this tidbit is by browsing all conferences, a time-consuming proposition.

The Café also offers a complete conference menu, with the ability to click to find out what the five most recent discussion topics were. In both "Hear Say" and the conference menu, a link to registration is provided. Once you've been lured by the promise of limericks, culinary arts, or polymorphous pleasure (whatever that is), you can sign up when the impulse strikes.

Find out more

Horn, Stacy. *Clicks, Culture, and the Creation of an Online Town.* Warner Books, 1998.

Kim, Amy Jo. *Global Villagers: Community-Building on the Web.* Peachpit, 1998.

Sterne, Jim. *What Makes People Click: Advertising on the Web.* Que, 1997.

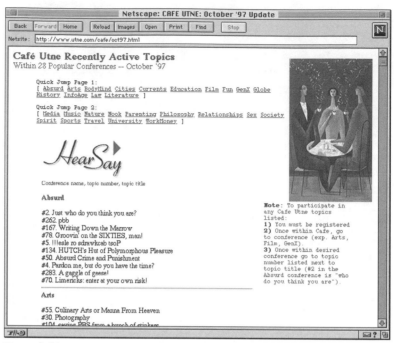

Figure 8-11. *"Hear Say" at Café Utne lets you eavesdrop on 28 of the most popular conferences before you enter.*

More than anything else, Café Utne shows a focus on the dynamics of conversation and how to facilitate it on the Web. They're one of the few community spaces in which you feel that the site's creators, leaders, and mentors are as much a part of the mix as its users. This human focus may help to explain its success, and certainly helps make it a supportive and welcoming space.

Recap

As more and more developers understand the importance of social interactions in webspace, "community" is fast becoming a buzzword. But communities are not all equal. The best web communities balance sophisticated technical solutions with "soft and mushy" social attributes. These successful web communities are centered around member interaction, participation, and content co-creation, not simply around more common site-to-user dialogues. Giving members a role in the community's future may mean you have to be extra responsive to your site's growth, but it's the best way to build the important "social scaffolding" web communities need.

## CHAPTER NINE

NAVIGATION DESIGN FOR ENTERTAINMENT SITES

*Before I compose a piece, I walk around it
several times, accompanied by myself.*

—Eric Satie

In this chapter

- Laying the groundwork
- Outlining specific goals
- Who's doing it right: Urban Diary
- Who's doing it right: Riven Journals
- Who's doing it right: Crimson Empire
- Recap

What makes something entertaining? What knowledge do game developers, toy makers, and movie directors share? Looking at Walt Disney's entertainment empire can help shed some light on the subject.

When Disney first planned his theme parks, he had more than rides in mind. He set out to create environments, fantastic experiences orchestrated by his team of "imagineers." And he rigorously controlled his parks to ensure that guests were shielded from incidents that might mar their visit or burst the bubble of fantasy. This focus on an immersive experience is still a core part of Disney's approach to entertainment—and part of the reason "Disney" is synonymous with "fun."

Like Disney, developers can also foster this immersive experience. Our potential incidents have less to do with catching Goofy on a cigarette break and more to do with infrastructure. Most of the barriers to immersive entertainment on the Web are technical: incompatibilities, memory problems, lack of plug-ins, unstable technologies.

This presents a frustrating paradox, since entertainment sites are constantly being pushed toward CD-ROM–like sophistication. But the push for increasing functionality and the need to avoid conflicts are really two sides of the same coin. Each has an equal role in fostering an immersive experience.

For entertainment sites, more than any other type of site, *integration* is the operative word. Functionality and accessibility, art and

"Most of the barriers to immersive entertainment on the Web are technical: incompatibilities, memory problems, lack of plug-ins, unstable technologies."

mechanics, storytelling and exploration all become part of one immersive, integrated experience. Navigation itself becomes an entertainment vehicle—bound up with the experience, not separate from it. The best CD-ROM titles and theme parks approach navigation this way. The best entertainment sites do the same.

Laying the groundwork

Though there are as many ideas about what is "entertaining" as there are people to ask, there are some common goals and expectations that are shared. Visiting entertainment-oriented sites, people tend to have the "second tier" expectations listed in Table 9-1.

Table 9-1. *User goals and expectations: Entertainment*

First Tier (general navigation questions)	Where am I? Where can I go? How will I get there? How can I get back to where I once was?
Second Tier (purpose-oriented questions)	How do I begin? What's going to happen? Will I get tips or hints as I go along? Am I going to have to work at it? How will I know I'm finished?

How do I begin?

Beginnings and endings are crucial for any type of storytelling. Many entertainment experiences incorporate elements of storytelling, so learning about staging these important transitions in other media can offer valuable insight. Understanding the Web's own quirks, though, is essential.

Orchestrating the beginning sequence is the first and most crucial step for any performance. This is where you capture the audience—or where they leave for greener pastures. If you think movie directors or writers feel pressured about the first impression, it's nothing compared to the pressure we have as web developers. In a brief entryway, we need to begin the story, tell people what they might need from a technical standpoint, and offer cues on how to proceed. Itchy mouse fingers dictate that this be done within the space of a couple of screens. Hey, no pressure.

In Urban Diary, Joseph Squier shows a mastery of this focused entryway. His art piece begins with a space in which visitors can either begin immediately or pause for assistance. He begins the story on the first page, offering a hook to draw people in. And in the initial pages of the Diary itself, he offers simple clues to how it all works. This balanced approach meets the demands of a fickle and fast-moving web audience.

What's going to happen?

Any good mystery writer will tell you that you never give away the ending before it's time, but you always plant clues. Without some idea of the direction of the story, it's difficult for people to "buy into it," to feel any sort of real participation or concern. Giving people a sense of what might happen doesn't mean telling all. It can mean providing teasers, clues, or a game overview.

Previewing has a long tradition, from big top shows hawking what's inside to the movie previews that sell us on a story. If you play CD-ROM games, think about the clues offered by the packaging ("destroy aliens before they destroy Earth") or by the game's introductory screens. In Riven, the sequel to the popular game Myst, one of the first screens is of a character giving you your mission. If these teasers are done well, they offer just enough of the story to make it interesting and provide valuable first clues.

In the web-based *Star Wars* comic *Crimson Empire,* shown in Figure 9-1, a brief introduction to the story scrolls into the distance in typical *Star Wars* fashion. Without the benefit of this story background, people might lose valuable time trying to figure out the story's context, time period, or history. Providing a quick preview lets people focus on the story, not on logistics or minor details.

Will I get tips or hints as I go along?

With all of this focus on orchestrating the beginning, it's easy to forget that people may still need help once they're underway. Again, for entertainment sites, you don't want to tell them "click here to kill the dragon" or "look behind door #3 for the answer to the puzzle." That would definitely spoil the fun. But subtle hints along the way provide feedback to help people determine whether they are on the right path. Tips available for the asking keep people in the game when they might have left in frustration. Features like maps or shortcuts save time for players, some of whom may be on a timed connection.

The Riven Journals, designed as a web preview for the computer game, build in subtle hints by animating many navigationals and using status bar messages to provide feedback, as shown in Figure 9-2. The journals also use cookies to remember your place and progress with the puzzles, allowing people to forget about logistics and immerse themselves in the mysterious world of Riven.

"Giving people a sense of what might happen doesn't mean telling all. It can mean providing teasers, clues, or a game overview."

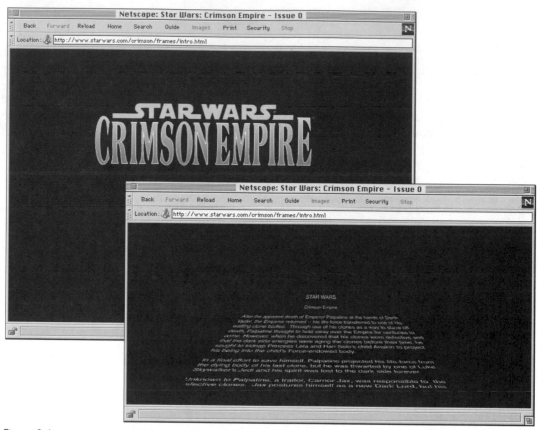

Figure 9-1. *In the web-based Star Wars comic Crimson Empire, the introduction to the story, which scrolls into the distance in typical Star Wars fashion, provides background information and a compelling first impression.*

Am I going to have to work at it?

When you're tired and looking for something relaxing and fun, would you settle for doing calculus? How about configuring new hardware? No? Most people wouldn't, and they won't want to work to understand an entertainment site either.

Puzzles can be great fun, but there's a fine line between mystery and frustration. People will want to focus on solving the game's mysteries, not on how to navigate or use basic tools. That quickly gets frustrating.

In the Riven Journals, you have to work to solve the tricky puzzles presented. The journals are mysterious, offering few clues that might give away the answers. However, they are not difficult to use. To explore or open a journal, you simply click on its cover. To page through, you click on the next page, or the forward arrow. To solve puzzles, you pull levers, push buttons, slide bars, and so on. All of

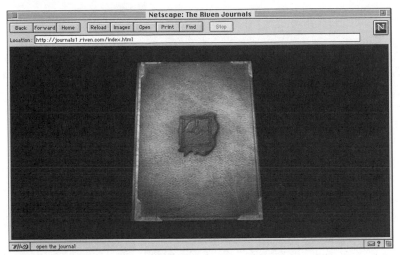

Figure 9-2. *The Riven Journals feature status bar messages on mouseover to provide clues.*

"There's a fine line between mystery and frustration. People will want to focus on solving the game's mysteries, not on how to navigate or use basic tools."

this feels fun and clever, but it's never hard. It never defies understanding—which is for the best, because the journals themselves often do. Visitors can focus on solving them, not on maneuvering around in them.

How will I know I'm finished?

"The end" is a dicey concept for hypermedia. Some sites exist simply to let people explore the space at random, without guidance or control—an entertaining look at the nature of hypermedia. But nothing can go on forever, and even a random exploration ends sometime. When people are ready to go, what will you leave them with? How will you stage their exit?

Some sites employ exit tunnels, a linear series of pages that "escort" people out of a site. Exit tunnels not only communicate that the end is near, but also help guide visitors on to a new destination. (David Siegel has one of the best examples of these on his personal site at *www.dsiegel.com.*) There are many other possibilities for exits, some as simple as having a screen that says "You're done" or "There's more next month; y'all come back now."

For entertainment sites, this feeling of completion is an important part of the experience, especially if you're presenting a game or puzzle. It's also a key part of providing well-designed navigation, since it serves as user feedback and designates the end of a path or route. Without a clear sense of when they're finished, people are likely to suffer from the common web malady of *abandonment-itis*—the sinking feeling that you've been left to fend utterly for yourself.

Control issues

Balance who has control — you or your visitors. You may have something to show them, but they also have to feel that they can get what they want quickly and easily.

The Riven Journals go beyond telling people when the larger puzzle is done, and tell them when each small puzzle has been finished. Within each of the five journals, there is a puzzle. When that puzzle is solved, a sound or animation plays, and a code is revealed within the journal. Each time you go back to reopen a journal you've solved, you'll see the code first, an easy way to avoid the problem of users going all the way to the end of a journal only to discover they'd already solved it. As for the larger puzzle's ending... well, you'll need to find that out for yourself.

Outlining specific goals

Filling in a third-tier of user goals and expectations can help you reduce the guesswork in designing an entertainment site. Entertainment on the Web can be as varied as it is in real life, and as difficult to define. Outlining specifics that relate to your site plan can help you refine your focus. It may also help you become the next big entertainment success story on the Web, if you follow the leads unearthed in your research.

Table 9-2 shows what third-tier goals and expectations might look like for a gaming site, such as an adventure or role-playing game.

Table 9-2. *User goals and expectations: Entertainment: Gaming*

First Tier (general navigation questions)	Where am I? Where can I go? How will I get there? How can I get back to where I once was?
Second Tier (purpose-oriented questions)	How do I begin? What's going to happen? Will I get tips or hints as I go along? Am I going to have to work at it? How will I know I'm finished?
Third Tier (topic- or audience-oriented questions)	What are the rules? What do I need in order to play? Is there a map of the game space? What if I make a mistake or change my mind? What if I need to leave in the middle? Can I store items or use them during the game? Can I play against someone? How do I win (or lose)?

Entertainment developers have it made when it comes to doing the research needed to highlight these third-tier goals. The best way to research user goals for an entertainment site is to *go have fun*. Keep one eye on what's happening "backstage," though. It'll offer clues about how someone crafted the experience, and why it works (or flops).

You might try some of the following methods:

- Pick up several CD-ROM titles that relate to your entertainment concept. (This is a costly proposition, but well worth it. If you know someone who is a game junkie, visit their house and ask to spend some time looking through their collection. Try your local library, too. Some libraries now circulate CD-ROMs.) Spend an afternoon looking at different game maps, or tool storage devices, or ways to present instructions. What feels comfortable and intuitive, and what feels cumbersome and hard to learn?

- Visit an amusement park (if you are anywhere near a Disney park, go there first). How is traffic control integrated into the experience, if at all? How are transitions between rides handled? How would you make things better if you were planning it?

- Go to several top web-based entertainment sites—try the ones mentioned in this chapter, as well as You Don't Know Jack (*www.bezerk.com*), Riddler (*www.riddler.com*), and zoeye (*www.spectacle.com/zoeye-/*). What technologies are in use, and how do they enhance or take away from the experience? How do these entertainment sites handle moving people around, providing instructions, starting and ending, and so on? What works and what doesn't?

- Go to a show or a storytelling event. Are these traditionally "passive" events really passive, or do any of them request audience participation? Are these events more or less immersive than the theme park you visited, and can you find out why?

- Talk with a storyteller, director, actor, or other performer and find out how they plan a performance. What role does timing play? What about space considerations or movement? How do they make transitions between scenes or acts or characters?

- If you have a little extra time, take a class on acting, stage design, or storytelling. In CD-ROM design and cell animation, artists are considered actors. A little extra training can't hurt. Find out for yourself what's involved in crafting a performance, and translate this onto the Web.

Supplement this research with user interviews and testing, since there's a lot you can learn about how people react to certain technologies, when they need help, what confuses them, and so on. Look for patterns that tell you not *what* people think is fun, but *why*. For

---

Software burden

Let the user know if they will need special toys to use your site. If your site can only be viewed with Netscape Navigator 4.0, Shockwave Flash, and RealVideo, it's best to inform people before they crash their machines.

Joseph Squier, Urban Diary

example, a Civil War textbook is probably not fun. A Civil War simulation game very well may be. Find out why this is the case, and your job is halfway done.

Who's doing it right: Urban Diary

Urban Diary, shown in Figure 9-3, is a series of beautifully assembled images that lead visitors through a puzzling diary. The work is an art piece, an exploration of found objects, and an experiment in creating art on the Web. Joseph Squier created the fascinating site as a part of his larger work, The Place (*www.art.uiuc.edu/ludgate/*).

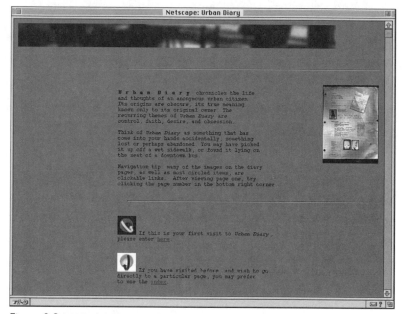

Figure 9-3. *Urban Diary provides subtle clues and beautiful images to help visitors explore its unfolding mystery.*

"I believe that people are intrigued by the mysterious, and often put off or bored by the obvious. I also know that there is a fine line between mystery and obscurity," Joseph explains.

Joseph brings this balanced approach to Urban Diary, which offers a blend of subtle guidance and flexible, user-driven exploration. One without the other would be frustrating, turning the piece into blunt recitation or impenetrable chaos. Urban Diary's balanced approach enhances the mystery of the story and encourages immersion.

Guidance

"Because the use of the Web is rising so dramatically, it is important to realize that a certain portion of the audience has probably arrived a bit disoriented, still trying to reach a comfort level with the navigational syntax that the rest of us so blithely take for granted," Joseph points out.

To address this need for guidance, Joseph included explicit directions up front. An entry page explains the basics of the site and offers the option of reading navigation tips. He also built in numerous subtle cues throughout the piece, as shown in Figure C-10.

"Once the audience enters Urban Diary, they must rely on their intuitions," Joseph says. "I gave a lot of thought to how I might use subtle navigational clues, ones that might even blend seamlessly with the imagery. I came up with the idea of circling things in pencil and underlining—something the anonymous author of the Diary might have done anyway."

Every link on early diary pages is hinted at in this way, but as viewers travel further into the piece, these clues are used less often. Joseph intended these initial pages to "educate" the audience in the Diary's approach to navigation. Once they have received the help they need, the cues are removed.

Joseph also shows a concern with timing, an essential ingredient for storytelling and something that's been largely missing from web entertainment so far. In order to control the pace at which the mystery begins to unfold, Joseph used an initial entry page that acts as a "foyer."

"You have to pass through the foyer to get to the main space," Joseph explains. "The purpose of that first page is to deliberately make people slow down. I've never liked the idea of 'surfing'—skimming the surface—and that's not what The Place is about. The Web does seem to encourage this skittish ricochet thing from site to site. I don't want people doing that at The Place.

"The foyer entrance is set to pause about 15 seconds before the main page is loaded. This is an important 15 seconds. It puts me in control for just a little bit, and makes people pause, take a breath. I know that some people don't stick around, but I figure that if they can't wait for a few seconds then they probably shouldn't be going into The Place anyway. I've made a choice about audience here. I'm not into universal appeal. I see the foyer as a screening mechanism."

Joseph's interest in timing probably has a lot to do with his background in video and photography. "When you're editing a time-based

Urban Diary
www.art.uiuc.edu/ludgate/ the/place/urban_diary/ intro.html

medium like video, or even when you're hanging an exhibition of photographs or paintings," he says, "there are complex issues concerning timing and pacing. These can be huge, exciting decisions. I'm looking for similar pacing mechanisms on the Web, and my 'foyer' is an example of one of my first and most satisfying discoveries in this area."

He also likens the purpose of the foyer to the way we are accustomed to beginning a book. "We almost never open the cover of a book and find the content starting right there on the first page—or starting on the cover. Most often, there are a few pages with little or nothing on them. You have to travel into the book a little bit before the real journey begins. Those first few quiet pages, while not containing content, serve an important function. They offer a buffer between the outside world and the inside of the book. We undergo a transition that clears our mind and helps us to focus on the experience waiting on those pages."

Flexibility

The subtle guidance that the Diary provides doesn't come at the expense of flexibility. The piece provides a rich and interesting space to explore. Return visitors can use a diary "map" or index, shown in Figure 9-4, to quickly jump to a particular page, while new visitors can explore as deeply or as superficially as they like.

To provide an exploratory experience that would not require a steep learning curve, Joseph used a visual approach. The Diary pages are large image maps. "I confess. I love image maps," Joseph says. "I find the use of text as a linking device to be a real yawner. My bias. I'm a visual artist. I prefer pictures over words. The idea of 'touching' an image on the screen and having that 'gesture' understood by the computer continues to fill me with amazement. It is one of the more intuitive forms of navigation that my mind can conceive.

"I also recognize my individual fascination is not necessarily a universal antidote," Joseph is quick to explain. "Image maps can take a long time to load, or may be completely out of the question for certain users with limited bandwidth. This is an extremely important consideration for designers. It goes back to my belief that designers need to think very carefully about their audience. In my case, I am willing to lose some of the audience at the lower end of the bandwidth spectrum. For some sites, that could be the worst of all possible choices."

Joseph has experimented with both client-side and server-side image maps for Urban Diary's navigation. "When I first started on Urban Diary, server-side maps were the only option. I had a conversion

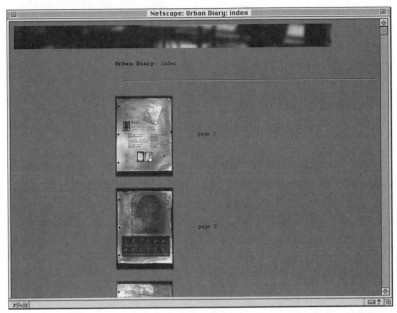

Figure 9-4. *Return visitors to Urban Diary can use a diary "map" to quickly jump to a particular page.*

experience with client-side maps. I find them infinitely more stream-lined and easier to create, and they seem to work faster than the server-side versions. There might be some excellent reasons to use server-sides, but I don't know about them."

"I think it's also important not to be completely seduced by the latest bells and whistles. The most successful sites continue to be those that rely on interesting ideas allied with solid design and architecture. Sites like these tend to use particular technologies because they make sense for, and add value to, the material."

Despite the seeming randomness of selecting options from the image maps, the Diary is surprisingly linear. It is similar both to a book and to an exhibit, and a fairly linear navigation scheme works well. "The Web promises all sorts of possibilities for non-linear structures," Joseph points out, "but that doesn't mean that older forms, like linearity, are no longer useful or interesting. I see this as a variation on the 'latest sexy web technology' syndrome, the notion that older, less glamorous devices should be shunned in favor of the Newer, Fresher, Better Thing."

For those who are curious about how the diary was assembled, Joseph offers an explanation as well as another mystery to explore. "The pages are physical objects. I scanned them. I keep them tucked away and get them out now and then. They're very delicate, fragile,

The Riven Journals

journals.riven.com

and to my mind, exquisitely beautiful. Urban Diary, by the way, originated with a bundled object I found many years ago on a rainy night, in an alley in downtown San Francisco. But that's another story...."

Who's doing it right: Riven Journals

The Riven Journals, shown in Figure C-11, were designed as a preview for the computer game Riven, the sequel to Myst. For the web preview, Organic Online created something remarkably like the CD-ROM game in feel and navigation. From the haunting background sound to the mechanical gadgets and puzzles, the Riven Journals echo their parent game brilliantly.

The result of this similar effort is that the web game is surprisingly immersive—something that is rarely found in this medium. The story, music, mystery, and mood come together to create this immersive feel, and the intuitive approach to navigation perfectly supports it.

Immersion

For a "worlds" game such as Myst or Riven, immersion is everything. Immersion is simply another way of saying suspension of disbelief, which is an essential ingredient in fantasy and storytelling. Without this suspension of disbelief, players will amuse themselves wondering how a certain tree was rendered. If they are immersed in the game, they will more likely try to climb it. Because entertainment is a two-part process—requiring both entertainer and audience—this high level of involvement is crucial.

From a navigation standpoint, the choices an entertainment developer makes can affect this suspension of disbelief. If it's necessary to stop the game in the middle and load some plug-in or other, the bubble is burst. If graphics take so long to load that the mood is lost, the bubble is burst. If navigation is not in context or is too hard to figure out, or the computer crashes in the middle, it's not going to feel very immersive. People will end up scrutinizing the trees.

To reduce some of these interruptions, Organic created very fast-loading graphics and avoided the use of plug-ins. By reusing some graphics throughout the site (such as the edges of journal pages), the pages are faster to load. Remaining graphics sport very small file sizes without compromising rich illustrations.

As much as possible is done using still images or GIF animation (for example, animating the buttons used to page through a journal, as shown in Figure 9-5). For puzzles requiring a higher degree of functionality, Java is used instead of Shockwave, providing a more accessible solution. The site also features optional background sound, but keeps audio files small and embedded, avoiding disrupting pop-up audio windows. These controlled measures help keep interruptions to a minimum. It's still a smoother experience on a high-speed connection, but even over a modem it feels compelling and trouble-free.

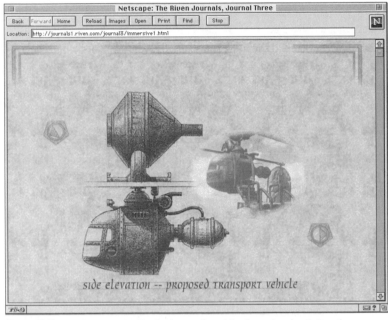

Figure 9-5. *At the Riven Journals, forward and backward controls (used to page through a journal) are animated to help suggest their purpose.*

Another important element in creating the feeling of an immersive experience is the lack of an intermediary. In many arcade and computer games, players view and participate in the action through a game interface that looks like a control panel. It's as if there is a window within the computer window, and the effect is usually to keep you one step away from the action (whether intentionally or unintentionally). In an immersive game such as Myst, there is nothing between players and the world except the glass of a computer monitor. The intermediary interface has been removed.

The Riven Journals take advantage of this same quality of immediacy, the quality which helped make Myst a best-selling computer game. Despite the fact that the journals are viewed in a browser, there is no other superficial interface to get in the way. People manipulate objects in an intuitive and direct way. To open or explore something, a user simply clicks on it. Game help appears at the

Cut to the chase

Many users will connect to your site from a modem, and some may have monthly time limits or hourly fees. If you have meaningless splash screens or other wasted real estate, they will only serve as barriers to navigation.

beginning, using the clever device of a sheet of paper plastered to a wall behind the journals.

The use of Java also contributes to the feeling of direct manipulation, since levers or buttons give satisfying feedback when they're used (see Figure 9-6). This sense of direct manipulation creates the illusion of space and of action—cause and effect—within that space.

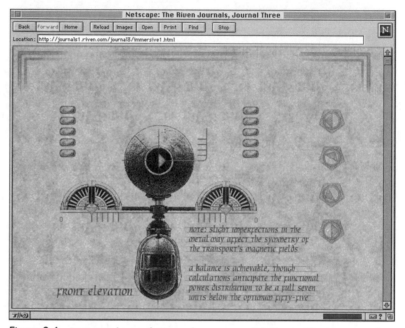

Figure 9-6. *Java puzzles are faster and more accessible than a Shockwave version might have been. The journals' mechanical controls offer satisfying feedback.*

The careful planning that went into the Riven Journals ensures that players can focus on the mystery of the journals, not on the mysteries of navigating the Web. The subtlest of cues separate the two—but the journals provide these cues without sacrificing an immersive experience. The journals are likely to do for web entertainment what Myst and Riven have done for CD-ROM entertainment: raise the bar for designing game spaces.

Who's doing it right: Crimson Empire

Navigation for entertainment sites doesn't need to be complex to work. In fact, the simplest methods often work best. For one web-based comic, a simple and intuitive approach to navigation offers the best way to tell a story.

The comic is *Crimson Empire*, shown in Figure 9-7, a *Star Wars* story written and illustrated by Dark Horse Comics, enhanced with animation and sound by Lucasfilm's Internet Division. Lucasfilm developed the web-based comic using Macromedia Flash. Though the need for a plug-in may turn away some visitors, the comic provides excellent user feedback.

Crimson Empire

www.starwars.com/crimson/

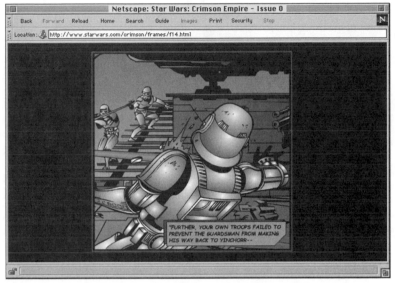

Figure 9-7. *Crimson Empire was developed by Dark Horse Comics and Lucasfilm's Internet Division, using Macromedia Flash to help tell the story.*

Feedback

Crimson Empire consists of a series of brief animation sequences presented in a linear fashion. On the Web, the typical way to navigate within a linear storyline is to find the inevitable "back" and "next" arrows. But *Crimson Empire*'s story frames are animated, not flat comic pages. Making sure people didn't accidentally click through prematurely meant finding a way to provide better user feedback. "Back" and "next" don't communicate anything about timing, inviting the possibility of mistakes.

Lucasfilm developed a simple approach to navigation that incorporates timing and feedback. When a frame is finished animating, a gray border appears around it, as shown in Figure C-12. Clicking on the image loads the next animation frame. It's simple and direct, providing excellent cues without interrupting the story.

Using this approach instead of the "back" and "next" arrows creates a feeling much more like a print comic. It's much better suited to the

Find out more

Garrand, Timothy. *Writing for Multimedia: Entertainment, Education, Training, Advertising, and the World Wide Web.* Focal Press, 1996.

Heinle, Nick. *Designing With JavaScript: Creating Dynamic Web Pages.* O'Reilly, 1997.

Laurel, Brenda. *Computers as Theatre.* Addison-Wesley, 1993.

Melcher, Ryan and Jeff Patterson. *The IUMA Guide to Creating Audio on the Web.* Peachpit, 1998.

Plant, Darrel. *Flash: Creating Animation for the Web.* Addison-Wesley, 1998.

Sinclair, Joseph. *Developing Web Pages for TV-HTML.* Charles River Media, 1998.

story, which is not simply a gallery of stills but a sequence of actions. Adding a thumbnail index similar to Urban Diary's or a text index of scene titles would be a helpful addition, especially for return visitors. Allowing people to jump to a particular scene in this way would offer the flexibility of interrupting the story and returning later.

Lucasfilm's simple, elegant approach to guiding users through the frames of *Crimson Empire* makes reading this web-based comic as fluid and fun as reading a print version. Their approach shows that "overengineering" is not always the best answer. Sometimes, simplicity is a better fit.

Recap

Entertainment developers have a particular challenge on the Web. Immersion is an important part of entertainment, but is difficult to achieve with the Web's current technical barriers. The best entertainment spaces control these technical limitations to minimize the potential for problems and interruptions. These sites also make navigation a part of the story, carefully crafting an entertainment experience that works for the Web.

## CHAPTER TEN

NAVIGATION DESIGN FOR IDENTITY SITES

Style ain't nothing but keeping the same idea from beginning to end. Everybody got it.
—August Wilson character

In this chapter
- Laying the groundwork
- Outlining specific goals
- Who's doing it right: Razorfish
- Who's doing it right: IBM
- Who's doing it right: powazek.com
- Recap

What do you stand for? How do you show it? You might adorn your car with bumper stickers, live by a certain social code, adopt a particular manner of speech, or dress a certain way. All of these factors—visual, verbal, social, and so on—contribute to how others perceive you. But what if you're trying to express yourself on the Web?

Psychologist Sherry Turkle says we are living in an "age of simulation." Online chat forums, 3D worlds, and MUDs create simulated environments, often simulated relationships. People have feuds, do business, play games, and even marry in cyberspace. CD-ROM software lets users "experience" life in another place or time. According to Turkle, these simulations can be as important to users as "RL"—real life.

This concept of simulation is especially important for anyone designing an identity site, regardless of whether it's a personal space or a large corporate endeavor. Your site is your alter ego in cyberspace, and visitors will judge you accordingly. Your interactions with users on the Web should be as compelling as those that occur off the Web, since you'll be judged by many of the same social standards. In both cases, a positive or negative experience can make a lasting impression.

Because the quality of the user experience often hinges on how people travel through a site, designing navigation means more than listing your site's sections and letting people do their thing. Imagine a

"Your interactions with users on the Web should be as compelling as those that occur off the Web, since you'll be judged by many of the same social standards."

corporate tour where people were left to wander about at random with only an org chart as a guide. As any marketing guru will tell you, that's bad public relations. Offer users guidance through your home in cyberspace just as you would if they came to your door. It's good manners, and it makes for a good experience.

Laying the groundwork

More than any other type of site, identity sites are about the developer's (or the client's) message. Still, the idea behind most identity sites is to be seen and understood—ideally by a large audience. It pays to be a little curious about why users are visiting, since it can help you make a better impression.

Visiting an identity site, users will tend to have the goals and expectations laid out in Table 10-1.

Table 10-1. *User goals and expectations: Identity*

First Tier (general navigation questions)	Where am I? Where can I go? How will I get there? How can I get back to where I once was?
Second Tier (purpose-oriented questions)	What do I know about this company (or person)? How can I find out about a product or service? How can I contact someone?

What do I know about this company (or person)?

How many web sites have you "landed on" only to quickly turn and leave? If it's more than you can count, you're not alone. People tend to make snap decisions about companies (or individuals) based on their web presence. This is nothing new, actually. People also tend to make snap decisions about companies based on their print materials.

Understanding identity issues is not just a job for graphic designers. On the Web, it's a job for programmers, marketers, customer service staff, site builders, and anyone else who gets their hands on your site. When a visitor drops in for a 10-second visit, all the pieces of your site should be working together to communicate who you are.

If someone crashes from a Java applet, has to wait while monster graphics download, or needs to sift through unintelligible marketing speak to find out about what you offer, you've said something about yourself—probably something you didn't want to say, such as "Nope, we never bother to test" or "Who cares what happens to you?" Paving the way for visitors speaks volumes about the kind of company (or person) you are.

In addition to a concern with the "big picture" or overall experience of your site, your specific navigation choices also help communicate certain qualities to visitors. IBM, for example, at one time featured a site mapping program called MAPA to allow visitors to dynamically generate a map from anywhere in the site. This small detail helped IBM stress its role as a technology leader. IBM also adds content, such as the resource for web developers shown in Figure 10-1, to help pull in visitors.

"Paving the way for visitors speaks volumes about the kind of company (or person) you are."

Figure 10-1. *More than just a piece of brochureware, IBM's site communicates that the company is a technology leader. Content such as this resource for web developers helps pull people in.*

For similar reasons, visitors to Disneyland are treated to a carefully crafted start-to-finish experience. Virtually every aspect of a visit is choreographed to reiterate the idea that Disney = Fun and Fantasy, from how visitors get around to what happens when a ride is over. You don't need Disney's resources to achieve this on the Web—but you do need their thoroughness.

How can I find out about a product or service?

Many visitors to identity sites come for inside information, to get news right from the horse's mouth. Honda doesn't sell cars on their site (*www.honda.com*), but it provides the best way to get detailed

One identity

Carry over any existing identity materials you have, such as a logo, onto the Web. Designing an entirely new web identity can confuse your users.

information about their product lines. Douglas Coupland's site (*www.coupland.com*) offers insight into his books and writings. A web developer's site might provide clients, rates, and services. How (or if) you provide this information says a lot about who you are.

Look at the case of two computer manufacturers. Winbook at one time had a site that was surprisingly information-free. You couldn't compare models, get reviews, or do much of anything. Dell (*www.dell.com*), on the other hand, allowed visitors to completely configure a dream system—encouraging people to get their hands on products, even if it was only "virtually." Dell's approach has helped win them a solid reputation and sometimes rabidly loyal customers, sending the message that "Dell does it right" (whether it's building computers or a web site).

Another approach to communicating your message is constructing meaning through organization. For example, think about your personal or business site. If you offer visitors the chance to browse through previous projects, have you organized it to guide prospective clients toward a particular conclusion or feeling? Or do you just have some randomly linked screen shots? Orchestrating how visitors navigate through this information can lend it extra value and significance.

How can I contact someone?

Strangely, a lot of companies have invested time and money in identity sites without ever including contact information. If you're going to make a good pitch, it makes sense to give your users every opportunity to follow up on it.

Making your street address, phone number, and email address easily available is not only about completing an online sales pitch, however. It's about other elusive qualities: trust and community. People are slow to trust an organization (or individual) on the Internet—with good reason, considering the number of Net scams reported. Providing ways to contact a real human in traditional, trustworthy ways (such as by postal mail or phone) can go a long way toward easing suspicious feelings.

Most people know their neighbors by face if not by name, and many people living in small communities are familiar with local merchants and community workers. Why not work to make yourself as well known and as trusted? Providing ample opportunities for contact is a simple place to start.

There's a flip side to encouraging contact, though. If you provide an email contact, make sure you respond to any messages within 48 hours, or this positive marketing opportunity can become a negative experience. If you decide you can't handle the volume of responses or the rapid turnaround time, you're better off providing only a snail mail address.

Outlining specific goals

The questions in the previous sections reflect typical user expectations for the majority of identity sites. A third tier added to your goals and expectations chart will help reveal yet another layer of user needs. In Table 10-2, a university is used as an example.

Table 10-2. *User goals and expectations: Identity: University*

First Tier (general navigation questions)	Where am I? Where can I go? How will I get there? How can I get back to where I once was?
Second Tier (purpose-oriented questions)	What do I know about this company (or person)? How can I find out about a product or service? How can I contact them?
Third Tier (topic- or audience-oriented questions)	What is the school's philosophy? What courses and programs are offered? Where can I find out about faculty members? What are the students like? How do I apply? How can I get there if I need to visit? How do I calculate costs?

A large percentage of visitors to a university site are applicants for admission, or are thinking of becoming applicants. These visitors usually have a very specific set of questions to ask of a variety of schools, and will sometimes rate responses based on trivial factors. If a particular university can answer their questions fairly easily, it bodes well for the entire process. A positive experience on the Web—especially for college applicants, who tend to make decisions on gut feelings—is a powerful factor in decision-making.

For a university, finding out about common third-tier expectations might involve questioning admissions staff, families, and enrolled students. For other identity sites, the audience may differ but the approach will be much the same. To find out more about third-tier expectations for your identity site, try some of the following methods:

- Ask people to write down traits or qualities that they consider positive for your type of identity site. For example, a hospital might have patients write down ideal qualities and find that

To link or not to link

Give some thought to whether you will link to other sites, and if so, how you will do it. This is particularly important on identity sites. A poorly placed or poorly labeled link to another site can sometimes leave users thinking that the new site is part of yours. Link selectively and provide link annotations if possible.

adjectives such as "clean" or "caring" were common. These traits can help you refine your site's tone and approach to interface design.

- Take a look at annual reports in print, on CD-ROM, and on the Web. How do these materials target a broad, usually anonymous audience of shareholders? How do they get their message across?

- Do some testing with small groups of users. Have people browse several identity sites and answer questions such as "What do you think of this company?" or "What does this company stand for?" What approaches or technologies disrupt the session or contribute to a negative experience (such as crashing)? What approaches contribute to a positive experience?

You may also want to try reading up on branding and identity issues in design, or even take a company tour for extra brain food. Balance these findings with what you want to communicate, and you'll begin to develop interactions that are meaningful for both you and your users.

Who's doing it right: Razorfish

"An identity site for a design company, particularly a digital one, is an interesting problem," according to Razorfish's Stephen Turbek, the company's information designer.

"There is the need to represent the company and to provide information to those who might be interested, but the form it takes is often read as much as the writing it contains. A site has to be both a functional tool and a living manifesto from the company."

Razorfish, whose site is shown in Figure C-13, has been creating just this sort of "living manifesto" since the early days of the Web. They've continually modeled possibilities for the medium both on their corporate site and within the Razorfish Subnetwork (RSUB), home to well-known destinations such as Typographic, Blue Dot, and The Virginator.

What's most exciting about Razorfish's approach is that they skillfully balance guidance and flexibility, cutting-edge technology and accessible browsing. In their hands, these qualities are not opposites, but ingredients that combine to shape the user experience.

On their corporate site, flexibility and guidance are clear strengths. A third quality—responsiveness—is also a powerful ingredient, and supports an idea that is becoming increasingly important in this medium: an interface should adapt to the visitor, and provide feedback about its changes.

Responsiveness

Responsiveness is roughly the idea that a user should expect a response, either immediate or long term, from a system. It's linked to ideas in human factors and industrial psychology, and helps to explain why telephones make musical sounds when we dial them. It also explains why waiting for downloads continues to be one of the most frustrating aspects of web use.

In web design, we've only begun to explore this idea of responsiveness, creating rollovers that mimic pushing buttons in the physical world or form output that thanks visitors for their submissions. There's a lot more we could do, and Razorfish shows two interesting approaches.

The most interesting is the frenzy meter, shown in Figure 10-2, a Java applet that "monitors bandwidth usage by animating during periods of heavy downloading." Sure, you could watch the status bar instead, but this is a much more intriguing approach.

Figure 10-2. *The "frenzy meter" at Razorfish animates during downloads.*

Stephen explains their development of the frenzy meter: "Because of the state of Java, particularly when we created the site, we didn't want to depend on a Java interface. However, as our programmers are very creative, we were able to make an interesting use of Java that added to the experience."

Stephen describes the frenzy meter as "a subtle addition that makes for a richer experience. The Java applet is actually measuring the data transfer happening on the client machine. As the transfer increases, the meter flickers more wildly." The frenzy meter also serves an additional navigation purpose, that of providing a quick link back to Razorfish's "epicenter," or core.

In addition to the frenzy meter, Razorfish employs rollovers to provide relevant highlights, as shown in Figure C-14. At the top of the screen, the Company and Case Studies sections feature small red "TVs" with mini-content cues. These cues, provided by rollovers, vary depending what area of the site you're in.

As Stephen explains it, "The square directly to the right of the section title shows the icon for the section you're currently in. The others randomly display other areas of the site that relate to that section. These links are based on our custom back end system, which allows us to define related items. These subtle choices expand the user's

Figure 10-4. *The four different options for visitors to Razorfish.*

options if they are interested, but do not limit or stand in for more obvious navigation possibilities."

Flexibility

Additions such as the TV rollovers make Razorfish both responsive and flexible. From the front door, users are given the opportunity to do things in a way that makes them feel comfortable. Opportunities exist for linear navigation, random exploration, and many options in between.

One of the things Razorfish was careful of when designing their site was browser and bandwidth accessibility. "Though we like to believe that everyone is connected to the Internet with a phat machine," Stephen points out, "we recognize that people's pipelines and browser capabilities differ."

To answer this need, the site offers users a choice at the front door, as shown in Figures 10-3 and 10-4. Users can pick the experience that suits them: S, M, L, or XL, with XL being the most resource-intensive. "We thought it was important to be up-front and honest about it," Stephen says of offering different versions of the site. "The same information is conveyed through every method. It's the richness of experience that varies."

Figure 10-3. *Razorfish offers four ways to experience their site: S, M, L, and XL, to fit capabilities of different users.*

Throughout the site this flexibility is apparent. "If this is to be an interactive medium," Stephen explains, "we shouldn't force the user into one path, but create enough to allow the user to find the way they want to navigate through the site."

They use a number of navigational approaches to accomplish this goal. In addition to providing a menu of topics, they also provide opportunities for linear navigation, suggest topics by animating short-cuts, and allow cross-linking to related areas. This variety is accomplished without HTML pages.

"We built a dynamic publishing system to handle the very specific needs our site had, including multiple levels of complexity, rich inter-activity, and relationships between sections," Stephen says. "Our site adjusts to every browser from WebTV to Netscape 4 and has proved to be a very workable system to expand and update."

Guidance

With the high degree of flexibility their site offers, Razorfish doesn't sacrifice guidance. Numerous small suggestions and tips help lead visitors to where they might want to go. Building in these contextual tips takes a bit more planning than simply implementing a forced linear march through your site, but it's well worth it—especially for a site with Razorfish's emphasis on user-driven movement.

One example of this guidance is that the two most common site areas—Company and Case Studies—appear highlighted at the top of the screen. This shows their importance and makes it easier for visitors to get what they need quickly. Another subtle example of guidance is in the blinking arrows at the bottom of the screen that allow for linear navigation, as shown in Figure 10-5. When you are able to "thumb through" a certain section, the arrows animate. At other times, they are still.

Figure 10-5. *Blinking arrows at the bottom of the screen allow for linear navigation within Razorfish's site.*

Razorfish also offers what they call the "vibe window," shown in Figure 10-6. This window, an animation box that rotates highlights from the Razorfish Subnetwork of sites, is intended in part as internal promotion. As Stephen explains, "By doing internal promotion, you can advertise to the user about features they may be interested in but didn't know about."

One of the best features of the vibe window is that it doesn't just toss you off to some new spot—an important consideration if you want to orchestrate the user experience. Before you are sent to the site high-lighted in the vibe window, an intermediate screen explains what you selected and where you will be going. For example, if you click

Dead end

Be careful about creating dead ends, such as "Under Construction" signs. If content is not ready to premiere but you'd like to let visitors know it's coming soon, a brief note on one of your finished pages should do the trick.

Figure 10-6. *The "vibe window" animates highlights from the Razorfish subnetwork of sites.*

on the vibe window when it shows a rotating graphic for "Disinformation," the following message appears:

> You have selected Disinformation, the subculture search engine. Disinformation is one of the most acclaimed and traveled sites on the World Wide Web. One of several titles found on The Razorfish Subnetwork, Disinformation is devoted to the proposition that "everything you know is wrong."

A small navigation icon prompts users to "Go to RSUB now." By providing this launchpad instead of simply linking without explanation, Razorfish can offer a more polished, seamless experience to visitors.

Stephen has some additional thoughts to offer on architecture and navigation. "I think that the organization of information should react more to the individual project at hand than to theory. By far the most important thing to do is to make sure that the project is really well defined. Nothing messes up a project more than last minute alterations to scope and purpose.

"One should always keep the person who is going to use the interface in mind," he continues. "Make sure they can make a mental model of the project and that the experience is both a useful and enjoyable one."

Who's doing it right: IBM

IBM's corporate site, shown in Figure C-15, is no skimpy marketing pamphlet. The site is enormous and information-rich, offering technology news, resources in multiple languages, a store, developer tips, and much more. Working with the San Francisco-based design firm

Would you like fish food with that?

Bringing visitors to an identity site takes effort. People who do come and absorb what you have to say are often those who would have come anyway: customers, friends, coworkers, peers. How do you get your fair share of all those other web users?

Part of the answer lies in how you market yourself. You probably wouldn't market yourself on a billboard the same way you would in a magazine, or present yourself on radio in the same way you would on television. The Web has its own marketing quirks, so you'll need to try some creative techniques.

Bringing visitors to an identity site takes effort. "Fish food" can help you draw new visitors to your site.

Rather than limiting yourself to "brochureware"—flat, traditional, marketing content—try creating "fish food" instead. Fish food, a term coined by David Siegel in *Creating Killer Web Sites* (Hayden, 1997), is added content designed for this medium and created with one purpose: to create ripples on the web fish tank and pull the guppies in.

If your company is a tax preparation service, your fish food might be a beat-the-IRS game. If your personal site features photos of your hernia operation, add a discussion board where people can share their experiences. Fish food doesn't replace your regular marketing duties, but it can help you draw new visitors to your site—as well as saving you from publishing the world's most expensive online brochure.

Studio Archetype, IBM has managed to bring this sprawling territory under one cohesive corporate umbrella.

IBM succeeds on the Web where many large corporations fail. They may have their hands in many simultaneous pies, but they present a consistent and united front. They've even managed to inject a friendly and personal tone, despite the challenging scope of their site. Their strengths are in branding, tone, and speed, three common problem areas for large corporate sites.

Branding

IBM has one of the most recognizable brands in any industry, and it's good business to leverage this on the Web. However, with many thousands of screens of information, branding becomes essential to navigation as well. How will visitors know they are still in IBM's corporate sphere, or if they've left for outside resources? With various departments and projects presenting a different "look and feel," it would be easy to lose the way.

But IBM has put as much thought into branding as they have into these many projects, and their site reflects a clear corporate identity

IBM

www.ibm.com

throughout. A distinctive top header featuring the well-known logo appears on every page. Variations on this header appear in subcategories and departments. The position of the logo is consistent throughout, reminding visitors that they are still within IBM's corporate home.

Style also plays an important part of establishing IBM's brand. The logo is strong enough to withstand numerous color changes (a testimony to the talents of designer Paul Rand), but cluttering the site with many differing typefaces or layouts could still sabotage it. Though some stylistic changes appear among areas of the site, basic stylistic traits stay the same, helping to contribute to an ongoing sense of location.

Speed

IBM uses a number of approaches to help visitors find what they want as quickly as possible. The site's scope could make finding a specific piece of information—such as whether a particular product has been released yet—extremely difficult and time consuming. IBM's many shortcuts allow visitors to jump quickly to what they need.

Visitors can search, browse a subject index (see Figure 10-7), or view a map of the site's contents. The search feature is particularly well organized. Typing a term in the search box and pressing the Go button yields an annotated list of results. For some topics on which there is a great deal of information, such as Java, the results list shows a link to a broad section rather than to every resource within it. Additional resources can also be displayed, and the number of results pages is clearly indicated by small page icons.

For people with browsers that support Dynamic HTML, added shortcuts are available in the form of rollovers, as shown in Figure 10-8. Passing your mouse over a site section shows a drop-down menu of options in that category, a simple and direct way to navigate the site.

A further way to encourage quick movement through the site is the use of *subsites*. Subsites, a term coined by Jakob Nielsen, are sections within your site that have their own look and feel and navigation. For IBM, subsites are an answer to the problem of information density (see Figure 10-9).

Each subsite—whether it deals with servers or shopping—echoes the look and feel of the parent site and features the IBM logo in a consistent location. Subsites allow IBM to present projects or product lines in specially constructed ways, without sacrificing cohesion and branding. They also mean that users don't need to navigate through several layers of confusingly "carbon copied" screens, and they

Figure 10-7. *Visitors to IBM's site can browse a subject index to help them find what they need quickly.*

Customize

If your site serves several audiences, try to give them each a comfortable, appropriate environment to move around in. Provide them with tools they will be able to use. This might entail using subsites (areas of your site that maintain a separate look and feel) for each audience.

Figure 10-8. *Users with browsers that support Dynamic HTML will find an extra shortcut at IBM's site: rollovers that display a drop-down menu when the mouse passes over them.*

lengthen the site's navigation breakdown point by periodically seeming to flatten the hierarchy.

Subsites usually rely on a hub navigation system, where users navigate among subsites by periodically jumping back up to the "hub" or core. For a site as rich and deep as IBM's, subsites introduce speed and the flexibility to better tailor the approach to the content.

Figure 10-9. *IBM makes excellent use of subsites, retaining their strong brand throughout but allowing for individualized approaches. IBM's branding system on the Web was developed by Studio Archetype.*

The danger with subsites is knowing when to spawn one. Not every category deserves its own subsite. IBM has wisely kept many central administrative sections safely within the hub (or core) of the site, spinning off sections when there is a need to address a special audience or need, such as shopping, annual reports, or resources for Java programmers.

Tone

IBM adds another essential ingredient to their corporate mix: a friendly and open tone. There are few corporations that will allow the average visitor anywhere near the CEO. Some companies make it hard to speak to anyone on staff. IBM goes beyond providing basic contact information and encourages you to email the top dog himself, CEO Lou Gerstner (see Figure 10-10).

Figure 10-10. *"Lou's page" encourages visitors to contact IBM's top dog, Lou Gerstner.*

Lou Gerstner stands in for IBM as much as or more than the logo does. Encouraging people to send him email helps build trust and increase customer loyalty. Giving him space on the site makes him a tangible part of IBM's web presence.

IBM also publishes their annual reports on the site, an open approach that (like Lou's email) also fosters communication and trust. Each of these reports acts like a subsite, featuring its own navigation and approach. With reports for 1994 through 1996, visitors can get a good sense of how the company's approach to the Web has evolved.

IBM is positioning themselves to be a force in e-commerce and Java development, and is one of the largest ad spenders on the Web. With a potentially huge volume of traffic being directed to the site by these marketing campaigns, IBM needs to show that they are more than just a corporate edifice. They need to show that they are a reliable technology partner, a source that is more trusted, competent, and congenial than competitors. Their web presence goes a long way toward accomplishing these goals.

Who's doing it right: powazek.com

"For me, powazek.com is the only place where, as a designer, I have no one to please but myself," Derek Powazek says of his personal site, shown in Figure C-16. "I have to please the client in my professional projects. I have to please the authors and audience in the fray. But with powazek.com, I just have to please myself."

Powazek.com
www.powazek.com

Derek, best known as the guy who runs "the fray" *(www.fray.com)*, uses powazek.com as a launchpad to his personal and professional projects. "It ties all my disparate projects together and provides one place where people can find out more about me as a person," Derek explains. The site's strength is its cohesion, particularly in the face of this diversity of resources.

Cohesion, the sense that a site is bound together, is a wonderful thing to find in this medium. For all its strengths, hypermedia is a sprawling, potentially boundless sort of thing. A cohesive approach—whether accomplished through design, structure, tone, or a combination of these—helps users to get a sense of location, of where they are in web space. Powazek.com shows that cohesion doesn't mean "dull sameness." Instead, it can enhance and showcase variety while limiting the chance of confusion.

Powazek.com features links to Derek's portfolio, his "home page" (for personal information), and to "the fray" and "kvetch," two of his larger projects. It also provides links to other temporary projects, including a page for a font he designed and a site created for a friend.

"The challenge I hit after a while was, with all these links on one page, how to communicate more about them visually," he explained. "Some links were external, some were internal. Some were major, some weren't." To provide the visual cues the site needed, Derek created bands of color separating internal links (his portfolio and home page) from external links (his major projects). Temporary projects are highlighted with animated boxes that pop in and out, drawing the visitor's eye.

Derek changes the page often, yet it remains cohesive and clear. In each version, he has maintained a consistent structure and a strong sense of personality. He also archives past versions of the page (see Figure C-17), encouraging people to explore the evolution of the site (and, in case you feel nostalgic, making it easy to go back to a particular design).

"Because the main powazek.com page is just links to my projects (and a few other pages)," he says, "I get a kick out of redesigning it all the time and playing with new design ideas there. I also leave all the past design experiments up there for people to see. In that way, it's like having a bit of my portfolio up front."

This open approach to design and experimentation says as much about Derek as his portfolio or resume (maybe more, actually). It balances intriguing variety with thoughtful structure to create a compelling experience for visitors.

Derek Powazek, powazek.com

Recap

If we're living in an "age of simulation," the way we craft identity sites becomes less a matter of providing corporate information than of shaping an experience. Thinking about how you want to be perceived is standard to most identity designs, but on the Web we need to add another component: understanding how the vagaries of the medium can affect this impression. Technical difficulties, inappropriate design, poorly planned navigation, and other factors can send messages you may not have intended. Your site is your alter ego in webspace, and a positive or negative experience can make a lasting impression.

Find out more

English, Marc. *Designing Identity: Graphic Design As a Business Strategy.* Rockport, 1998.

Olins, Wally. *Corporate Identity: Making Business Strategy Visible Through Design.* Harvard Business School Press, 1990.

Rogener, Stefan, Albert-Jan Pool, Ursula Packhauser, and E. M. Ginger. *Branding with Type.* Hayden Books, 1995.

Schulman, Martin A. and Rick R. Smith. *The Internet Strategic Plan: A Step-By-Step Guide to Connecting Your Company.* Wiley, 1997.

Sherwin, Gregory R., and Emily N. Avila. *Connecting Online: Creating a Successful Image on the Internet.* Psi, 1998.

Turkle, Sherry. *Life on the Screen: Identity in the Age of the Internet.* Touchstone Books, 1997.

## CHAPTER ELEVEN

NAVIGATION DESIGN FOR LEARNING SITES

Everything should be made as simple as possible, but not simpler.
—Albert Einstein

In this chapter

- Laying the groundwork
- Outlining specific goals
- Who's doing it right: DigitalThink
- Who's doing it right: National Geographic
- Who's doing it right: The Annenberg/CPB Project
- Recap

I love science museums. Ten dollars gets you enough tweaking, pulling, switching, pressing, poking, and learning to satisfy even the most extreme fidgeters. What makes most science museums great, however, is not that they have a lot of cool gadgets (though that's definitely part of the charm). Looking beyond the veneer of frenetic activity, someone has put a lot of thought into how to design a user-driven learning space.

Designing learning spaces on the Web is a lot like designing learning spaces in a museum. In both cases, audiences are transitory, move through at different paces, and have different backgrounds or experience to bring to the topic. Both museum and web learners tend to lose patience quickly, prefer quickly digested information, and want to try things for themselves. With its potential for encouraging interactivity and experimentation, the Web has a lot to offer these "casual" learners.

Not all learners are casual learners, however. Directed learners, like directed shoppers, have much more concrete goals and often need more in-depth information. Your friend may have a passing interest in how Java works, but as a professional developer you may need to know it—and fast. You may be in a situation where your employer demands that you learn it. Your approach to learning the topic will probably not be the same as your friend's.

Depending on whether they are casual or directed learners, people may have different requirements when it comes to how a topic is

"Learning is often cumulative. Recommending a starting point helps ensure that learners don't miss out on crucial information."

presented. People may also have different learning styles, or preferences for particular teaching methods. But despite these important differences, learners still share some fundamental needs and desires, especially when it comes to learning online. These common learning needs should help you lay the groundwork for all learning sites, whether you're in the business of offering corporate training or unveiling the mysteries of the dinosaurs.

Laying the groundwork

Taking a few years off to study educational theory would go far toward telling you what learners need—but you're not likely to find a client who will sit patiently by while you get your degree. Luckily, there's a simpler alternative that can still offer valuable insights: learn from learners themselves. By observing and interacting with them, particularly with those who are participating in web-based learning, we can find out about their preferences, behaviors, needs, and wishes.

Observing learners on the Web, you'll find that they typically have the "second tier" expectations shown in Table 11-1.

Table 11-1. *User goals and expectations: Learning*

First Tier (general navigation questions)	Where am I? Where can I go? How will I get there? How can I get back to where I once was?
Second Tier (purpose-oriented questions)	Where should I begin? Do I need special knowledge or tools? How do I know what you say is true? How can I get information that's right for me? How can I try it for myself? What if I want to learn more (or less)? What if I have questions?

Where should I begin?

One of the great things about hypermedia is that you can go almost anywhere from almost anywhere. It's also one of hypermedia's biggest drawbacks. Where do you start if there is no logical beginning, middle, or end? If there are a dozen possible routes, how do you know which one is right for you? Exploration stops being fun when all guidance goes out the window.

Most people, once they're oriented, can become much freer in their explorations. It's a bit like a toddler who continually heads back to "home base" (a parent) during his explorations. Learners are the same. Offer them some initial guidance about how to begin, and they will be able to roam more freely and confidently.

Learning is also often cumulative—that is, each lesson or experience builds on a previous one. How can I appreciate the beauty of Urdu poetry when I haven't mastered the grammar? What's the point of learning Java if you've never laid eyes on the Web? Some things just need to happen in progression. Recommending a starting point helps ensure that learners don't miss out on crucial information.

One option for designing a learning site with a clear starting point is to use a linear entryway. This doesn't mean you're trapped in linearity throughout the site (though a linear approach seems to work well to present core concepts). For example, The Annenberg/CPB Project Exhibits use an initial splash screen—with only one possible route into the site—to introduce the topic to visitors. Later screens build in flexibility of movement.

Do I need special knowledge or tools?

I remember desperately wanting to take clarinet lessons in fourth grade. Fresh from a bad experience with violin lessons, I walked into the school music room and signed up for clarinet. When I showed up for the first class, I was the only one without a clarinet. Those lessons didn't last long, because no one bothered to state the obvious: You have to bring your own instrument, kid. Duh.

Normally, if you sign up for an art class, you're told what supplies to bring. Take a language class and you'll be told where to find the text-book. A class on programming or networking may have particular prerequisites. In all of these cases, students are told what they need to have or know before they join a class.

Telling people what they'll need saves time (theirs and yours) and avoids potential problems such as inadequate equipment or insufficient background knowledge. Removing these potential barriers means learners can focus on the topic at hand, not on unnecessary problems.

DigitalThink, a site specializing in web-based training, saves users time and angst by creating an area for "setting up your computer for a DigitalThink course," shown in Figure 11-1. This setup area offers instructions for gearing up on different platforms. They also state clearly in their course catalog whether students should buy a book, and where the book can be found. This detailed information helps keep students informed of additional costs or setup tasks, which in turn helps them make better decisions about whether to sign up for a course.

"Give most people a chance to doubt your authority, and they'll ricochet back into the search engine they came from."

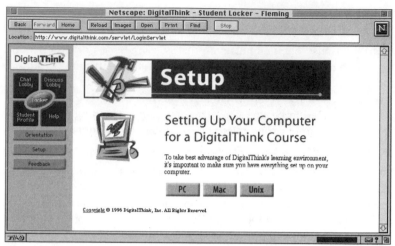

Figure 11-1. *DigitalThink offers instructions for setting up your computer for a course.*

How do I know what you say is true?

Like it or not, the Web has a reputation as untrustworthy. Partly this is because there is a lot of garbage and misinformation out there—in the world, not just in cyberspace. Mixed feelings about the Web's trustworthiness are also in response to a lack of source information, the clear communication of who's behind a site.

If you think that mistrust doesn't have much to do with navigation, go find some parents who are searching the Web for homework information for their kids. Questions about source, worries about bias, and doubts about accuracy (which can be founded on the smallest spelling error) are effective ways to spook visitors. Give most people a chance to doubt your authority, and they'll ricochet back into the search engine they came from.

Having a trusted and recognizable name, such as National Geographic or The Annenberg/CPB Project, certainly helps—but only if it's displayed prominently. Providing names of producers and content creators is also part of gaining trust. It shows that someone stands behind the information, and that some care was taken in putting it together. You'd be surprised at how far these simple measures will go toward establishing the trust a learning site needs.

How can I get information that's right for me?

If directed and casual learners have different needs, and people in general have different learning preferences (or learning styles), then part of your job becomes building in flexibility and alternatives. Even if you're presenting corporate training to a group of people with the same skill set and experience, you may need to use different training techniques to reach all of your users.

Usually this means offering opportunities for visual learners to view pictures or diagrams, for verbal/textual learners to hear and read explanations, and for active learners to learn by discovery or activity. It sounds pretty daunting, but it's not as hard as it seems. Providing these different opportunities will make learners feel more at ease right from the start and will help ensure that they aren't turned away by an approach that doesn't address their needs. An added benefit is that, similar to museum design, incorporating this flexibility can make your learning site a richer and more exciting space.

DigitalThink, for example, uses several methods to help communicate a subject to students. Text forms the bulk of it, but is well organized and separated across pages to make it more digestible. Figures and illustrations are being used more and more, and new features such as Java "flipbooks" increase discovery opportunities for active learners.

With personalization on the rise, it's increasingly likely that learners will be able to design their own learning experiences, complete with video, audio, images, or activities—or devoid of them, if they desire. Exploring how we can better offer flexible, customized learning on the Web should offer some intriguing solutions.

How can I try it for myself?

If I were to tell you that you could make a lightbulb glow with only a battery and two wires, would you believe me? Or would you need to try it for yourself? If you see a cool example of code or an article on a new browser stunt, don't you want to see for yourself if it really works?

Learning something new seems to demand that it be tested or tried. People learning a new language will often go out of their way to find others who speak it. New site designers will often take on clients for free in order to try out their newfound skills. The announcement of a new browser or software feature often precedes a lot of successful and not-so-successful experimentation. The need to try things for ourselves is a natural response, one we can address in exciting ways on the Web.

The Annenberg/CPB Project Exhibits, for example, build in frequent opportunities for hands-on experimentation in a topic. People learning about Russia can calculate the cost of living in Moscow,

"Students need to know there is help in case they have problems or fail to grasp a concept."

while those learning about the Middle Ages can try their hand at medieval doctoring. Exploring an exhibit on statistics in polling, learners are asked to participate in a poll and can see how others have responded.

These opportunities for discovery help people to synthesize new information, or to integrate it into their experience and thinking. Like science museums, where hands-on is a way of life, sites that encourage this sort of discovery make people a more central part of their own learning process. Opportunities appear in context, so that people don't need to wander far afield in search of ways to test their knowledge.

What if I want to learn more (or less)?

In creating a book or video, you're pretty much locked in to what and how much you present. Unless you're working for Cliff's Notes, you're probably not offering a condensed version and an in-depth version of your product. On the Web, building in layers of information is a much more feasible proposition.

But why bother taking the time to do this? Remember that you may have both casual and directed learners visiting your site. Providing a concise route for more casual learners (who tend to skim the surface) helps to hold their interest and pull them through your site. In-depth information, which most directed learners will demand, can be made available in a separate layer or route. Serving these needs separately encourages both your casual and directed users to stick around.

National Geographic for Kids uses a similar idea in their Cyber Tiger module. Kids can create a new home for a Siberian tiger using facts about its habitat and behavior. Additional information is provided in small chunks throughout the module in a "Wild File" that is linked to from certain pages, as shown in Figure 11-2. The alternative would be to make kids read long passages of text in order to proceed with an activity, an almost sure-fire way to lose them.

What if I have questions?

The ability to question an instructor is part of what makes "in-person" learning effective, and one of the reasons why distance learning has been slow to get off the ground. It's a rare class that winds down without a question asked, since even the most skilled instructor simply can't predict what is in every student's mind.

Students need to know that there is help in case something goes wrong, in case they fail to grasp a concept, or in case they have questions about extending their knowledge or applying their skills. If

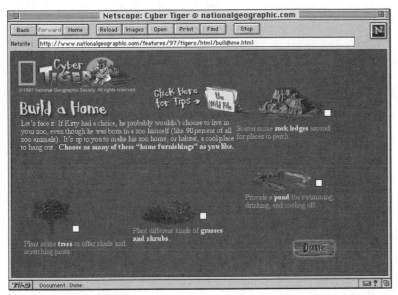

Figure 11-2. *National Geographic's Cyber Tiger offers kids the chance to find out more by clicking on a "Wild File."*

you're selling courses on the Web, you may find that prospective students have another set of questions having to do with how learning works online, or how they can talk to an instructor, or what happens if they have technical difficulties. Like shopping sites, if you answer these questions before they are asked, users are more likely to give you their trust—and their business.

Outlining specific goals

For learning sites, many of your most important decisions (and most exciting developments) will be made in response to your specific audience and focus. For example, if you're introducing dinosaurs to adults, you'll present it quite differently than if you're introducing the same topic to kindergartners. If you're planning a site to be used by one teacher in one classroom, you'll approach it in a very different way than you would if the site were geared toward the public Web.

For me, these differences are part of what makes web development exciting. Just when you think you've done the definitive site on a topic, someone throws in a new and interesting twist. Answering the challenges of these specific audiences and topics makes for a richer, more enjoyable experience for users. The alternative is a cookie-cutter approach to site design, which doesn't make for very good service.

To help target your development challenges, go back to your goals and expectations chart and fill in a third tier representing topic- or audience-oriented questions. For a site on learning a language, these third-tier goals might look like the ones in Table 11-2.

Table 11-2. *User goals and expectations: Learning: Language*

First Tier (general navigation questions)	Where am I? Where can I go? How will I get there? How can I get back to where I once was?
Second Tier (purpose-oriented questions)	Where should I begin? Do I need special knowledge or tools? How do I know what you say is true? How can I get information that's right for me? How can I try it for myself? What if I want to learn more (or less)? What if I have questions?
Third Tier (topic- or audience-oriented questions)	How do I know if I'm saying the words right? What if I come across a word I don't know? How can I try out my new conversation skills? Is there anything I need to know about the culture in order to learn the language?

If you can address both these second- and third-tier questions, as well as serve people's basic navigation needs, your site will almost take care of itself. Using these questions as a guide is the key to identifying your real challenges, and brainstorming user-centered solutions.

There are a few things you can do to beef up your knowledge of learners' behaviors and goals, especially where specific audiences and topics are concerned. To find out what these third-tier goals are for your learning site, try adding some of these research tasks to your development schedule:

- Take a class. If you're planning a language learning site, for example, go take a class on a language you plan to offer. Within the first few meetings, you should have a sense of what your own learning needs are. Listen to other people's questions in class and see if you can find shared concerns. Interview classmates if you can.

- Talk to teachers. Whether it's approaching your language instructor in the previous scenario or arranging to meet with a public school teacher, talking to teachers is sure to yield results. Ask them what the most frequently asked questions are in their topic, or what support materials they use. Find out not only what they do, but what they don't do—and find out why, if you can.

- Arrange a test to find out for yourself how learners react to the Web. Have co-workers, friends, or hired temps or testers (if you can get them) look at several learning sites. What do people tend to like? What do they dislike? How much text can they read and absorb? Do their behaviors change if they are directed (or very task-focused) learners or if they are learning for the enjoyment of it? One-on-one tests allow you to gain much better insight into individual behaviors, so try to plan your testing around these one-on-one meetings.

- Research current thinking in education. Are there new practices you can incorporate into your site? Are there methods that might be particularly well suited to the Web? Pick up a few books and magazines on teaching and training, and see what professionals are talking about. If you don't feel qualified to integrate these new methods but have some money to spare, think about bringing in an expert advisor or educational consultant.

- Look at CD-ROMs, books, and videos that are geared toward helping someone learn about your topic. If you're presenting dinosaurs, look at science CD-ROMs, or glossy illustrated children's books, or a PBS video. How do they present the information to different audiences? What's effective and what's not?

- Go to museums, especially science museums or those that offer "hands-on" learning. How did the exhibit designers create learning spaces for a moving audience? What exhibits are the most popular? How do museums blend experimentation and guidance?

- Read training manuals and other self-guided instruction materials. Look at help screens in various software applications. Are there approaches that seem to work well? What might turn people off about training manuals?

As always, use interviews and tests to augment your research, and look for patterns in what you find. Particularly in education, there are plenty of excellent resources to be found.

Who's doing it right: DigitalThink

DigitalThink (Figure 11-3), a web-based training source, has been getting a lot of attention lately. They've been lauded for providing "a surprisingly personal experience" (*Training with Multimedia*) and for being "the first truly collaborative learning site" (*New Media*). When the INVISION awards for excellence in multimedia handed them a gold medal in 1997, one judge described the site as "one of the best examples of Web-based training today."

DigitalThink

www.digitalthink.com

Figure 11-3. *DigitalThink has been called "one of the best examples of web-based training today" because of its simplicity, support, and flexibility.*

Online training is nothing new. So what makes DigitalThink different?

Adjectives like "personal" and "collaborative" begin to tell the story. The site's strengths are simplicity, support, and flexibility—which also happen to be among the top concerns for people in search of Web-based training.

Simplicity

In a medium already famous for "information overload," simplicity is a rare and wonderful find. It's easy to want to include everything on a site, since media boundaries and storage limits seem vague. But selectivity separates the wheat from the chaff these days, and keeping the approach simple and direct is part of this equation.

This is especially true when the audience is learners, who should not have to learn a complex site system before learning the topic at hand. If you have an hour to spend learning Java on the Web, and you spend half of that time trying to figure out how the site works and the other half downloading components you need, you're not going to get very far.

"Simple" and "information-rich" are not necessarily opposites. A carefully structured site can appear simple and approachable though it provides a large amount of valuable information. A poorly structured site can make the smallest piece of information seem hopelessly complex. DigitalThink excels at the former—distilling large amounts of information into a simple and approachable format.

Chris Gollmer, DigitalThink's Creative Director, explains their approach. "From a design standpoint, both instructionally and graphically, we were trying to present the information in the simplest way possible and make it really easy to learn."

One of the ways DigitalThink accomplished this was to develop a course model and apply it across topics, maintaining consistency and reducing the chance that repeat students would need to relearn the site system each time they took a class.

Chris Gollmer, DigitalThink

"Once we had a system in place, it was easy to adapt it to any course," Chris says. "They share the same features—they all have audio, they all have chat, they all have exercises and quizzes—it's just the content that changes. The model allows us to be flexible enough that we can handle different kinds of courses, whether they're information technology or lifestyles courses."

Part of keeping the experience simple and direct is managing download time. "One of the big limitations for most of our students is bandwidth," Chris explains. DigitalThink was able to keep graphics small and fast by limiting the site's color palette and using "flat" art (illustration that features large areas of a color). They also limited the number of graphics to reduce unnecessary downloads, and recycled headers, footers, and navigation icons across the site so that many graphics can be loaded from the browser cache as a user progresses through the course.

The site also features intuitive navigation graphics. Buttons and bars look pressable—they suggest their purpose, as shown in Figure 11-4. Flat art used for tips or illustration is therefore less easily confused with navigation graphics. DigitalThink has continued to improve on the intuitiveness of their navigation graphics throughout their courses. In earlier incarnations, the directional arrows were often indistinguishable from the header art. "We did have some issues where the arrows were getting lost in the art—they were too decorative and not functional enough." Figure 11-5 shows some early sketches for the navigation bar.

Support

From a "locker" where you can store course information to a setup area that shows you how to configure your computer for a course, DigitalThink offers excellent support features for learners. Removing potential obstacles, such as worries over course signup or materials, means visitors are more likely to sign up for and successfully complete a course.

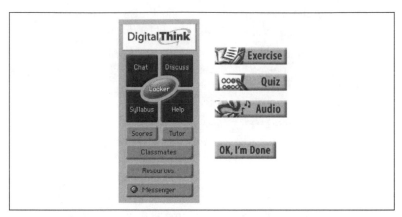

Figure 11-4. *Buttons in DigitalThink's navigation toolbar look pressable—they suggest their purpose.*

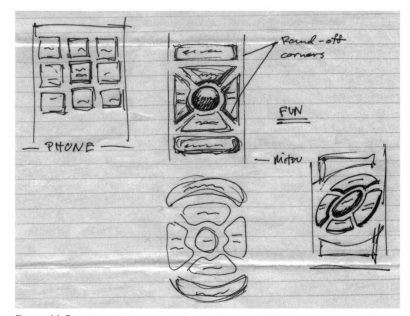

Figure 11-5. *Chris Gollmer's early sketches for DigitalThink's navigation toolbar.*

Possibly the most impressive support feature is the ability to email an actual human, a course tutor who is available to answer any questions you might have during the course. The Tutor button is always available in the control panel on the left-hand side of the screen, and instructions for how and when to contact the tutor are also given.

Students can also communicate with classmates, a terrific way to take advantage of the knowledge of people who may be farther along in the same course. By selecting the Classmates button from the control panel, you can see who else is online at the same time you are, and how far they've come in the course. Privacy is protected by giving each student a DigitalThink email address instead of providing their actual contact information.

To store course and personal information, each student has a "locker," shown in Figure 11-6. This removes the problem of having to remember which courses you've signed up for, and then trying to remember how to get back to them. Returning students simply visit the locker, log in, and view their courses. The idea could easily be extended in the future to provide access to books or tools, a place to store course notes, or other helpful features.

Design tip

Balance providing alternatives with maintaining an uncluttered interface. Too many doors can be as frustrating as too few.

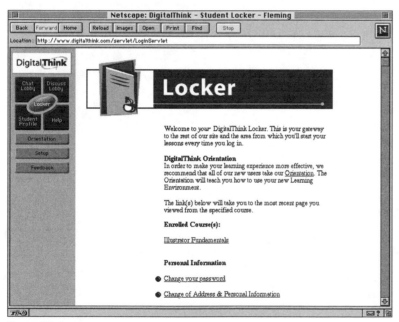

Figure 11-6. *Each student at DigitalThink has a "locker" for storing their course and personal information.*

Chris describes how they came up with the idea for the locker. "Originally we had wanted to call it the 'homeroom,'" he says, "but we decided the real philosophy behind the company is not K–12 learning. It's adult training. We decided that 'homeroom' was really not appropriate. The only other thing we came up with was the locker. That was your place to hang out in school. It was your place to keep everything."

Design tip

Try not to overengineer.
With learning sites particularly, technical experimentation is much less important than getting results. Try the simplest method first before using potentially troublesome new technologies.

Flexibility

Most people won't sit down and complete a course in one day. With the wealth of information presented in each course, it would be very difficult to do, even if you wanted to. To offer students the flexibility of completing a course in stages, DigitalThink uses a course syllabus—but with a twist.

DigitalThink's syllabi are no ordinary course outlines. Once a course is underway, they track your progress through the outline using a database, shown in Figure 11-7. Click on the Syllabus button in the control panel while in the middle of a course and a pop-up window appears. An outline shows visited topics and your current location within the course. The syllabus allows instant access to any topic in the course. Students can leave in the middle of a course and later take up exactly where they left off.

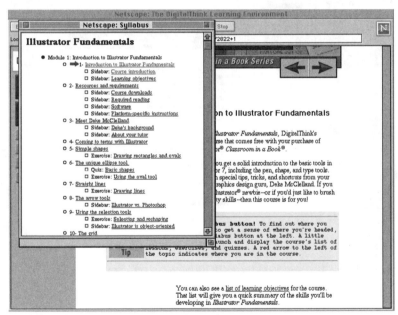

Figure 11-7. *DigitalThink's syllabus offers an outline of the course and tracks your progress through it.*

This powerful feature is not the only sort of flexibility that the site offers. They are one of the few sites to offer a rich multimedia experience for learners, an important part of addressing various learning styles and preferences. DigitalThink uses audio, Java-based exercises, and illustrations to complement the text in each course.

"From the very beginning we wanted to have audio, mainly because it adds another multimedia aspect to the course," Chris says. "Originally we'd used Shockwave and had a lot of problems with that, so eventually we switched over to Real Audio. It's much more stable, and it seems to have become the web standard for audio."

Describing their experience with Shockwave, Chris says, "The Shockwave audio files weren't that great, and they were making certain platforms crash. One of those was the Mac. We ran into some other problems with Java and Shockwave, some conflicts that made it a big headache."

They then tested using Real Audio, and found it worked better for their setup. All their courses were then "retrofit" with Real Audio. "It's been great since then. I know a lot of other people who say great things about Shockwave. I'm not badmouthing Macromedia, because I think they make a great product. It just didn't work out for us."

DigitalThink also uses Java to add hands-on exercises and other interactive components. "New things that we're implementing now are Java flipbooks," Chris explains. "You can flip through a sequence of events at your own pace and learn the concept at the speed you want to." A Java flipbook is shown in Figure 11-8.

> **Design tip**
>
> Keep pages readable. Clear, large fonts help, as does good contrast between text and backgrounds. Busy background patterns can make it very difficult for people to read and can be needlessly distracting. For text that users will spend more than a few seconds reading, use FONT SIZE=3 or above. If text is created as a graphic, make sure it doesn't dither (become speckled) and that it's large enough to read on all platforms.

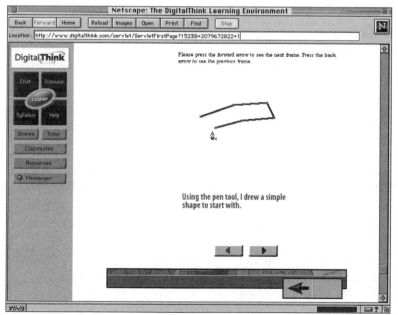

Figure 11-8. *A Java "flipbook" allows students to flip through a sequence of events (such as an exercise) without leaving the page.*

**National
Geographic
for Kids**

*www.nationalgeo-
graphic.com/kids/*

They're also using Java to enhance the course experience with roll-overs. "For example, if you're trying to learn Java and there's a whole bunch of code listed," Chris says, "you can rollover different lines of code to pop up a window that will tell you what that code actually does." The team is also using new simulation applets which mimic the experience of doing an exercise.

"The simulation applets are up and running with great feedback so far from our students," Chris says. "They are used quite extensively in one of our Administering Microsoft NT courses and the applet provides a very realistic working environment." Part of DigitalThink's process when creating a new course is to conduct beta testing for one to two weeks before the course is launched. 10 to 20 beta testers take the course and offer feedback, which is incorporated into the course before launch.

Because of their strong orientation toward providing what learners need, DigitalThink is leading the pack in web-based training. Most of their courses cover technical topics, but a recent wine tasting course, co-created with Virtual Vineyards, has proven a positive test of their model.

Who's doing it right: National Geographic

National Geographic's site (Figure C-18) has consistently been ranked as one of the Web's best learning sites since it premiered over a year ago. It's also one of the few mainstream learning sites to offer content for children, an audience that has its own needs and behaviors when it comes to web use.

"Educational content on the Web can be presented quite differently than what's possible in print," Dorrit Green, National Geographic's director of children's content, says of their approach to designing for this medium. "In the online environment, information can be non-linear and multidimensional with users directing the action. We try to use the interactive capabilities of the Web to create an immersed, first-person experience, putting the kid on assignment for National Geographic."

Kids are put off by many of the same things that adults find frustrating. "One of the most basic frustrations is the feeling of not having a grounding," Dorrit explains, "of having gotten away from your home base. You don't know where you are, either in terms of the structure or the scope of the content.

"For example, if a particular feature is dependent on a rather narrative story line, it can be frustrating and confusing to have too many opportunities to stray off track. Kids like to feel that they're making progress. They like to have a sense of how much farther they have to go until they've completed the task, story, or game."

Building on their knowledge of what kids look for on the Web, National Geographic has created learning modules that excel at providing guidance, both visually and structurally.

Guidance

One of their modules, Cyber Tiger, is a particularly good example of how guidance can help make learning fun (see Figure C-19). Cyber Tiger's entrance page offers only one route into the site, then builds slowly in complexity from that point onward.

To being their online exploration, young visitors are prompted to name their tiger first, a nice way to focus their attention and personalize the experience. Once inside the tiger module, the activity (planning and furnishing a new zoo home for a tiger) is also very focused, with few distracting asides.

One of the best and fastest ways to present guidance is through visual cues. This becomes especially important if your audience isn't famous for sitting down and reading the instructions before plunging in. As Dorrit points out, "Kids are much bolder in their approach. Unless they're inexperienced with computers, kids tend to sit down and plunge right in. They want the immediate gratification of clicking, playing, and exploring. Kids don't have much patience for reading instructional material, so it's important to construct content— whether it's editorial, navigational, or visual—that's as intuitive as possible."

Throughout the module, visual cues, from animation to color usage, help draw kids through the steps in building their tiger's home. An animated tiger draws the eye to the starting point, and each following step is similarly highlighted. These visual cues are immediately understandable, creating an obvious path through the module.

This guidance doesn't come at the expense of exploration. In fact, it works with it to create a richer, more entertaining experience. Dorrit explains the way the Ghosts in the Castle, another learning module for kids, was designed. It includes both a linear and a more exploratory approach.

"We set up two different options for navigation so that kids with different styles could have a choice. One method is linear. The user starts at one area of the castle and moves from room to room by finding and clicking on the castle's resident mouse (the rodent variety, not the computer peripheral). Moving through this way, the

The Annenberg/ CPB Project Exhibits Collection

www.learner.org/exhibits/

user starts at the gatehouse of the castle and ends up in the dungeon."

The alternative navigation system allowed for a more random approach. "We used an illustration of a miniature castle that's constructed in segments. The user can click on different parts of the castle to jump around and explore different rooms." But regardless of which navigation method a user chooses, guidance is still offered.

In the case of the more exploratory method, Dorrit explains that "the miniature castle navigation bar serves to show the user, by highlighting, how much of the castle has been explored. When the entire castle strip is highlighted, you know you've completed the tour."

Offering a few words of advice to people who are planning sites for youth, Dorrit cautions, "Keep in mind at all times that kids' attention spans are even shorter than adults' are! Generally, it's helpful to present main text information as HTML text (rather than text in an image) so that it loads as quickly as possible. You lose a certain amount of control over style and length, but it's an important consideration."

Dorrit also recommends designing for modem users, since they continue to make up a large part of the web audience. "Remember that not everybody out there has the latest, most powerful hardware. We try to create material for a standard 28.8 modem. There are also a significant number of people still using 14.4 modems. Make your content accessible to everyone, at least on some level. Feedback that we've gotten indicates that kids often don't want to bother with downloading and installing plug-ins, so if you're using things like Real Audio, QuickTime VR, and Shockwave, do so judiciously. Always offer alternative material so that kids who don't have the bells and whistles won't be short-changed."

Last but not least, Dorrit stressed the importance of "good, substantive content. The online medium offers unprecedented opportunities to serve up really worthwhile material in ways that kids will find irresistible."

Who's doing it right: The Annenberg/CPB Project

The Annenberg/CPB Project is known for its high-quality videos, which are used for teaching in schools, colleges, and libraries, and are frequently broadcast on public television for casual learners. In 1997, the Project decided to bring the same educational mission to the Web, and the Exhibits Collection is the result (see Figure 11-9).

Figure 11-9. *The Annenberg/CPB Project Exhibits Collection offers an accessible and hands-on approach to casual learning on the Web.*

Each exhibit in the collection explores one topic from one of the many Annenberg/CPB Project video series; for example, volcanoes, Russia, or the environment. Through participatory activities and supporting links, students and casual learners can move at their own pace through a topic (see Figure 11-10).

A large part of the Project's audience has always been teachers at the high school and college levels, who use the video materials in their classrooms. The series are also popular with libraries and other public educational institutions. In designing educational exhibits for the Web, the exhibits team expected that these populations would continue to form a core part of the audience. Knowing that many schools and libraries still accessed the Web with text-only browsers (such as Lynx) or "antique" browser versions, the challenge for the exhibits team was to build interactivity that would be within reach of this core audience group.

The strengths of the Exhibits Collection are its accessibility and its consistency, which help reduce the chance of errors or confusion interrupting the exploration of a topic.

Accessibility

In outlining accessibility goals, it's tempting to take one of two easy roads out. The first road, designing for only the latest browser versions, is obviously problematic. The second road, attempting to design for every browser ever made, is equally problematic. In both cases, these arbitrary decisions would better be replaced by some simple research into the intended audience's typical setup.

Though libraries and schools are increasingly reaping the benefits of educational technology grants, it's still very common to find text-based web browsers installed. Even those libraries and schools that do have the latest equipment and browsers may not install plug-ins (for reasons of security, institutional policy, or other reasons). To serve this audience, it's best to target specific design tasks: make sure

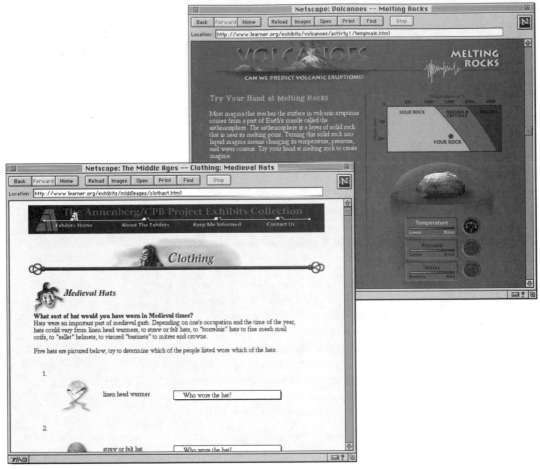

Figure 11-10. *In each exhibit at the Annenberg/CPB Project, learners can try hands-on activities such as identifying medieval headwear or melting volcanic rocks.*

that the majority of the site is usable on a text-only browser, and make sure that plug-ins are kept to a minimum.

In the Exhibits Collection, as much as possible is accomplished with CGI and GIF animation. JavaScript is also occasionally used but kept to a minimum, and in some cases an alternative version of a hands-on activity is given. Shockwave, Java, and frames are generally not used, since many users find these technologies problematic.

In most cases, taking the extra time to brainstorm a "low-tech" version of a learning activity yields a solution that would actually work better than the "high-tech" version. For example, in an exhibit on Russia, an "interactive atlas" was used to present country information throughout the exhibit. The navigation challenge for this feature was how to send users back to the exact page they came from, since it was possible they could access the atlas from any number of pages.

Normally, this would be done with frames, or by launching a small window with JavaScript. Either of these could work well for some audiences, but for a wider appeal a different approach was needed. Edward Piou, the site's programmer, used HTTP referer logs to achieve the same effect, with maximum accessibility.

When you access a new file or page, referer logs tell the server what page you just came from. Developers usually use referer data to track where their visitors are coming in from (i.e., from a search engine, etc.). In this case, Edward used the same information to force the atlas to "remember" what page a user had just come from. He wrote a CGI script that essentially retained this referer information until a user was ready to leave the atlas, at which point they could "close" the atlas and return directly to the page they had come from. It's a seamless approach, and requires no additional windows or frames that might hamper printing.

Consistency

With a new exhibit premiering each month, the need for consistency is great. The benefit for visitors is that they can better focus on the learning experience, and not on repeatedly learning how to use an exhibit. The benefit for developers is that they don't need to reinvent the wheel each month.

Consistency doesn't have to mean dullness, though it can if it's taken to extremes. Core elements can follow predetermined guidelines, but still be original and fun. A typical exhibit, for example, consists of:

- A splash screen introducing the core question or concept to be explored, usually through an animation or other compelling approach.

- An introductory screen providing a more traditional text introduction, and outlining the exhibit content.

- Several content sections, with an opportunity to explore more in-depth information in each.

- Several activities, offering a chance to synthesize concepts through trial, discussion, interpretation, or questioning.

- Related resources, including links and books on the topic. Links are also integrated into content sections.

To help maintain a consistent approach, an architecture model for a typical exhibit was created. Some layout and design elements are also carried through, but a great deal of flexibility remains. Color, some

Find out more

Hall, Brandon. *Web-Based Training Cookbook.* Wiley, 1997.

McCormack, Colin, and David Jones. *Building a Web-Based Education System.* Wiley, 1997.

Porter, Lynnette R. *Creating the Virtual Classroom: Distance Learning with the Internet.* Wiley, 1997.

aspects of layout, typography, activities, and other areas can be tailored to the topic at hand. The result is a compelling learning experience, designed to appeal to a wide audience of casual adult learners.

Reaction to the Exhibits Collection has been excellent. Yahoo! named one exhibit, "The Middle Ages," a Pick of the Year for 1997. Teachers have responded with thanks for the accessible approach. With a new exhibit premiering every month, the model is still being tested, but so far has proved very resilient. Like DigitalThink's flexible and extensible model, The Annenberg/CPB Project Exhibits Collection provides the welcoming stability many learners need.

Recap

Designing learning spaces on the Web often means taking into account transitory audiences, brief attention spans, or users with different backgrounds and approaches. The Web has plenty to offer as a learning space, but for many learners it can still be a difficult environment. When people have to learn how to navigate, use a tool, or download an accessory, they won't have much time or energy left to learn the topic at hand. Successful learning spaces offer guidance and assistance to help overcome these barriers. They balance rich features with an accessible approach, creating a supportive experience for learners.

## CHAPTER TWELVE

NAVIGATION DESIGN FOR INFORMATION SITES

The best way to be boring is to leave nothing out.

—Voltaire

In this chapter

- Laying the groundwork

- Outlining specific goals

- Who's doing it right: MSNBC on the Internet

- Who's doing it right: Lycos

- Who's doing it right: Computers.com

- Recap

Info-glut, information anxiety, information overload: why is it disturbing to have so much information? Stock figures, daily news, medical research, and government records are at our fingertips, so why aren't we all better off for it? Why are so many people lost in a rising tide of information?

In part, it's because we have collectively given more thought to what we provide than to how we provide it. Making the full text of congressional activities available online is a swell idea, but it's only the first step in getting it to users. Providing access to a rich mine of data via the Web sounds cutting edge, but it's not necessarily so—at least not without giving some thought to how people will search it, store it, move through it, manipulate it, and present it to suit their own needs.

Understanding these factors is fundamental to navigation design. If you understand how people will want to use those congressional reports, you can begin to construct avenues through the information. You become an interpreter of information, not simply a warehouser of data, making connections between information objects to meet user goals.

Sites whose main purpose is to provide information face serious pressure when it comes to navigation design. They need to be faster, cleaner, better organized, more up-to-date and content-rich than any other type of site. Users depend on it, because they depend on the information—in some cases, urgently.

"If you understand how people will want to use information, you become an information interpreter instead of a data warehouser."

Laying the groundwork

"Information" is a vague term, and can be applied to a variety of topics and approaches. Most sites provide information of some kind or another. For some sites, however, providing information is at the core of what they do. It's not in the service of commerce, entertainment, or marketing. The information itself is the product.

Looking at sites that show this core concern with providing information, we can learn a lot about how traditional information-seeking translates to the Web. Generally, people in search of information on the Web will have the "second tier" expectations shown in Table 12-1.

Table 12-1. *User goals and expectations: Information*

First Tier (general navigation questions)	Where am I? Where can I go? How will I get there? How can I get back to where I once was?
Second Tier (purpose-oriented questions)	How will I know if a site has what I'm looking for? How do I find the exact information I need? What if I'm not sure what to look for? Will the information be right for me? Can I trust this information? Can I store what I find for later use?

How will I know if a site has what I'm looking for?

Before you offer up any other information to users, there's one key item you need to address: the scope of your site. Most people in search of a particular piece of information begin by evaluating their options. What resources are available? Which is most likely to have the answer? You'll save your users—and probably yourself—a lot of wasted time if you explain your scope up front.

It might be clear from the name of your service that you offer medical information, but you still need to explain what kind, who it is intended for, where it comes from, and so on. If you're well-branded like *Encyclopedia Britannica*, people probably have a good idea what to expect. If you're not, you might want to first explain what the boundaries of your site are, either up front or in a FAQ. Because navigating for information usually occurs across sites, helping users make the most of their time only reflects positively on you.

A scope note doesn't have to be exhaustive to be effective. CNET's Computers.com explains itself with one succinct subtitle: "Computers.com: What to buy. Where to get it." That's enough to tell someone who's looking for computer industry news that Computers.com isn't going to be the best place to start.

Providing a clear statement of scope is part of helping visitors to predict outcomes and make decisions. There are other ways to help visitors predict whether your site will be of use. Tools such as a site map, a site index, or a table of contents provide an overview of your site that is essential for predicting usefulness. These tools will allow users to see, almost at a glance, whether your site will meet their needs.

How do I find the exact information I need?

What does the word "sasquatch" mean? When was the Magna Carta signed? How tall is the Empire State building? These are all specific questions that will have reasonably exact answers. People looking for this sort of information generally want to be able to type terms directly into a search box. There's no reason they should have to wade through a thicket of subject headings to get to what they need when they already have the terms needed to yield answers.

This search-oriented approach is one specific kind of information-seeking behavior. It's not the only kind, but it's certainly common enough that you'll need to make these visitors happy. It's much like shopping at Amazon.com for that novel you've been waiting anxiously for these past six months. You probably know the title, and don't want to have to browse the new releases (or, god forbid, the whole fiction section) to find it. Being able to search is an essential feature of information sites, because seeking precise information is an integral part of our behavior.

Allowing people to limit searches makes searching with terms (usually a dicey business) much more effective. Lycos, for example, allows users to limit where they search for a term (the Web, Usenet, etc.), to search only within a page's title, or to search a set of results. Computers.com, like Yahoo!, lets you limit a search to the category you're currently in. For keyword searching—which has a well-deserved bad reputation—limiting offers a way to increase effectiveness without giving up the simple and familiar search box.

Besides the vagaries of the search box, there's another way you can serve these very directed users: by providing shortcuts. For information sites, shortcuts are crucial. Shortcuts can take the form of a pull-down menu to popular site sections, a table of contents, or a scrolling highlights box. The shortcuts you develop should offer added value to your users. MSNBC on the Internet, for example, organizes their site into sections or departments. To provide a more

> *"For information sites, shortcuts are crucial. Shortcuts can take the form of a pull-down menu, a table of contents, or a scrolling highlights box."*

rapid alternative to browsing section news, they also include "Quick News," a shortcut designed to offer the top stories from all sections in a compact format.

What if I'm not sure what to look for?

There's another type of information-seeking behavior that is just as common and less easily served by a search box. In the search for exact information—for facts, really—you have a lot to go on already. The question—"When was the Magna Carta signed?"—holds the answer, or at least the key to getting it. More commonly, however, that key is missing.

Think of the way young children ask questions. They tend to ask questions like, "Why is the sky blue?" or "Where do bees go in the winter?" Try typing that sort of thing into a search box, and you're likely to get gibberish in return. But in the library where I used to work, this sort of open-ended question was par for the course. And if you think kids can come up with some incredible questions, wait until you see what adults ask. "Where do you keep late-19th century American fiction written by women?" was the sort of humdinger you might be faced with on any given day.

Computers hate questions like that, and so did I. Most search engines, local or web-wide, are not designed to answer that kind of question. It's why your average web developer, wondering how to make a link open in a new window or which audio format will work best, posts that sort of thing to a discussion list instead of heading over to the friendly neighborhood search site. It's a Catch-22: if you don't know the answer, it's tough to know how to phrase the question.

For this sort of searching, browsing is sometimes a good way to begin. Advanced search features that allow you to search across fields (such as title or description) also help. If there's a chance that some portion of your audience will have this sort of open-ended question—and people being people, there probably is—you might want to brainstorm new ways of allowing access to your pool of information.

Will people want to search with natural language, for example? Are there alternative ways to help people get to what they need, ways that don't involve hit-or-miss keywords? Will sophisticated subject trees or 3D information spaces or Java-based knowledge maps be the answer? Right now, human intervention still works best for this type of question. Live chat with a peer or research intermediary might end up being the most manageable solution.

Will the information be right for me?

There's more information available to us than most of us could ever use. Yet despite the fact that we're swimming in a sea of information, we may not get the answers we need. Differences in skill level, language, bias, depth, and other factors can shrink this vast sea to puddle-like proportions, a small oasis of usable information.

Imagine for a moment that you're a 10-year-old kid who wants to find out about black holes. Searching for "black holes" (on the Web or elsewhere) will surely turn up lots of results, but many of them will be all wrong for you. You might turn up conference proceedings in which the latest mathematical proofs about black holes are heatedly discussed. You might turn up a religious text offering an alternate view of heavenly bodies. How do you reach the nuggets of information that will suit your needs?

Two of the best approaches to serving this need for personalized information are tailoring information to an audience and allowing filtering. In stores, libraries, schools, and elsewhere, tailoring to an audience is expected. On the Web, we can take this one step further, offering different versions of a site for different audiences. Yes, it's more time-intensive, but it allows the ability to target the very specific information needs of a particular audience.

Similarly, content filtering is another way to increase the chance that people will find relevant information. By allowing people to enter information about their interests, or to filter out things they definitely aren't interested in, you decrease the amount of unusable information they have to sift through. There's some exciting stuff being done at the moment with collaborative filtering, too, in which the combined ratings of a group of users can be used to establish relevance.

Lycos, for example, incorporates this type of community rating system into their search site. Lycos users can view Community Guides (see Figure 12-1)—lists of sites in a topic area that have been ranked according to how users rated them. MSNBC on the Internet offers a similar idea, allowing readers to view which articles are most popular at the moment. MSNBC on the Internet's ratings, like Lycos's community ratings, are based on user input.

Can I trust this information?

It might not seem like a navigation issue, but concerns about trustworthiness are often enough to keep people away from information—and at the worst, away from your site. There are a few things that have crept into the public consciousness about the Internet, and one of them is the gnawing sense that Internet information is untrustworthy. You could try to argue that a lot of the information on the Net is

"We're swimming in a sea of information, but very little of it may actually be useful."

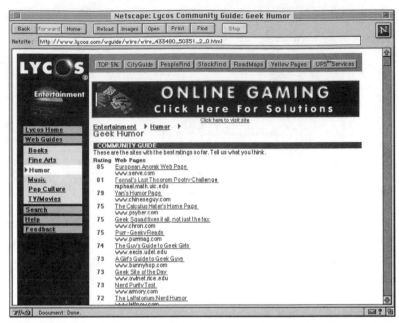

Figure 12-1. *Lycos's Community Guides show visitors how sites have been ranked by other users.*

usually as accurate as its print cousins, but you're better off showing than telling.

In order to show that your site's information is trustworthy (assuming it is), you need to show source. Where does this information come from if it's been repurposed? Who is the author or collector? Why should we trust that person? How often is the information updated? You can answer these questions fairly easily with just a few simple additions, including date, author, and origins.

Dating information is possibly the most essential of these additions, as much to protect yourself as to make it easier for users to find relevant material. Computers.com, for example, allows users to sort product reviews by date, a valuable aid if you're looking for only the most recent head-to-head tests.

For someone wanting to track the progress of a big industry court case, dates are a necessary framework. For your site, dates ensure you aren't accidentally presenting outdated information as though it were fresh. Particularly in areas such as medicine or business, timeliness is no small concern.

Can I store what I find for later use?

Anyone who regularly uses their browser's bookmarks knows there's got to be a better way. If your bookmarks are like my bookmarks (and for your sake I hope they're not), they're a tangled mess of random-looking sites, some collected into categories, some dangling afterthoughts. Bookmarks are handy to a point, but the lack of a sensible way to sort or present them seriously limits their usefulness.

For people doing research on the Web, storage is a huge issue. If you're spending a full day scouring webspace for resources, you're going to be looking for a place to dump things. If you've found a terrific article that everyone else in the office should read, you're going to want to pass it along. Unfortunately, neither storage nor delivery is currently very advanced on most information sites.

Ideally, people should be able to store information from various stages in the process. What was that search that turned up the best answers? If you can store it, you needn't bother about reconstructing it. What was that related topic or pathway I wanted to explore? If you can record it somewhere, you'll be more likely to come back to it. Many sites are now encouraging users to store their preferences, to some degree. Being able to store the final product itself—the information—will be a valuable next step.

"For people doing research on the Web, storage is a huge issue. People may want to store searches, results, and filtering preferences for later use."

Outlining specific goals

Despite shared user goals about finding information, there are still some important differences. A site offering legal information will have a different approach than one that offers entertainment industry news, and thankfully so. Not only will the goals and concerns of site developers differ in these cases, the goals of users will too. Nevermind how many sidebars you've seen in your day—there is no generic template for information sites.

To find out what user goals are specific to a certain type of information or content, you need to dig deeper than the typical second-tier goals outlined in Table 12-1. Your third tier will require some research to flesh out, but the potential returns (in visitors, income, or prestige) are sure to make it worthwhile. Table 12-2 shows what these third-tier goals might look like for a site providing health and medical information.

Table 12-2. *Goals & expectations: Information: Health & medicine*

First Tier (general navigation questions)	Where am I? Where can I go? How will I get there? How can I get back to where I once was?

Table 12-2. *Goals & expectations: Information: Health & medicine (continued)*

Second Tier (purpose-oriented questions)	How will I know if a site has what I'm looking for? How do I find the exact information I need? What if I'm not sure what to look for? Will the information be right for me? Can I trust this information? Can I store what I find for later use?
Third Tier (topic- or audience-oriented questions)	Is this information up-to-date and accurate? Does it reflect any particular stance or bias? Is it for doctors or patients? Can I search for a certain condition or illness? Can I limit my search to information that will apply to my situation or needs (by age, gender, etc.)? Is there a glossary available? Can I talk to an expert who can help me make sense of this information?

To find out more about these third-tier goals for information sites, you might try some of the following methods:

• Look at other media designed to provide similar information. If you're in the business of providing news via the Web, look at news sources elsewhere. What limitations do TV or newspapers have that you might not have on the Web? How do these other media allow people to navigate through information, if at all?

• Find out about people's storage habits. How do people usually store this type of information, if they store it? Can you devise something that will make their miles of file cabinets obsolete? Can you make it easier for them to share information with others? What do people want to be able to do with the information they store?

• Visit a library. Find one that relates to your content area, if you can. How have they organized the information? Are there shortcuts or special displays that might indicate frequent user demands for a certain kind of information? Talk to a librarian. Find out about frequently asked questions and the most common ways people want to find information. Are there ways you can expand upon library services to better meet the needs of users?

• If you have a search engine on your site, check the logs to see what sort of things people are searching for. Is there anything that might suggest a new way of allowing people to navigate through information? Do the search logs show that users expect you to offer a certain area of content?

- Interview users about your content area. Ask them what they'd like to know, and how they'd want to find it. Ask them to envision the ideal way to navigate through the information, if they could have anything they wanted.

- Conduct user tests. Ask people to use a handful of sites (ideally in your content area) to find a piece of information. What do people like, and what's frustrating? What features are heavily used, and what are ignored?

- Browse magazines and newsletters in your content area. Letters to the editor can reveal common questions and concerns. How are these publications organized? What conventions and terms are shared? What else can you tell about what readers might be asking for?

MSNBC on the Internet

www.msnbc.com

For information sites, focus on searching for patterns in how people want to find information. If you're offering news, do people always want to be able to limit by geographical location or timeliness? If you're offering medical information, do they usually want to search by disease? Understanding these preferences means you can build the routes that people need, and makes you a more informed interpreter and guide.

Who's doing it right: MSNBC on the Internet

When the Interactive Bureau redesigned MSNBC on the Internet's site (see Figure C-20), they faced a complex, information-rich news site that would need to be updated several times daily. The resulting design is both controlled and flexible, an excellent blend of scalable architecture and well-planned information design.

The site's main strength is in managing the complexity of a frequently updated news site. With numerous content departments, rotating advertisements, multimedia add-ons, opportunities to interact and personalize the experience, and more, MSNBC on the Internet might have fallen into chaos. Instead, it is an approachable, direct, and well-organized information source.

Managing complexity

Until fairly recently, just providing information via the Web was a laudable pursuit. It was enough to be one of the forward-thinking few who recognized the power of the Web for mass communication. Those days are gone, replaced with a new challenge: providing increasingly complex layers of information, and making it all seem simple.

With sites as complex and information-rich as MSNBC on the Internet, that's no small challenge. Interactive Bureau addressed this by creating a multi-layered site that maximizes on-screen real estate, provides excellent cues and labels, and builds in supporting features such as collaborative filtering.

The front door of the site, MSNBC on the Internet's "cover," has a tightly constructed layout that offers content departments in a navigation bar, but also rotates hot news items. Special features scroll across the top of the screen, while top headlines appear in a rotating sidebar, as shown in Figure 12-2. The cover packs all of this information, in addition to the main cover story and a rotating banner ad, onto the screen without the need for scrolling. It's a fine example of above-the-fold design, and nicely reduces the potential sprawling chaos of the front door.

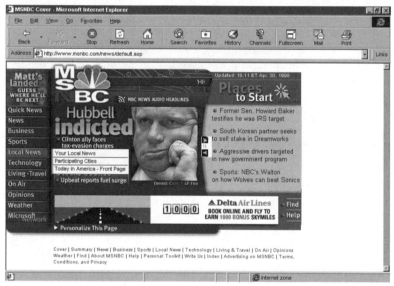

Figure 12-2. *On MSNBC on the Internet's "cover," rotating highlights (on the right side of the screen) act as shortcuts to news stories that might otherwise be buried.*

Rotating highlights act as shortcuts, allowing users to jump immediately to an article or feature without navigating through hierarchical levels. MSNBC on the Internet makes excellent use of these highlights, rotating them not only at the top level but on each department main page. Each department features these highlights and a lead story—much like the front door—but departments also include a complete listing of current stories in that area. The effect is that the site gets progressively more content-rich and complex as you navigate through it, rather than presenting its content all at once.

Accompanying most articles there are related stories, interactive supplements, multimedia components, and supporting Internet links, as shown in Figure 12-3. This could make articles a headache to read, but thankfully these materials are well laid out and labeled. Supporting links are labeled with an icon to show whether the material is an external site, interactive feature, and so on. These asides are kept marginal, separated from the body of an article to avoid confusion. Rather than avoiding complexity, the site incorporates it and manages it well.

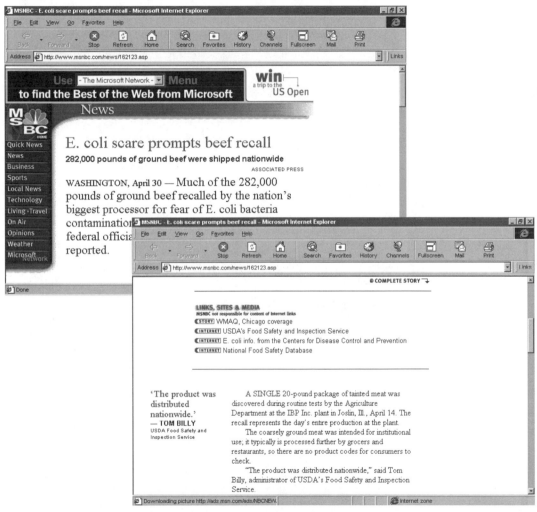

Figure 12-3. *Related stories, links, and multimedia components are shown in story margins at MSNBC on the Internet.*

Lycos

www.lycos.com

Another excellent feature of the site is its ad integration. For many sites, ads are an element that defies integration, appearing unrelated to content or even to the site itself. MSNBC on the Internet had good ad integration before the redesign, and Interactive Bureau retained that important trait. In the new version, as in the old version, ads are built into the layout of each page, not simply tacked on afterward.

Ironically, Microsoft Internet Explorer users face a slightly harder time of it than Netscape users, though it's in the guise of greater functionality. MSIE users are shown a frustrating message about security options the first time they visit the site. Luckily for MSIE users, the message doesn't appear again.

MSNBC on the Internet's site offers the complexity news junkies demand, but presents it within a carefully constructed framework. It's an excellent piece of information design, and shows that it's possible to have information-rich environments within the confines of the screen.

Who's doing it right: Lycos

What do you need to offer if your site is a launchpad to the entire Web? What do you do if your audience includes newbies and Net vets alike, and they're using every browser and platform under the sun? Over several years and several redesigns, the staff at Lycos has given this some serious thought. They've had to. For search sites, competition is steep—and design challenges are often even steeper.

"Lycos is in a tough spot, as all of the search sites are," says the site's creative director, Doren Berge. "Everyone turns to you to help find the way around the Net, but you have levels of users. You have the ones who are coming on for the very first time, and the Net vets. From a business standpoint the real target is the millions of people pouring on every month. We want to get them and hold their hands, but without patronizing our advanced users. That's a tall order."

To address this diversity, Lycos has built a stable of alternatives (see Figure 12-4). These multiple ways of accessing information are one of the things that sets Lycos apart from its search siblings, and one of its strengths as an information site.

Alternatives

For information sites, providing alternative paths through information is essential. There are few types of information that would suggest only one way to access them. Add to this the fact that people have differing approaches to finding information, and things start to get interesting.

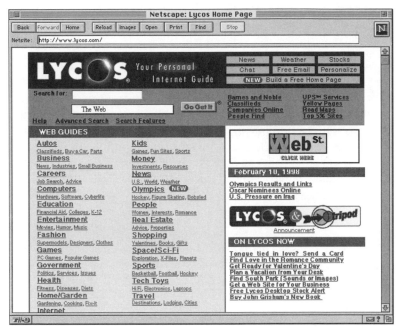

Doren Berge, Lycos

Figure 12-4. *To serve its wide spectrum of users, Lycos offers multiple ways of accessing information.*

For Lycos, which serves millions of users each month, managing this diversity is serious business. They might decide to offer a Yahoo-style browsable index, but if they do it at the loss of search flexibility, they've lost part of their audience. They might decide to offer high-tech search features, but if they alienate new users, they can't stay in the game. The trick is in achieving a balance, something Lycos has managed nicely.

Lycos is also caught in the muddle that many search sites are facing these days: are they portals or destinations? Most search sites seem to want to be both, another factor that makes providing alternatives crucial.

"A lot of people only want the search box," Doren explains. "They don't want anything to get in the way. So we want to offer that, but at the same time, we want to create a destination as well. It can really be a quagmire."

Lycos wants to be a destination site partly because advertising is their primary source of revenue, and ad views (or impressions) are an important factor in determing success in this business model. "Our challenge is to deliver a successful search experience along with valuable content that keeps users on the site as long as possible, and hopefully encourages them to return again and again," Doren says.

"These objectives obviously conflict with each other. Combining these objectives into one cohesive experience is a challenge facing all of the navigation hubs."

A search box—still the first thing visitors will expect from a search site—appears at the top of the screen, with search help and tips only a click away. People can limit a search easily by using a drop-down menu underneath the search box. On inside pages, once you've run a search, you can continue to refine it (see Figure 12-5). The ability to search your results set, search by title, search by URL, or even search within a particular site offers flexibility and increases the probability of finding what you need (see Figure 12-6). Results can be displayed by page title or URL.

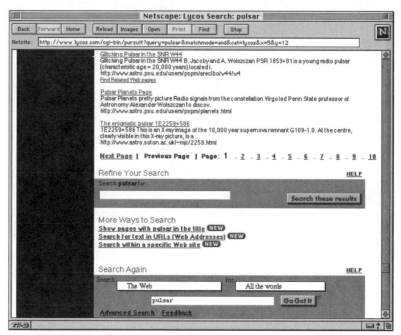

Figure 12-5. *At Lycos, users can refine a search or try a new one directly from the results page.*

For people who are not interested in the search box, Lycos provides a number of browsable options. The core browsing feature is their Web Guides. Web Guides are collections of resources organized by category, similar to Yahoo!'s approach. You can also view Community Guides, which feature community ratings of content that you can contribute to, or browse selected reviewed sites in the Lycos Top 5%—both strong community-oriented features that offer an alternative to the sometimes "unfeeling" search box.

With this feature-rich approach, Lycos has to make careful use of its screen real estate. "A prominent element of our navigation has been the left navigation bar," Doren says. "A lot of people say that a left navigation bar is old, but the truth is it's part of a visual vocabulary. People understand it. People are already looking for it. We have a lot of information that needs to be on every page. We update the site several times a day, including subsections. So you need to rely on clichés."

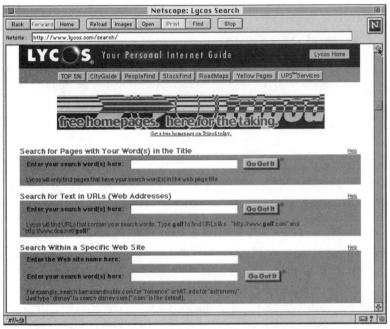

Figure 12-6. *Searching by URL, title, or within a particular domain helps boost the relevancy of results at Lycos.*

"Browser compatibility is without question my biggest nightmare," Doren continues. "We're working on browser detection to serve up variations of the site, but the site itself is enormous. It's not really practical to deliver different versions for every platform, browser, and version. We monitor what browsers are coming in, and it's all over the map. We're always searching for that middle ground. Many users will have a broken experience, something that's not terrific. We try to take that into account."

To better determine why some users might have a "broken experi-ence," Lycos frequently conducts user tests. "There's a huge value in testing," Doren explains. "During each redesign, we build a proto-type and take it into testing. We learn something every time we do it.

I can't stress the value of testing enough. As product designers we just get too close to what we're doing. User testing is always an eye-opening experience."

Throughout multiple redesigns, Lycos has shown a constant focus on growth, experimentation, and responsiveness to user needs. Whatever the future holds for search sites, Lycos's flexible approach will help ensure that new users can take their time getting there, while Net vets busy themselves blazing the trail.

Who's doing it right: Computers.com

CNET's yellow sidebar is by now the stuff of web legend, more recognizable even than their red button logo. But CNET's large network of sites is anything but hackneyed. Recent subsite spin-offs show the valuable lessons CNET has learned during its reign as one of the top Web destinations.

Computers.com, shown in Figure C-21, is one of these recent spin-offs and is a central source for information about computing equipment. The site offers articles and product reviews for a wide range of must-have toys, from digital cameras to servers. The site's strengths are its speed and filtering capabilities.

Speed

Computers.com has eleven product categories and numerous reviews, tips, asides, and external links. It could easily be a time-consuming proposition to wade through this wealth of information. Computers.com circumvents this problem by building in features designed to increase the speed and effectiveness of your equipment quest.

One of the simpler features designed to increase speed and navigability is the presence of recursive paths. You've probably seen recursive paths or directories on Yahoo!. For example, on Computers.com, if you've clicked on the Cameras category, then selected Video Cameras, you'll see text links showing the path you took and giving you a simple route out:

`Home >> Cameras >> Video Cameras`

This sort of recursive path is part of what makes Yahoo! a popular and navigable site, and CNET puts this simple feature to good use on Computers.com. There may be fancier and more high-tech methods of solving this problem, but recursive directories are still the fastest way to navigate through levels of hierarchy.

Computers.com also features a Quick Search box, available on every page, as shown in Figure 12-7. From any category, you can run a search in case you aren't finding the product you need. You can limit your search to the current category only, an excellent feature that is also reminiscent of Yahoo!.

Figure 12-7. *Computers.com offers shortcuts such as a Quick Search feature and recursive categories.*

CNET's network of sites has strict rules about download times, and Computers.com is no exception. Across CNET, 20–25 K per page is the norm, a brutal but necessary requirement for a popular information site. On Computers.com, download times are kept to a minimum by making extensive use of table background color, recycling headers across pages, and keeping graphics small and simple.

Filtering

Knowing that most computer shoppers tend to look for equipment by platform, price, or other features, Computers.com lets users filter product information accordingly. Within the Cameras: Still Photo section, for example, you can filter by platform, price, number of photos stored, and viewfinder type.

Faced with an otherwise daunting amount of product information to search through, most users can show much better results by filtering. The filtered results are much more manageable to browse through, and likely to be much more relevant, as shown in Figure 12-8.

Find out more

Dillon, Andrew. *Designing Usable Electronic Text: Ergonomic Aspects of Human Information Usage.* Taylor & Francis, 1994.

Rosenfeld, Lou, and Peter Morville. *Information Architecture for the World Wide Web.* O'Reilly, 1998.

Sano, Darrell. *Designing Large-Scale Web Sites: A Visual Design Methodology.* Wiley, 1996.

Shenk, David. *Data Smog: Surviving the Information Glut.* Harper, 1997.

Veen, Jeffrey. *Hotwired Style: Principles for Building Smart Web Sites.* Wired, 1998.

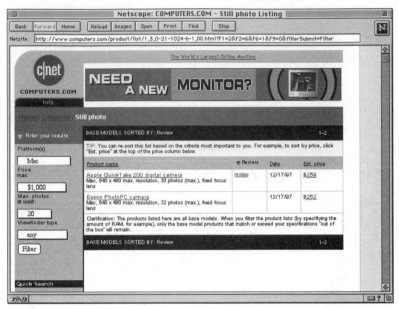

Figure 12-8. *Filtering can reduce your results to a much more manageable and relevant set of products.*

People can also change the way product listings are displayed, choosing to show matching products by price, for example, instead of by name. Enabling this tailored display of information means users don't need to scroll long lists to find products in their price range or ones that have been recently reviewed.

CNET excels at creating tightly focused spaces, or subsites, within its larger network. Computers.com is one of the more successful examples of CNET's commitment to speed, flexibility, and user goals. It's an excellent addition to a bustling information network.

Recap

To meet users' needs and demands, information sites must be faster, cleaner, better organized, more up-to-date, and more content-rich than any other type of site. Information sites are often caught between the pressures of designing for ease of use and providing rich and complex content. Successful sites balance ease of use and complexity, as well as incorporating "value-added" features that help users not only find but interpret, store, and share information. Understanding how people will want to use information is crucial to finding this balance.

TECHNICAL TIPS

This appendix presents a series of technical tips for implementing some of the design ideas discussed in the book.

Using forms for navigation

Using forms to get feedback from your visitors is common, but they're also useful for navigation. Redirect forms offer space-saving drop-down menus for large sites, and allow frequently changing options to be updated more easily.

You can add a redirect form to your site that works with JavaScript or CGI. JavaScript is slightly faster, since it doesn't need to send an additional message to the server, but CGI is more accessible. Below is a simple CGI redirect script you can use for navigation.

Part 1: The form

To include the script in your pages, you'll need to create a form. Do this by adding the following code to your HTML. Make sure that the path to the cgi-bin is correct for your server, or it won't work.

```
<FORM METHOD="POST" ACTION="/cgi-bin/redirect.pl">
<SELECT NAME="Location">
<OPTION VALUE="http://www.whitehouse.gov/">The White House
<OPTION VALUE="http://www.webreview.com/">Web Review
<OPTION VALUE="http://www.amazon.com/">Amazon.com
</SELECT>
<BR>
<INPUT TYPE="SUBMIT" VALUE="Go">
</FORM>
```

In this appendix

- Using forms for navigation
- Targeting frames
- The META refresh tag
- Creating fast-loading graphics
- Cracking up: An alternative to image maps

Part 2: The script

The CGI script, redirect.pl, is below. Make sure to check that the path to Perl is /usr/local/bin/perl. Save it as redirect.pl in a text editor such as NotePad, and transfer it to your cgi-bin as ASCII text. Once it's there, you'll need to make sure it's executable. Talk to your server administrator about how to do this at your location.

```
#!/usr/local/bin/perl
# This program sends a "redirect" message to the user's browser, pointing
# it off to a URL based on the information that was input to the CGI.
# Written 4/28/97 by ep Productions, Inc. Permission granted to
# use, redistribute, modify, etc., so long as this header is intact.
# http://www.eppi.com/
# Save the location the user chose to the variable 'location'.
# We input using the CGI.pm perl package, from http://www.perl.com/CPAN/
use CGI;
$cgi = new CGI;
$location = $cgi->param('location');
# A default location, if the HTML form didn't supply a location
if ($location eq '') {
        $location = "http://www.eppi.com/eppi/";
}
# Print the http headers that redirect the browser
print "Status: 302 Moved Temporarily\n";
print "Location: $location\n\n";
exit;
```

This script was written by Edward Piou of ep Productions, Inc. (*www.eppi.com*), a Washington, D.C.-area Internet development firm. Feel free to use this script in web projects, but please keep the copyright header intact.

Targeting frames

"Frames made my son cry," a fellow web designer once remarked. I'm sure quite a few adults have wanted to do the same when faced with four or five scrolling boxes dissecting their screen.

Why do users dislike frames so much? Frames are often badly targeted, eat up screen real estate, and can take longer to load. Users often can't get accurate cues from the location line, and they may have trouble printing, bookmarking, and saving pages. Still, despite good reasons to be cautious about using frames, they can actually offer solutions for some sites. Understanding targeting is a key step in designing frames that work.

Step 1: Name your frames

Each window in a frameset can be easily named. By naming each frame, you can target how documents should appear inside windows with great precision. Look at this example of a screen split into two frames, top and bottom:

```
<HTML>
<HEAD>
<TITLE>Targeting Test</TITLE>
```

```
</HEAD>
<FRAMESET ROWS="80, *">
   <FRAME SRC="top.html" NAME="topframe">
   <FRAME SRC="bottom.html" NAME="bottomframe">
</FRAMESET>
</HTML>
```

In this example, the top frame is appropriately named *topframe* and
the bottom is named *bottomframe*. Navigation buttons that appear in
topframe can be targeted to load HTML documents into *bottomframe*. This is crucial, since the default action for frames is to load a
new document into the same frame the link appears in. In other
words, if you don't specify a target, links in *topframe* would load
documents into *topframe*.

Step 2: Target a frame

Looking at the links in top.html (the file that makes up the contents
of the navigation frame called *topframe*) gives you a better idea of
how targeting works. In the example below, there are three links that
we want to load into the window *bottomframe*. There are two ways
to do this:

- Add a target attribute to each anchor tag. The file top.html would
  contain the following targeted links:

  ```
  <A HREF="red.html" TARGET="bottomframe">
    <IMG SRC="red.gif" BORDER=0></A>
  <A HREF="yellow.html" TARGET="bottomframe">
    <IMG SRC="yellow.gif" BORDER=0></A>
  <A HREF="green.html" TARGET="bottomframe">
    <IMG SRC="green.gif" BORDER=0></A>
  ```

In this example, the three files, red.html, yellow.html, and green.html,
would each load into the window called *bottomframe*. Because we
want all our files in this example to load into the same window, there
is a faster way to do this, as explained below.

- Add a BASE TARGET tag. Within a particular frame, the BASE
  TARGET tag sets a default window to load all links into.

  ```
  <BASE TARGET="bottomframe">
  <A HREF="red.html"><IMG SRC="red.gif" BORDER=0></A>
  <A HREF="yellow.html"><IMG SRC="yellow.gif" BORDER=0></A>
  <A HREF="green.html"><IMG SRC="green.gif" BORDER=0></A>
  ```

With one BASE TARGET in each file, you can save the time and effort
needed to add target information for a long list of menu options.

Step 3: Understand "magic" targets

There are several predefined target names you can use as well. These
are always preceded by an underscore and are set names that
shouldn't be altered. These "magic" targets, as they're often called,
are listed below.

```
TARGET="_blank"
```
This will cause a new window to be launched and the file red.html to be loaded into it.

```
TARGET="_self"
```
This will cause the file red.html to load into the window where the link appears. If the link is in the window called *topframe* then the file will load there.

```
TARGET="_parent"
```
This will cause the file red.html to load into the window of its parent frameset—in this case, it will fill the entire window. If you placed this link inside one frame of a nested frameset, it would replace the nested frameset.

```
TARGET="_top"
```
This causes the file to fill the entire browser window, obliterating all frames.

To use this in your code, add the target name to an anchor tag:

```
<A HREF="red.html" TARGET="_blank"><IMG SRC="red.gif" BORDER=0></A>
```

For more information on frames (including basic tutorials), try these sites:

Framing the Web
www.webreference.com/dev/frames/

Let's Talk Targeting
www.webmonkey.com/webmonkey/html/96/36/index2a.html

Changing Two Frames at Once
www.hotwired.com/webmonkey/geektalk/97/02/index4a.html

The META refresh tag

You've probably been to at least one page that whisked you off it, seemingly by magic. This nifty trick is accomplished with the META refresh tag. The refresh tag forces a new page to load within a specific time period. For site developers wanting to experiment with forced movement across a site, it offers some interesting applications.

The refresh tag should be used carefully, since moving people along before the previous page's content loads can be self-defeating. Web users have a wide variety of connections, from T1 lines to some very clunky modems, and it's difficult to predict exactly what the right timing is. Too slow, and your T1 users will be able to have a nap while they wait for the next page. Too fast, and your modem users may have no idea what was on that blank page they just came from.

The best safeguard (besides lots of testing on different systems) is to provide a manual link somewhere on the page. This means speed users don't need to wait, and anyone experiencing trouble with the tag can simply bypass its forced march. Make sure to include this link so that users whose browsers don't support the META tag can continue through your site.

To use the META refresh tag in your pages, add one of the following lines of code inside the <HEAD> tag:

```
<META HTTP-EQUIV="Refresh" CONTENT="20">
```

This will cause your page to reload in 20 seconds. To load a different page, you need to specify the file that will replace the existing page, like this:

```
<META HTTP-EQUIV="Refresh" CONTENT="20; URL=secondpage.html">
```

In this example, the page will refresh in 20 seconds, replacing the existing page with a new page called secondpage.html. You can play around with the timing of this tag, but it's generally not a good idea to go below 20 seconds or so. This allows users a little leeway in case they have a slow connection or want to print the page, view your source, or read any text you've included. It also lets them use the browser's Back button without being trapped in a loop of instantly changing pages.

The punctuation for this tag may seem a little odd, with no quote after URL=, but make sure this is how you reproduce it. The time limit and target URL are both enclosed inside the CONTENT quotes. There is no </META> tag "off switch."

For more information about the META refresh tag, try the Web Developer's Virtual Library META tag pages at *WWW.stars.com/Authoring/ HTML/Head/meta.html.*

Creating fast-loading graphics

Graphics can be serious bandwidth hogs, causing delays and frustration for users. Sure, we could start designing "graphics-free" sites (as some people amazingly propose), but that's not much of a solution. A better approach is to understand what can be done to make graphics smaller, faster, and more efficient. There are a number of things you can do to achieve this goal:

- *Reduce physical size.* Reducing the physical size, or dimensions, of an image is a good first place to start. Instead of creating an image that fills the screen, experiment with creating a smaller image to get a similar design effect. Every inch you can trim from your image is a file size savings.

- *Reduce colors.* The smaller the number of colors in an image, the smaller its file size. In an image editing program such as Adobe

Photoshop, you can reduce the number of colors in each image's palette. In creating your artwork, make sure to use browser-safe colors (the 216 colors that display consistently on both 256-color Mac and 256-color PC monitors). But don't stop there. Instead, shoot for saving files with *less* than these 216 colors. An image created using four browser-safe colors and saved as an Exact Palette 4-color GIF will be three or four times as fast as the same image saved as a Web Palette 216-color GIF. In the second case, the image is carrying around 212 extra colors it doesn't need. Other ways to reduce colors include posterizing an image, using flat art (illustration) instead of photos, and using black and white wherever possible.

- *Reduce dithering and anti-aliasing.* Images that are "fuzzy" (dithered) or photorealistic usually sport much larger file sizes. By reducing dithering, you can reduce file sizes. To do this, avoid saving files with "diffusion" in Photoshop, and always try to work with web safe colors from the start when creating artwork for the Web. Doing so will mean less need for masking unsightly color shifts with dithering effects. Also, in creating text as an image file, you might choose to leave text aliased, or pixelated (see Figure A-1) instead of smoothing the edges with anti-aliasing. This can reduce file sizes by half, though it does looks jaggy. Experiment with different effects to find the balance between attractive images and small file sizes.

Figure A-1. *Anti-aliasing (on the left) and aliasing (on the right). Aliasing makes for smaller file sizes, though it does look jaggy.*

Figure A-2. *The image on the right was saved as a JPEG. Not only is it larger than the GIF on the left, it looks a lot worse.*

- *Use the right file format.* If you are working with a photo, use a compression format meant for photos (JPEG). If you're working with an illustration or with text as an image, use one meant for drawings (GIF). Saving an image with an inappropriate format can double or triple the image's file size, not to mention causing unpleasant color shifts and other effects (see Figure A-2).

- *Use image compression tools.* There is an increasing number of excellent image compression tools available specifically for web design use. BoxTop Software has some of the best, including Image Vice, a power tool for crunching web images. These tools are available for both JPEGs and GIFs. They can buy you file savings even after you've reduced size, color, and everything else you can think of.

- *Add image WIDTH and HEIGHT tags.* Once you've created your speedy images, make sure to include image width and height (in pixels) in your code. This tells the browser the dimensions of the images it will need to download, which lets the browser begin to display a page before images are finished loading. To do this, insert tags into your code as in the following example:

```
<IMG SRC="yourfile.gif" WIDTH="100" HEIGHT="100">
```

- *Recycle graphics wherever possible.* In terms of speed, the next best thing to using no images is to use images that are cached. Cached images are the ones that have already been downloaded (for example, the images from the screen you just left). The web browser stores these images in its cache for short-term use. Reusing certain images across your site will make pages seem to load faster, since the browser will pull them from the cache instead of from the Net.

For more about web safe colors and fast-loading graphics, pick up Lynda Weinman's *Designing Web Graphics 2e* (New Riders, 1997) or *Photoshop for the Web* by Mikkel Aaland (O'Reilly, 1998).

Cracking up: An alternative to image maps

Image maps are one way to construct a clickable landscape, but they do have their drawbacks. Server-side image maps are always "hot," with little guidance about what areas are really going to get you somewhere. With their cues in the status bar, client-side maps are better. But if you want to provide precise mouseovers, or include a small animation inside a layout without creating a huge file, you can't do much with a client-side image map either. For this type of precision, there is a better option: carving up your image files and reassembling them with HTML, as shown in Figure A-3.

Splitting a large image into smaller pieces (forced into position with tables or alignment tags) allows you much finer control over your layout. It also means that some "quiet" areas of the image can be replaced with simple and fast-loading spacer tags. Very localized mouseovers suddenly become possible. There is a greater server load initially, but if you recycle graphics across screens this can be minimized.

Figure A-3. *Forcing two smaller images to seamlessly align below a top cell.*

How to do it: Tables

Tables are an excellent way to precisely force a layout. Once you have your image carved up into smaller pieces, you only need to know an extra trick or two to reassemble it in a table. Most of the code is exactly the same as an ordinary table layout.

```
<TABLE CELLPADDING=0 CELLSPACING=0 BORDER=0 WIDTH=200>
<TR>
<TD><IMG SRC="top.gif" WIDTH=200 HEIGHT=100 BORDER=0></TD>
</TR>
<TR>
<TD><IMG SRC="bottomleft.gif" WIDTH=100 HEIGHT=100 BORDER=0>
 <IMG SRC="bottomright.gif" WIDTH=100 HEIGHT=100 BORDER=0></TD>
</TR>
</TABLE>
```

In this case, what you might not have picked up on from simply glancing over the code is the importance of deleting all carriage returns inside your <TD> cells. If you press Return while coding those lines, Netscape will insert space between images. Despite the fact that we're all told that carriage returns will be ignored, in this case they are the key to a working layout. You'll also need to make sure that CELLPADDING and CELLSPACING are set to 0, and that you've set WIDTH attributes for each cell and for the whole table.

Depending on your layout, you might also need to add ALIGN and VALIGN tags to your table cells. Adding an ALIGN tag, such as ALIGN=RIGHT, to your <TD> tag will ensure your images are positioned correctly. VALIGN=TOP (used in the <TR> or <TD> tag) will cause an image to align at the top of a cell, and VALIGN=BOTTOM will do the opposite.

How to do it: Image alignment tags

For simple layouts that don't require complex tables, you can use plain old IMG ALIGN tags to get the job done. This works well if you need to wrap images to the left or right of a larger image. The secret here is in making sure to set the HSPACE and VSPACE to 0, as well as in adding a <BR> tag to force the images to wrap. You'll also need to add a <NOBR> tag so that aligned pieces don't wrap on smaller monitors. Your code will look like this:

```
<NOBR>
<IMG SRC="left.gif" WIDTH=100 HEIGHT=200 BORDER=0 ALIGN=LEFT HSPACE=0
  VSPACE=0>
<IMG SRC="righttop.gif" WIDTH=100 HEIGHT=100 BORDER=0>
</NOBR>
<BR>
<IMG SRC="rightbottom.gif" WIDTH=100 HEIGHT=100 BORDER=0>
```

GLOSSARY

ALT attribute
Used inside the <IMG> tag, the ALT attribute specifies alternate text that will seen by users in the event that images don't display. Example: <IMG SRC="cows.gif" ALT="cows">

banner ad
An advertising graphic with a rectangular or "banner" shape, usually 468 × 60 pixels in size.

bit depth
A measurement of the number of colors used in an image or monitor. An average monitor might have 256 colors (8-bit). Monitors that offer millions of colors to display with are increasingly common, however.

browser compatibility
A judgment of how well a site looks and functions on different web browsers, such as Microsoft Internet Explorer and Netscape Navigator.

browser-safe palette
A palette made up of the 216 colors considered "safe" for web design. These 216 colors are the only colors common to both 256-color Macintosh and 256-color Windows computers, and will display consistently in most web browsers on both systems. This palette is also called the Netscape 216-color palette, or the web palette.

CGI
Stands for Common Gateway Interface, a way to present dynamically generated information on the Web. CGI scripts commonly process forms, dynamically build pages, and accept user input.

chat
Real-time discussion over the Web.

client
Software that receives and interprets data from a server. Netscape Navigator is a web client, for example.

client-side image map
An image map that stores map coordinates on the client side; that is, in the HTML document itself rather than in a separate coordinates file on the server.

contextual interview
An interview conducted in the user's everyday environment; that is, at the user's desk, in his or her classroom, etc.

cross-platform
Functioning well on a variety of computer platforms, such as Macintosh and Windows.

database-driven

Describes a site that relies on a database to generate pages. Many shopping catalogs are database-driven, and so are many large content sites.

distance learning

Organized, directed learning that takes place on the Web, via email, or in other "virtual" forums.

Dynamic HTML

A hybrid technology for creating interactive web pages. Dynamic HTML combines Java-Script and cascading style sheets so that every element on a page can be controlled by a script.

dynamic site map

A site map that is generated on demand by a web server, rather than frozen in a static format.

entry tunnel

A series of screens that form a linear path into a site.

ethnographic methods

Descriptive methods used in anthropology to record customs, activities, and other social traits.

exit tunnel

A series of screens that offer concluding material or direct visitors to other web resources.

extranet

The distributed network formed when external users or clients are allowed remote, password-protected access to an internal web such as an intranet. Often used to refer to a password-protected web site, such as a *project site*.

e-zine

Short for electronic magazine. Also called web zine.

focus group

A group of people—selected because they are part of the intended audience—who are asked to offer opinions and ideas about a product or service.

front door

The first screen of a site.

hierarchies of information

The organization of information into families or categories. Information hierarchies show relationships among topics.

hit logs

See *server logs*.

horizontal scrolling

Scrolling sideways within a web browser's window. When a site has content that is wider than the browser window, users must scroll horizontally to see it.

icon

A small, graphical representation of a concept, such as a picture of a house that signifies "Home."

image map

An image that has clickable "hot" zones that act as links to other files. See also *client-side image map*.

interaction design

A field of design that is concerned with crafting interactions between people (users, publishers, or others) with technology as a mediator. Interaction design borrows heavily from storytelling, theatre, and psychology.

interface

The combined screen elements that separate the user from the complex workings of a program or machine.

interstitial advertising

Advertising that interrupts the flow of a site or story to present a sales pitch.

labels

Names; terms used to describe menu options, site categories, or other elements.

location line

The part of a browser's display that shows the address (URL) of the site currrently being viewed.

mappings
> The clear relationship between a tool and its purpose, which allows users to predict the results of using that tool.

metaphor
> Using a familiar concept to describe an unfamiliar one, as when an online store calls the device used to collect purchases a "shopping cart."

META refresh
> An HTML tag that causes a web page to reload or be replaced by a second page after a timed period.

micronavigation
> Navigation that occurs within an individual page element, such as within a *banner ad*.

netography
> A list of Internet resources.

newbie
> Slang for new Internet user.

participatory design
> A design approach in which users participate actively in the design of a product, service, structure, or environment. Users are considered part of the design team, rather than external testers.

project site
> A password-protected web site used to share information among project team members.

prototype
> A working model that is not yet finished but that represents the major technical, design, and content features of the site. Prototypes are used for testing.

push media
> Content that is "pushed" at the viewer, such as news delivered directly to your desktop by the PointCast Network. Email is sometimes considered "push media."

recursive path
> A clickable pathway from the current location to the original starting place, or from a broader topic to a narrower one, that facilitates backwards movement. For example, *Computers >> Operating Systems >> Macintosh*.

remote
> A device, somewhat like a television's remote control, that is created with JavaScript and placed on a user's desktop. Remotes often contain navigation options or shortcuts.

resolution
> A measurement of image or monitor quality that is based on the amount of information displayed per square inch. An average 14" monitor displays about 72 dots per inch (dpi).

rollover
> A JavaScript technique in which one image is replaced by a second image when a mouse is passed over it.

semiotics
> The study of constructing or communicating meaning, either in spoken language or visual language.

server
> Software that "serves" files to users on request. Web server software makes possible file storage, transfer, and other site-related tasks. The physical computer where a site's files are located is also referred to as the server.

server logs
> Records of activity for a site or domain. Server logs track visitor information, any errors that might occur, and other events.

site architecture
> The structure of a web site. Reflects how information is organized, including categories, subsites, labeling, and other relationships.

site flow
> The flow of movement through your site. Site flow usually represents the way an average user will move through your site's space.

site map
> A visual representation of the contents of your site, often in the form of a flowchart.

specs
> Short for specifications, which outline the design and technical requirements for building a site or product.

splash screen
> A simple, focused introductory screen that serves as a "cover" or tunnel into the rest of your site.

status bar
> The bottom half-inch of a web browser window. The status bar shows the progress of downloading pages and can reveal information about items on mouseover.

storyboard
> A sequence of sketches showing major actions or outlining a story. Storyboards are commonly used in moviemaking, television, and advertising.

streaming media
> Media such as video or audio that can be viewed as they are are being downloaded to your computer. Non-streaming media can't be viewed until they have finished downloading.

style guide
> A record of the design, technical, and content decisions made during the development process. A style guide lists what fonts or colors are in use, how files should be named, what editing style is preferred, and so on.

subsite
> A subsection of a larger site. A subsite has its own look and feel and navigation scheme.

TARGET
> The TARGET attribute allows designers to specify where a document will load: in a new window, in a certain frame, and so on.

usability
> An indication of whether a product or site is "usable," that is, whether the intended audience finds the product easy to use and helpful in completing the goals at hand.

user experience
> The sum of all interactions and events, both positive and negative, between a user and a web site.

visual hierarchies
> The meaningful organization—by position, color, size, movement, and so on—of visual elements on a page or screen. Visual hierarchies show relationships among page elements.

VRML
> Virtual Reality Markup Language. A language used to create 3D worlds accessible via the Internet.

walkthrough
> A skeletal, text-only version of a site that allows designers to test basic navigation.

NETOGRAPHY

V isit the sites listed here for more information about topics covered in this book. Obviously, sites change frequently, so make sure to check the web version of this netography for updates and additions (*www.squarecircle.com/navigation/*). You can also find the netography on the CD-ROM, which you can use as a launchpad to the sites mentioned in this book.

Navigation

Designing Navigation Systems

www.webreview.com/wr/pub/98/02/20/arch/index.html

An excerpt from *Information Architecture for the World Wide Web* (O'Reilly, 1998), a book by web architects Lou Rosenfeld and Peter Morville.

The Navigation and Usability Guide

webreview.com/wr/pub/98/05/15/thing/index.html

Web Review article offering tips for designing more usable, navigable sites.

Designing Site Navigation

www.webreference.com/dlab/9705/index.html

Web Reference article explaining navigation principles through site critiques.

In this appendix

- Navigation
- Usability and user testing
- Organization of information
- Information and interaction design
- Process
- Document markup and scripting
- Graphics production
- Content
- Surveys and demographics
- Browsers
- Accessibility

Design That Offers a Sense of Place

www.internetworld.com/print/1997/07/14/undercon/19970714-design.html

Article describing the "you are here" factor in web design.

Problems with Navigating in Web Applications

www.emdash.com/webapps_new/webapps.htm#section-list

Article presenting common navigation problems on the web and techniques for avoiding them.

ACM Digital Library

www.acm.org/dl/

Search conference proceedings and full-text articles in the Association for Computing Machinery's Digital Library (search for keyword "navigation"). Requires free registration.

Plumb Design Visual Thesaurus

www.plumbdesign.com/thesaurus/

A concept map that allows users to navigate through related terms.

Web Page Design for Designers: Navigation

www.wpdfd.com/wpdnav.htm

Article offering tips on navigation design.

Principia Hypertextica

world.std.com/~wij/web-design/navigability.html

Some tips on navigability from a mathematics educator's guide to web design.

Usability and user testing

Usable Web: Guide to Web Usability Resources

www.usableweb.com/

A large collection of resources on usability, navigation, site architecture, and much more. Collected and maintained by Keith Instone.

useit.com: Usable Information Technology

www.useit.com/

Jakob Nielsen's site offers articles and resources in usability, tips on how to conduct user tests, and his well-known Alertbox column.

User Interface Engineering

world.std.com/~uieweb/

UIE's site offers many articles on user testing, as well as research summaries from their own usability studies.

Web Review: Usability

webreview.com/wr/pub/Usability

Articles on usability from Web Review magazine.

Organization of information

Web Review: Web Architect

www.webreview.com/universal/previous/arch/

Articles on site architecture by Web Review's web architects, Lou Rosenfeld and Peter Morville.

Hypertext Now!

www.eastgate.com/HypertextNow/

Articles and other resources on structuring documents in hypertext.

Beyond Bookmarks: Schemes for Organizing the Web

www.public.iastate.edu/~CYBERSTACKS/CTW.htm

Ideas and perspectives on organization schemes for the Web.

The WDVL: Resource Location

www.wdvl.com/Location/

Resources on site structure and navigation from the Web Developer's Virtual Library.

Information and interaction design

HCI Index

is.twi.tudelft.nl/hci/

Selected resources in human-computer interaction.

View Source Magazine: Human Interface

*developer.netscape.com/viewsource/index_
frame.html?content=archive/archivelist.html#humaninterface*

Netscape's DevEdge Online features several articles on human-computer interaction topics.

Bad Human Factors Designs

www.baddesigns.com/

A scrapbook of unusable designs, from buttons that won't push to containers that won't open.

Microsoft Developer Network News Online: The Human Factor

www.microsoft.com/devnews/topics/humanfactor.htm

Articles on human factors in web design.

Apple Web Design Guide

applenet.apple.com/hi/web/intro.html

Apple's guide to user-friendly web design.

W3: User Interface

www.w3.org/UI/

Information on the World Wide Web Consortium's User Interface team and their research and publications.

Anchor: Web Index: User-Centered Design

www.ahref.com/index/catlisting.html?cat_id=16

A collection of resources on user-centered design.

The On-Line Visual Literacy Project

www.pomona.edu/visual-lit/intro/intro.html

A survey of visual elements and principles such as shape, line, motion, etc.

BUILDER.COM: Voices: Dan Shafer

www.builder.com/Programming/Shafer/index.html

Tips and advice from user-centered design advocate Dan Shafer.

Salon | The Data Artist

www.salonmagazine.com/march97/tufte970310.html

Salon Magazine article on Edward Tufte, author of *Envisioning Information*.

A Unified Field Theory of Design

www.vivid.com/form/unified/unified.html

An article on information/interaction design by vivid studios' Nathan Shedroff.

Nathan Shedroff's World

www.nathan.com/

Nathan Shedroff built this personal site to feature his work as well as other interaction and information design resources.

Erik Spiekermann on Information Design

www.metadesign.com/metaculture/articles/info.htm

Meta Design's Erik Spiekermann explains information design basics.

Digital Storytelling Conference

www.dstory.com/

The site for the annual digital storytelling conference held in Crested Butte, Colorado.

ACM Interactions Magazine

www.acm.org/interactions/

The web site for the print magazine on interaction design offers selected articles online.

First Monday

www.firstmonday.dk/index.html

Web magazine featuring regular articles on information design, site planning, and other web topics.

Communication Arts

www.commarts.com/

Web site for the print magazine of the same name. Selected articles and resources available on the Web.

Process

Secrets of Successful Web Sites

www.highfive.com/secretsites/

The site for David Siegel's excellent project management book. Features his "project profiler."

Studio Archetype: Process

www.studioarchetype.com/process/quickview.html

Outlines DADI (Define, Architect, Design, Implement), the design process used by Clement Mok's firm, Studio Archetype.

vivid studios: Form + Function

www.vivid.com/form/

A detailed look at the design process used by vivid studios, which specializes in interaction design.

How CNET Does It

www.builder.com/Business/HowCnet/?st.bl.bus.feat

Article offers an inside look at how CNET produces their site.

Creating Your Site's Style Guide

webreview.com/wr/pub/98/02/06/webmaster/index.html

Web Review article that offers an overview of site style guides.

Yale C/AIM Web Style Guide

info.med.yale.edu/caim/manual/contents.html

The well-known guide to web style. From Yale University.

Sun Guide to Web Style

www.sun.com/styleguide/

A "cookbook for helping people create better web pages," Sun's style guide offers numerous site-building guidelines.

Defining Your Site's Mission

webreview.com/wr/pub/97/09/26/feature/mission.html

Web Review article offering advice on defining your site's mission and goals.

Art and the Zen of Web Sites

www.tlc-systems.com/webtips.shtml

Site-building tips from writing to marketing.

Innovating

www.innovating.com/

Articles and tips on creativity, including workplace innovation.

Innovation Network: Articles & Reports

www.thinksmart.com/articlesandreports.html

Articles on organizational and personal creativity.

Anchor: Creativity

www.ahref.com

Article on the basics of creativity theory, with related web resources.

NetMarketing

netb2b.com/

How to market your site and draw in visitors. From Ad Age magazine.

Document markup and scripting

Weblint

www.weblint.com/

Verify your HTML code.

Webcoder.com

www.webcoder.com

Javascript and Dynamic HTML resources by Nick Heinle, the author of *Designing With JavaScript*.

BUILDER.COM: Web Authoring

www.builder.com/Authoring/?st.bl.gp.tb.auth

Articles and features on HTML and other authoring topics, from CNET's BUILDER.COM.

Web Review: HTML

webreview.com/wr/pub/HTML

Articles on HTML from Web Review magazine.

NCSA Beginner's Guide to HTML

www.ncsa.uiuc.edu/General/Internet/WWW/HTMLPrimer.html

The popular guide to HTML from the National Center for Supercomputing Applications (NCSA).

Webmonkey: HTML Tutorial

www.hotwired.com/webmonkey/teachingtool/

A browsable collection of HTML tutorials. Includes their teaching tool, "Monkey See, Monkey Do."

XML.com

xml.com/

Everything you ever wanted to know about XML (eXtensible Markup Language).

The CGI Resource Index

www.cgi-resources.com/

Index of CGI resources, including canned scripts and tutorials.

Graphics production

Lynda.com

www.lynda.com

Resources on color and the browser-safe palette by the author of *Designing Web Graphics*.

Web Site Garage

www.websitegarage.com

Tools to reduce GIFs, check download times, and perform other optimization tasks.

BoxTop Software

www.boxtopsoft.com

Makers of Image Vice and other image optimization products.

Adobe

www.adobe.com

Makers of Photoshop and Image Ready, as well as other products.

Terry Morse Software: Myrmidon

www.terrymorse.com/

Convert Quark, PageMaker, Word, or other Mac files to HTML layout.

Limit Yourself: Small and Safe Color Palettes

www.tripod.com/web_tech/lifesupport/columns/gifgirl/970218.html

Gif Girl, Tripod's design columnist, tackles optimizing images by reducing color palettes. Includes how to load the browser-safe palette.

BUILDER.COM: Get Animated!

www.builder.com/Graphics/Webanim/?st.bl.graph.feat

Article explaining how to create GIF animations.

Macromedia: Flash Support Overview

www.macromedia.com/support/flash/

Support and tutorials for Flash developers.

Content

Writing Well for the Web

webreference.com/content/writing/

Four-part Web Reference article on writing for the web.

Editing for the Web: Creating Compelling Hypertexts

www.towson.edu/~lieb/updates/chapter12/writing.html

Editing tips adapted for the Web.

How to Write for the Web

www.useit.com/papers/webwriting/writing.html

A paper by Jakob Nielsen describing principles for writing on the Web.

Contentious

www.contentious.com

An e-zine for web writers, editors, and content planners.

Online-Writing

clio.lyris.net/cgi-bin/lyris.pl?enter=online-writing&text_mode=0

A discussion list for writers, editors, and others involved in writing for the Web.

What is good hypertext writing?

kbs.cs.tu-berlin.de/~jutta/ht/writing.html

Thoughts and impressions on what makes good writing on the web. Includes a list of "dangerous words" such as click, cool, and surf.

Wired Style

www.hotwired.com/hardwired/wiredstyle/

A site for the book *Wired Style: Principles of English Usage in the Digital Age.* Offers tips, mini-articles, and jargon.

Surveys and demographics

GVU WWW User Surveys

www.gvu.gatech.edu/user_surveys/

Bi-annual surveys of Internet users by Georgia Tech's Graphics, Visualization, and Usability Center.

NUA Internet Surveys

www.nua.ie

Ireland-based Internet company that posts regular news and survey results by email.

Jupiter Communications

www.jupiter.com

Market research and demographics firm that sells statistical reports.

Relevant Knowledge

www.relevantknowledge.com

Provides regular studies of Internet demographics (many for a fee), including most visited sites.

Nielsen Media Research

www.nielsenmedia.com

Internet usage information and other media statistics.

Browsers

BrowserCaps

www.browsercaps.com/

Find out which browsers support certain HTML features (tables, forms, fonts, and so on).

BROWSERS.COM

www.download.com/Browsers/

Read reviews of browser features and versions, and download software and plugins.

BrowserWatch

browserwatch.internet.com/

Get the latest stats on who's winning the browser war.

BrowserXpress

www.techweb.com/tools/browse/browserxpress.html

News and views on web browser software.

Accessibility

Principles of Universal Design

www2.ncsu.edu/ncsu/design/cud/multi/udprinc/udprincx.html

Design principles for physical and virtual spaces, emphasizing accessibility and ease of use.

W3C Web Accessibility Initiative

www.w3.org/WAI/

Describes an initiative put forth by the World Wide Web Consortium (W3C) to promote web accessibility measures.

NCAM

www.wgbh.org/wgbh/pages/ncam/

WGBH's National Center for Accessible Media offers tips on designing for visually impaired and deaf users.

typo.com: websense

www.typo.com/websense/websense.html

Tips on contrast, ALT tags, readability, and other topics adapted from Crystal Waters's book, *Universal Web Design*.

Microsoft's Accessibility and Disabilities Site

microsoft.com/enable/

Resources on accessible technology (including site building) from Microsoft.

Bobby

www.cast.org/bobby/

Tool that will analyze how accessible your site is to user with disabilities and those using older browser versions.

What Does Your HTML Look Like in Lynx?

www.miranova.com/~steve/Lynx-View.html

Find out how Lynx users will experience your site.

BIBLIOGRAPHY

Aaland, Mikkel. *Photoshop for the Web*. O'Reilly & Associates, 1998.

Adams, James L. *Conceptual Blockbusting: A Guide to Better Ideas*. Addison-Wesley, 1986.

Albers, Josef. *Interaction of Color*. Yale, 1963.

Brand, Stewart. *How Buildings Learn: What Happens After They're Built*. Penguin, 1995.

Carroll, John M., ed. *Scenario-Based Design: Envisioning Work and Technology in System Development*. Wiley, 1995.

Cooper, Alan. *About Face: The Essentials of User Interface Design*. IDG, 1995.

Dillon, Andrew. *Designing Usable Electronic Text: Ergonomic Aspects of Human Information Usage*. Taylor & Francis, 1994.

Dinucci, Darcy, Maria Giudice, and Lynne Stiles. *Elements of Web Design, 2e*. Peachpit Press, 1998.

English, Marc. *Designing Identity: Graphic Design As a Business Strategy*. Rockport, 1998.

Flanders, Vincent, and Michael Willis. *Web Pages That Suck: Learn Good Design by Looking at Bad Design*. Sybex, 1998.

Garrand, Timothy. *Writing for Multimedia: Entertainment, Education, Training, Advertising, and the World Wide Web*. Focal Press, 1996.

Gelernter, David. *Machine Beauty: Elegance and the Heart of Technology*. Basic Books, 1998.

Gloor, Peter A. *Elements of Hypermedia Design: Techniques for Navigation and Visualization in Cyberspace*. Springer Verlag, 1996.

Hall, Brandon. *Web-Based Training Cookbook*. Wilcy, 1997.

Heinle, Nick. *Designing With JavaScript: Creating Dynamic Web Pages*. O'Reilly, 1997.

Horn, Stacy. *Clicks, Culture, and the Creation of an Online Town*. Warner Books, 1998.

James, Geoffrey. *Success Secrets from Silicon Valley: How to Make Your Teams More Effective (No Matter What Business You're In)*. Times, 1996.

Jamison, Brian, Josh Gold, and Warren Jamison. *Electronic Selling: Twenty-Three Steps to E-Selling Profits*. McGraw-Hill, 1997.

Johnson, Steven. *Interface Culture: How New Technology Transforms the Way We Create and Communicate*. HarperCollins, 1997.

Kim, Amy Jo. *Global Villagers: Community-Building on the Web.* Peachpit, 1998.

Lakoff, George, and Mark Johnson. *Metaphors We Live By.* University of Chicago Press, 1983.

Laurel, Brenda. *Computers as Theatre.* Addison-Wesley, 1993.

Lefkon, Wendy, ed. *Walt Disney Imagineering: A Behind the Dreams Look at Making the Magic Real.* Hyperion, 1996.

McCormack, Colin, and David Jones. *Building a Web-Based Education System.* Wiley, 1997.

Melcher, Ryan, and Jeff Patterson. *The IUMA Guide to Creating Audio on the Web.* Peachpit, 1998.

Mok, Clement, ed. *Graphis New Media 1.* Graphis, 1996.

Mok, Clement. *Designing Business: Multiple Media, Multiple Disciplines.* Macmillan, 1996.

Moody, Fred. *I Sing the Body Electronic: A Year With Microsoft on the Multimedia Frontier.* Viking, 1995.

Mullet, Kevin, and Darrell Sano. *Designing Visual Interfaces: Communication Oriented Techniques.* Prentice Hall, 1995.

Nielsen, Jakob, and Robert L. Mack. *Usability Inspection Methods.* Wiley, 1994.

Nielsen, Jakob. *Usability Engineering.* AP Professional, 1994.

Norman, Donald. *The Design of Everyday Things.* Doubleday, 1990.

Olins, Wally. *Corporate Identity: Making Business Strategy Visible Through Design.* Harvard Business School Press, 1990.

Peppers, Don, and Martha Rogers. *The One to One Future: Building Relationships One Customer at a Time.* Doubleday, 1997.

Plant, Darrel. *Flash: Creating Animation for the Web.* Addison-Wesley, 1998.

Porter, Lynnette R. *Creating the Virtual Classroom: Distance Learning With the Internet.* Wiley, 1997.

Reeves, Byron, and Clifford Nass. *The Media Equation: How People Treat Computers, Television, and New Media Like Real People and Places.* Cambridge University Press, 1996.

Rogener, Stefan, Albert-Jan Pool, Ursula Packhauser, and E. M. Ginger. *Branding with Type.* Hayden Books, 1995.

Rosenfeld, Lou, and Peter Morville. *Information Architecture for the World Wide Web.* O'Reilly, 1998.

Rubin, Jeffrey. *Handbook of Usability Testing: How to Plan, Design, and Conduct Effective Tests.* Wiley, 1994.

Sano, Darrell. *Designing Large-Scale Web Sites: A Visual Design Methodology.* Wiley, 1996.

Schrage, Michael. *No More Teams! Mastering the Dynamics of Creative Collaboration.* Doubleday, 1989.

Schuler, D., and Aki Namioka. *Participatory Design: Principles and Practices.* Erlbaum, 1993.

Schulman, Martin A., and Rick R. Smith. *The Internet Strategic Plan: A Step-By-Step Guide to Connecting Your Company.* Wiley, 1997.

Schwartz, Evan I. *Webonomics: Nine Essential Principles for Growing Your Business on the World Wide Web.* Broadway Books, 1997.

Sellers, Don. *Getting Hits: The Definitive Guide to Promoting Your Website.* Peachpit, 1997.

Shenk, David. *Data Smog: Surviving the Information Glut.* Harper, 1997.

Sherwin, Gregory R. and Emily N. Avila. *Connecting Online: Creating a Successful Image on the Internet.* Psi, 1998.

Siegel, David. *Secrets of Successful Web Sites: Project Management on the World Wide Web.* Macmillan, 1997.

Sinclair, Joseph. *Developing Web Pages for TV-HTML*. Charles River Media, 1998.

Spiekermann, Erik, and E.M. Ginger. *Stop Stealing Sheep & Find Out How Type Works*. Hayden Books, 1993.

Sterne, Jim. *Customer Service on the Internet: Building Relationships, Increasing Loyalty, and Staying Competitive*. Wiley, 1996.

Sterne, Jim. *What Makes People Click: Advertising on the Web*. Que, 1997.

Sullivan, Louis H. *Kindergarten Chats and Other Writings*. Dover, 1980.

Tufte, Edward. *Visual Explanations*. Graphics, 1997.

Turkle, Sherry. *Life on the Screen: Identity in the Age of the Internet*. Touchstone Books, 1997.

Veen, Jeffrey. *Hotwired Style: Principles for Building Smart Web Sites*. Wired, 1998.

Waters, Crystal. *Universal Web Design: Hands-On Instruction of Design Alternatives*. New Riders, 1997.

Waters, Crystal. *Web Concept and Design, 2e*. New Riders, 1997.

Web Site Usability: A Designer's Guide. User Interface Engineering (self-published), 1997.

Weinman, Lynda. *Designing Web Graphics*, 3e. New Riders, 1998.

Wurman, Richard Saul. *Information Architects*. Graphis, 1996.

Yesil, Magdalena. *Creating the Virtual Store: Taking Your Web Site from Browsing to Buying*. Wiley, 1996.

A

accessibility features, 201
advertising, community sites, 137
Amazon.com, 113–118
  accessibility features of, 114
  customization ability of, 116
  feedback feature of, 116
  flexibility of, 116
  speed of, 114
Annenberg/CPB Project, 200–204
  accessibility features of, 201
  consistency of, 203
architecture (see site architecture)
audience, defining, 32–34
  information gathering and, 79
  multiple, 33
  narrowing of and, 32
  (see also users)

B

back links, 17
Berge, Doren, 216
beta-testing, 40
brainstorming, 88
branding features, 175
Bumgardner, Jim, 129

C

Café Utne, 146–148
  mentoring feature, 146
  previewing feature of, 147
CNET, 220–222
  filtering feature of, 221
  speed of, 220

communities, building, 127
community sites
  advertising and, 137
  Café Utne, 146–148
  feedback on, 131
  Firefly, 143–146
  goals of, 134–136
  groundwork for, 128–134
  help and, 133
  learning about people on, 133
  participation in, 129
  privacy and, 131
  rules of, 130
  sceneServer, 138–143
  trust issues and, 132
complexity, management of, 213
Computers.com, 220–222
  filtering feature of, 221
  speed of, 220
consistency features, 14, 203
containers, 140
content, organization and, 48–51
context, navigation and, 17
contextual interviews/
        storytelling, 82
Crimson Empire, 162
  feedback feature of, 163
Cyber Tiger, 199

D

deep site structure, 54
design, 34–37
  action on web and, 71
  familiarity and, 35

interaction and, 73
  participatory, 37
  psychology of, 71–74
  redesign tips and, 95
  usability engineering and, 35
design comps, 93
detection, 19
DigitalThink, 185, 191–198
  flexibility features of, 196
  simplicity of, 192
  support features of, 193
disposable camera studies, 83

E

entertainment sites
  beginning, 150
  clues, teasers, overviews, 151
  Crimson Empire, 162
  ease of use of, 152
  finishing on, 153
  goals for, 154
  groundwork for, 150–154
  Riven Journals, 160–162
  tips, hints and, 151
  Urban Diary, 156–160
exit tunnels, 153

F

FAO Schwarz, 122–125
  site ease of use and, 123
Faris, Jim, 39
feedback
  community sites and, 131
  features, 163

feedback (*continued*)
    navigation and, 16
    sceneServer, 140
filtering features, 221
financial information, security, 106
Firefly, 143–146
    portabilty of, 144
    searchability feature of, 145
flexibility features, 158, 172, 196
focus groups, 39
forms, 21
    navagation, 223
frames, 224–226
frenzy meters, 171

G

Garden Escape, 118–122
    community feature of, 119
    customer support and, 119
    previewing feature of, 121
Gerstner, Lou, 178
Gollmer, Chris, 193
Graphics Visualization and
            Usability surveys, 31
graphics, fast-loading, 227
Green, Dorrit, 198
Grice, H. Paul, 74
growth (see maintenance, growth)
guidance features, 157, 173, 199
GVU surveys, 31

H

heuristics, testing and, 36
hierarchies, visual, 64

I

IBM, 174–179
    branding feature of, 175
    speed feature of, 176
    tone of, 178
identity sites
    contact information and, 168
    goals for, 169
    groundwork for, 166–169
    IBM, 174–179
    information features of, 167
    powazek.com, 179
    Razorfish, 170–174
    snap decisions about, 166
image maps, alternatives to, 229
immersion features, 160

implementation, 96–99
    backend, 98
    content preparation, editing, 97
    interface design and, 97
    troubleshooting and, 98
indexes, 57
information gathering
    audience and, 79
    climate, competition and, 81
    communication methods, 84
    mission, goals, history, 78
    process of, 78–84
    project resources and, 80
    standards and, 80
    user goals, expectations and, 82
information sites
    Computers.com, 220–222
    goals of, 211–213
    groundwork for, 206–211
    helping users and, 208
    locating exact information, 207
    Lycos, 216–220
    MSNBC, 213–216
    personalized information, 208
    statements regarding, 206
    storage capability of, 210
    trustworthiness of, 209
infrastructure building, 51–58
interface designs, 21
interfaces, visual messages and, 63

K

Kim, Amy Jo, 127

L

labels, 23
launching, 99–101
    marketing and, 100
    quality assurance testing, 99
learning sites
    Annenberg/CPB
            Project, 200–204
    beginning, 184
    depth of, 188
    DigitalThink, 191–198
    flexibility of, 186
    goals of, 189–191
    groundwork for, 184–189
    interactiveness of, 187
    National Geographic, 198–200
    questions, asking and, 188
    special knowledge, tools, 185
    trustworthiness of, 186

linking, 169
Lycos, 216–220
    alternatives offering feature, 216

M

maintenance, growth, 101–103
    links and, 102
    new content, features and, 102
    periodic testing and, 103
    server logs and, 102
mapping site flows, 91
marketing, 100
mentoring features, 146
META refresh tags, 226
metaphors, visual messages, 67
Mok, Clement, 3, 22, 65
MSNBC on the Internet, 213–216
    managing complexity and, 213
Muller, Michael, 37

N

National Geographic, 198–200
    guidance features of, 199
navigation
    alternatives and, 18
    consistency of, 14
    context and, 17
    defined, 2
    economy of time, action, 19
    feedback and, 16
    forms, 223
    labels for, 23
    learning, 14
    principles of, 13
    site's purpose and, 26
    users' goals and, 26
Nielsen, Jakob, 36, 38, 176
Norman, Donald, 71

O

organization
    content and, 48–51
    need for, 45
    standards and, 47
    subjectivity and, 46

P

portability features, 144
powazek.com, 179
pre-design testing, 39
previewing features, 147

privacy
    community sites and, 131
    shopping sites and, 107
problems, identifying, 85
process
    implementation and, 96–99
    information gathering, 78–84
    launching and, 99–101
    maintenance, growth, 101–103
    prototyping and, 91–96
    six-phase approach to, 75–77
    strategy and, 84–91
profiles, 8–10
project profilers, 79
prototypes, 91–96
    building, testing of, 94
    design comps and, 93
    final architecture plans and, 95
    mapping site flow and, 91
    production specification
        outlines, 96
psychology of design, 71–74
pull-down menus, 57

Q

Quebe, 87

R

Razorfish, 170–174
    flexibility of, 172
    guidance feature of, 173
    responsiveness feature of, 171
redesigns, tips for, 95
responsiveness features, 171
Rettig, Marc, 82, 139
Riven Journals, 160–162
    immersion feature of, 160

S

scenarios, 10
sceneServer, 138–143
    feedback feature of, 140
    flexibility of, 140
Schrage, Michael, 88
searchability, 57
    features, 145
security, financial information, 106
shadowing, 83
shallow site structure, 54
Shedroff, Nathan, 48, 66

shopping sites
    Amazon.com, 113–118
    FAO Schwarz, 122–125
    financial information
        security, 106
    finding items on, 108
    Garden Escape, 118–122
    groundwork for, 106
    guidance, advice for, 108
    merchants' goals and, 112
    outlining goals of, 110–113
    previewing products on, 109
    privacy and, 107
    problems, returns and, 110
    users' goals and, 111
shortcuts, 21, 56
Siegel, David, 79, 153
simplicity features, 192
simulation, 165
site, 206
site architecture
    building infrastructure, 51–55
    conceptual design and, 59
    deep, shallow, 54
    interfaces and, 64
    process of, 58
    production, operations and, 62
    research and, 58
    shortcuts and, 56
site maps, 57
social scaffolding, 127
speed features, 176
Squier, Joseph, 150, 156
standards, 47
    information gathering and, 80
strategy, 84–91
    brainstorming and, 88
    content organization and, 90
    defining concept, scope and, 89
    design, technical
        alternatives, 90
    media, use of and, 87
    models, using, 86
    problem identification and, 85
Studio Archetype, 3
subsites, 176
support features, 193
surveys, 31, 33

T

table of contents, 57
teaching, 30
terminology, 24

testing, 36
    administrators of, 41
    equipment and, 43
    evaluation of, 43
    focus groups and, 39
    format of, 42
    participant selection and, 40
    periodic, 103
    quality assurance, 99
    timing of, 39
tone of sites, 178
tours, 141
troubleshooting, 98
Tufte, Edward, 69
Turbek, Stephen, 170
Turkle, Sherry, 165

U

Urban Diary, 156–160
    flexibility feature of, 158
    guidance feature of, 157
user testing (see testing)
User-Interface Engineering, 39
users
    clients versus, 6–8
    discovering goals of, 111
    experience of, 2
    goals of, navigation and, 26
    information gathering and, 82
    navigation alternatives and, 18
    needs of, 4–6
    profiles of, 8–10
    surveys of, 31, 33
    technological challenges, 29
    terminology of, 24
    (see also audience, defining)

V

visual hierarchies, 21
visual messages, 21–23, 63
    clarity versus chaos and, 69
    explanations and, 69
    form, function and, 70
    hierarchies and, 64
    metaphor and, 67
    show and tell and, 68

W

Web
    movement through, 1
    users' experience of, 4–6

Jennifer Fleming (*jennifer@squarecircle.com*) owns Square Circle Solutions, a Boston-area company specializing in user experience consulting and information design. Square Circle Solutions' client list includes Tripod, The Annenberg/CPB Project, EBSCO Publishing, and Shareholder Direct. Jennifer is a frequent speaker at industry conferences and has taught courses in web and computer design topics for United Digital Artists, the Massachusetts College of Art, and Naugatuck Valley Community Technical College. Jennifer has a Master's degree in library and information science and an undergraduate degree in fine arts.

About the Author

Web Programming

CGI Programming on the World Wide Web

By Shishir Gundavaram
1st Edition March 1996
450 pages, ISBN 1-56592-168-2

This book offers a comprehensive explanation of CGI and related techniques for people who hold on to the dream of providing their own information servers on the Web. It starts at the beginning, explaining the value of CGI and how it works, then moves swiftly into the subtle details of programming.

Dynamic HTML: The Definitive Reference

By Danny Goodman
1st Edition July 1998
1088 pages, ISBN 1-56592-494-0

Dynamic HTML: The Definitive Reference is an indispensable compendium for Web content developers. It contains complete reference material for all of the HTML tags, CSS style attributes, browser document objects, and JavaScript objects supported by the various standards and the latest versions of Netscape Navigator and Microsoft Internet Explorer.

Frontier: The Definitive Guide

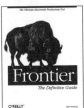

By Matt Neuburg
1st Edition February 1998
618 pages, 1-56592-383-9

This definitive guide is the first book devoted exclusively to teaching and documenting Userland Frontier, a powerful scripting environment for web site management and system level scripting. Packed with examples, advice, tricks, and tips, *Frontier: The Definitive Guide* teaches you Frontier from the ground up. Learn how to automate repetitive processes, control remote computers across a network, beef up your web site by generating hundreds of related web pages automatically, and more. Covers Frontier 4.2.3 for the Macintosh.

JavaScript: The Definitive Guide, 3rd Edition

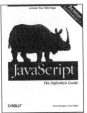

By David Flanagan & Dan Shafer
3rd Edition June 1998
800 pages, ISBN 1-56592-392-8

This third edition of the definitive reference to JavaScript covers the latest version of the language, JavaScript 1.2, as supported by Netscape Navigator 4.0. JavaScript, which is being standardized under the name ECMAScript, is a scripting language that can be embedded directly in HTML to give web pages programming-language capabilities.

Learning VBScript

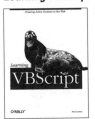

By Paul Lomax
1st Edition July 1997
616 pages, includes CD-ROM
ISBN 1-56592-247-6

This definitive guide shows web developers how to take full advantage of client-side scripting with the VBScript language. In addition to basic language features, it covers the Internet Explorer object model and discusses techniques for client-side scripting, like adding ActiveX controls to a web page or validating data before sending to the server. Includes CD-ROM with over 170 code samples.

Graphics/Multimedia

Lingo in a Nutshell

By Bruce Epstein
1st Edition November 1998
634 pages, ISBN 1-56592-493-2

This companion book to *Director in a Nutshell* covers all aspects of Lingo, Director's powerful scripting language, and is the book for which both Director users and power Lingo programmers have been yearning. Detailed chapters describe messages, events, scripts, handlers, variables, lists, file I/O, Behaviors, child objects, Xtras, browser scripting, media control, performance optimization, and more.

Graphics/Multimedia

Director in a Nutshell

By Bruce A. Epstein
1st Edition March 1999
658 pages, ISBN 1-56592-382-0

Director in a Nutshell is the most concise and complete guide available for Director®. The reader gets both the nitty-gritty details and the bigger context in which to use the multiple facets of Director. It is a high-end handbook, at a low-end price—an indispensable desktop reference for every Director user.

QuarkXPress in a Nutshell

By Donnie O'Quinn
1st Edition June 1998
546 pages, ISBN 1-56592-399-5

This quick reference describes every tool, command, palette, and sub-menu in QuarkXPress 4, providing users with a detailed understanding of the software so they can make informed choices and reduce time spent learning by trial-and-error.

Encyclopedia of Graphics File Formats, 2nd Edition

By James D. Murray & William vanRyper
2nd Edition May 1996
1154 pages, Includes CD-ROM
ISBN 1-56592-161-5

The second edition of the *Encyclopedia of Graphics File Formats* provides the convenience of quick look-up on CD-ROM, up-to-date information through links to the World Wide Web, as well as a printed book—all in one package. Includes technical details on more than 100 file formats. The CD-ROM includes vendor file format specs, graphics test images, coding examples, and graphics conversion and manipulation software. An indispensable online resource for graphics programmers, service bureaus, and graphic artists.

Photoshop in a Nutshell

By Donnie O'Quinn & Matt LeClair
1st Edition October 1997
610 pages, ISBN 1-56592-313-8

Photoshop 4's powerful features make it the software standard for desktop image design and production. But they also make it an extremely complex product. This detailed reference defines and describes every tool, command, palette, and sub-menu of Photoshop 4 to help users understand design options, make informed choices, and reduce time spent learning by trial-and-error.

Perl

The Perl Cookbook

By Tom Christiansen & Nathan Torkington
1st Edition August 1998
794 pages, ISBN 1-56592-243-3

This collection of problems, solutions, and examples for anyone programming in Perl covers everything from beginner questions to techniques that even the most experienced Perl programmers might learn from. It contains hundreds of Perl "recipes," including recipes for parsing strings, doing matrix multiplication, working with arrays and hashes, and performing complex regular expressions.

Learning Perl, 2nd Edition

By Randal L. Schwartz & Tom Christiansen
Foreword by Larry Wall
2nd Edition July 1997
302 pages, ISBN 1-56592-284-0

In this update of a bestseller, two leading Perl trainers teach you to use the most universal scripting language in the age of the World Wide Web. Now current for Perl version 5.004, this hands-on tutorial includes a lengthy new chapter on CGI programming, while touching also on the use of library modules, references, and Perl's object-oriented constructs.

O'REILLY®

TO ORDER: **800-998-9938** • *order@oreilly.com* • *http://www.oreilly.com/*

OUR PRODUCTS ARE AVAILABLE AT A BOOKSTORE OR SOFTWARE STORE NEAR YOU.

FOR INFORMATION: **800-998-9938** • **707-829-0515** • *info@oreilly.com*

Perl

Learning Perl on Win32 Systems

By Randal L. Schwartz, Erik Olson &
Tom Christiansen
1st Edition August 1997
306 pages, ISBN 1-56592-324-3

In this carefully paced course, leading Perl trainers
and a Windows NT practitioner teach you to program in
the language that promises to emerge as the scripting
language of choice on NT. Based on the "llama" book,
this book features tips for PC users and new, NT-specific
examples, along with a foreword by Larry Wall, the creator of Perl, and Dick
Hardt, the creator of Perl for Win32.

Mastering Regular Expressions

By Jeffrey E. F. Friedl
1st Edition January 1997
368 pages, ISBN 1-56592-257-3

Regular expressions, a powerful tool for manipulating
text and data, are found in scripting languages, editors,
programming environments, and pecialized tools. In
this book, author Jeffrey Friedl leads you through the
steps of crafting a regular expression that gets the job
done. He examines a variety of tools and uses them in
an extensive array of examples, with a major focus on Perl.

Learning Perl/Tk

By Nancy Walsh
1st Edition January 1999
376 pages, ISBN 1-56592-314-6

This tutorial for Perl/Tk, the extension to Perl for
creating graphical user interfaces, shows how to use
Perl/Tk to build graphical, event-driven applications
for both Windows and UNIX. Rife with illustrations, it
teaches how to implement and configure each Perl/Tk
graphical element.

Perl Resource Kit—UNIX Edition

By Larry Wall, Nate Patwardhan, Ellen Siever,
David Futato & Brian Jepson
1st Edition November 1997
1812 pages, ISBN 1-56592-370-7

The *Perl Resource Kit—UNIX Edition* gives you the
most comprehensive collection of Perl documentation
and commercially enhanced software tools available
today. Developed in association with Larry Wall, the
creator of Perl, it's the definitive Perl distribution for
webmasters, programmers, and system administrators.

The *Perl Resource Kit* provides:

- Over 1800 pages of tutorial and in-depth reference documentation
  for Perl utilities and extensions, in 4 volumes.
- A CD-ROM containing the complete Perl distribution, plus hundreds
  of freeware Perl extensions and utilities—a complete snapshot of the
  Comprehensive Perl Archive Network (CPAN)—as well as new software
  written by Larry Wall just for the Kit.

Perl Software Tools All on One Convenient CD-ROM

Experienced Perl hackers know when to create their own, and when they
can find what they need on CPAN. Now all the power of CPAN—and more—
is at your fingertips. The *Perl Resource Kit* includes:

- A complete snapshot of CPAN, with an install program for Solaris and
  Linux that ensures that all necessary modules are installed together.
  Also includes an easy-to-use search tool and a web-aware interface
  that allows you to get the latest version of each module.
- A new Java/Perl interface that allows programmers to write Java classes
  with Perl implementations. This new tool was written specially for the
  Kit by Larry Wall.

Experience the power of Perl modules in areas such as CGI, web spidering,
database interfaces, managing mail and USENET news, user interfaces,
security, graphics, math and statistics, and much more.

Perl

Programming Perl, 2nd Edition

By Larry Wall, Tom Christiansen &
Randal L. Schwartz
2nd Edition September 1996
670 pages, ISBN 1-56592-149-6

Coauthored by Larry Wall, the creator of Perl, the
second edition of this authoritative guide contains
a full explanation of Perl version 5.003 features. It
covers Perl language and syntax, functions, library
modules, references, and object-oriented features,
and also explores invocation options, debugging, common mistakes, and
much more.

Perl Resource Kit—Win32 Edition

By Dick Hardt, Erik Olson,
David Futato & Brian Jepson
1st Edition August 1998
1,832 pages, Includes 4 books & CD-ROM
ISBN 1-56592-409-6

The *Perl Resource Kit—Win32 Edition* is an essential
tool for Perl programmers who are expanding their
platform expertise to include Win32 and for Win32
webmasters and system administrators who have
discovered the power and flexibility of Perl. The Kit contains some of
the latest commercial Win32 Perl software from Dick Hardt's ActiveState
company, along with a collection of hundreds of Perl modules that run
on Win32, and a definitive documentation set from O'Reilly.

Perl in a Nutshell

By Stephen Spainhour, Ellen Siever &
Nathan Patwardhan
1st Edition January 1999
674 pages, ISBN 1-56592-286-7

The perfect companion for working programmers,
Perl in a Nutshell is a comprehensive reference guide
to the world of Perl. It contains everything you need
to know for all but the most obscure Perl questions.
This wealth of information is packed into an efficient,
extraordinarily usable format.

Mastering Algorithms with Perl

By Jon Orwant, Jarkko Hietaniemi &
John Macdonald
1st Edition August 1999 (est.)
480 pages, ISBN 1-56592-398-7

There have been dozens of books on programming
algorithms, but never before has there been one that
uses Perl. Whether you are an amateur programmer
or know a wide range of algorithms in other languages,
this book will teach you how to carry out traditional
programming tasks in a high-powered, efficient, easy-to-maintain manner
with Perl. Topics range in complexity from sorting and searching to statistical
algorithms, numerical analysis, and encryption.

Advanced Perl Programming

By Sriram Srinivasan
1st Edition August 1997
434 pages, ISBN 1-56592-220-4

This book covers complex techniques for managing
production-ready Perl programs and explains methods
for manipulating data and objects that may have
looked like magic before. It gives you necessary
background for dealing with networks, databases,
and GUIs, and includes a discussion of internals to
help you program more efficiently and embed Perl within C or C within Perl.

How to stay in touch with O'Reilly

1. Visit Our Award-Winning Web Site

http://www.oreilly.com/

★ "Top 100 Sites on the Web" —*PC Magazine*
★ "Top 5% Web sites" —*Point Communications*
★ "3-Star site" —*The McKinley Group*

Our web site contains a library of comprehensive product information (including book excerpts and tables of contents), downloadable software, background articles, interviews with technology leaders, links to relevant sites, book cover art, and more. File us in your Bookmarks or Hotlist!

2. Join Our Email Mailing Lists

New Product Releases
To receive automatic email with brief descriptions of all new O'Reilly products as they are released, send email to:
listproc@online.oreilly.com
Put the following information in the first line of your message (*not* in the Subject field):
subscribe oreilly-news

O'Reilly Events
If you'd also like us to send information about trade show events, special promotions, and other O'Reilly events, send email to:
listproc@online.oreilly.com
Put the following information in the first line of your message (*not* in the Subject field):
subscribe oreilly-events

3. Get Examples from Our Books via FTP

There are two ways to access an archive of example files from our books:

Regular FTP
- ftp to:
  ftp.oreilly.com
  (login: anonymous
  password: your email address)
- Point your web browser to:
  ftp://ftp.oreilly.com/

FTPMAIL
- Send an email message to:
  ftpmail@online.oreilly.com
  (Write "help" in the message body)

4. Contact Us via Email

order@oreilly.com
To place a book or software order online. Good for North American and international customers.

subscriptions@oreilly.com
To place an order for any of our newsletters or periodicals.

books@oreilly.com
General questions about any of our books.

software@oreilly.com
For general questions and product information about our software. Check out O'Reilly Software Online at **http://software.oreilly.com/** for software and technical support information. Registered O'Reilly software users send your questions to: **website-support@oreilly.com**

cs@oreilly.com
For answers to problems regarding your order or our products.

booktech@oreilly.com
For book content technical questions or corrections.

proposals@oreilly.com
To submit new book or software proposals to our editors and product managers.

international@oreilly.com
For information about our international distributors or translation queries. For a list of our distributors outside of North America check out:
http://www.oreilly.com/www/order/country.html

O'Reilly & Associates, Inc.
101 Morris Street, Sebastopol, CA 95472 USA
TEL   707-829-0515 or 800-998-9938
        (6am to 5pm PST)
FAX   707-829-0104

O'REILLY®

TO ORDER: **800-998-9938** • **order@oreilly.com** • **http://www.oreilly.com/**
OUR PRODUCTS ARE AVAILABLE AT A BOOKSTORE OR SOFTWARE STORE NEAR YOU.
FOR INFORMATION: **800-998-9938** • **707-829-0515** • **info@oreilly.com**

Titles from O'Reilly

WEB

Advanced Perl Programming
Apache: The Definitive Guide, 2nd Edition
ASP in a Nutshell
Building Your Own Web Conferences
Building Your Own Website™
CGI Programming with Perl
Designing with JavaScript
Dynamic HTML: The Definitive Reference
Frontier: The Definitive Guide
HTML: The Definitive Guide, 3rd Edition
Information Architecture
    for the World Wide Web
JavaScript Pocket Reference
JavaScript: The Definitive Guide, 3rd Edition
Learning VB Script
Photoshop for the Web
WebMaster in a Nutshell
WebMaster in a Nutshell, Deluxe Edition
Web Design in a Nutshell
Web Navigation:
    Designing the User Experience
Web Performance Tuning
Web Security & Commerce
Writing Apache Modules

PERL

Learning Perl, 2nd Edition
Learning Perl for Win32 Systems
Learning Perl/TK
Mastering Algorithms with Perl
Mastering Regular Expressions
Perl5 Pocket Reference, 2nd Edition
Perl Cookbook
Perl in a Nutshell
Perl Resource Kit—UNIX Edition
Perl Resource Kit—Win32 Edition
Perl/TK Pocket Reference
Programming Perl, 2nd Edition
Web Client Programming with Perl

GRAPHICS & MULTIMEDIA

Director in a Nutshell
Encyclopedia of Graphics
    File Formats, 2nd Edition
Lingo in a Nutshell
Photoshop in a Nutshell
QuarkXPress in a Nutshell

USING THE INTERNET

AOL in a Nutshell
Internet in a Nutshell
Smileys
The Whole Internet for Windows95
The Whole Internet: The Next Generation
The Whole Internet User's Guide & Catalog

JAVA SERIES

Database Programming with JDBC and Java
Developing Java Beans
Exploring Java, 2nd Edition
Java AWT Reference
Java Cryptography
Java Distributed Computing
Java Examples in a Nutshell
Java Foundation Classes in a Nutshell
Java Fundamental Classes Reference
Java in a Nutshell, 2nd Edition
Java in a Nutshell, Deluxe Edition
Java I/O
Java Language Reference, 2nd Edition
Java Media Players
Java Native Methods
Java Network Programming
Java Security
Java Servlet Programming
Java Swing
Java Threads
Java Virtual Machine

UNIX

Exploring Expect
GNU Emacs Pocket Reference
Learning GNU Emacs, 2nd Edition
Learning the bash Shell, 2nd Edition
Learning the Korn Shell
Learning the UNIX Operating System,
    4th Edition
Learning the vi Editor, 6th Edition
Linux in a Nutshell
Linux Multimedia Guide
Running Linux, 2nd Edition
SCO UNIX in a Nutshell
sed & awk, 2nd Edition
Tcl/Tk in a Nutshell
Tcl/Tk Pocket Reference
Tcl/Tk Tools
The UNIX CD Bookshelf
UNIX in a Nutshell, System V Edition
UNIX Power Tools, 2nd Edition
Using csh & tsch
Using Samba
vi Editor Pocket Reference
What You Need To Know: When You Can't
    Find Your UNIX System Administrator
Writing GNU Emacs Extensions

SONGLINE GUIDES

NetLaw   NetResearch
NetLearning   NetSuccess
NetLessons   NetTravel

SOFTWARE

Building Your Own WebSite™
Building Your Own Web Conference
WebBoard™ 3.0
WebSite Professional™ 2.0
PolyForm™

SYSTEM ADMINISTRATION

Building Internet Firewalls
Computer Security Basics
Cracking DES
DNS and BIND, 3rd Edition
DNS on WindowsNT
Essential System Administration
Essential WindowsNT System Administration
Getting Connected:
    The Internet at 56K and Up
Linux Network Administrator's Guide
Managing IP Networks with Cisco Routers
Managing Mailing Lists
Managing NFS and NIS
Managing the WindowsNT Registry
Managing Usenet
MCSE: The Core Exams in a Nutshell
MCSE: The Electives in a Nutshell
Networking Personal Computers with TCP/IP
Oracle Performance Tuning, 2nd Edition
Practical UNIX & Internet Security,
    2nd Edition
PGP: Pretty Good Privacy
Protecting Networks with SATAN
sendmail, 2nd Edition
sendmail Desktop Reference
System Performance Tuning
TCP/IP Network Administration, 2nd Edition
termcap & terminfo
The Networking CD Bookshelf
Using & Managing PPP
Virtual Private Networks
WindowsNT Backup & Restore
WindowsNT Desktop Reference
WindowsNT Event Logging
WindowsNT in a Nutshell
WindowsNT Server 4.0 for
    Netware Administrators
WindowsNT SNMP
WindowsNT TCP/IP Administration
WindowsNT User Administration
Zero Administration for Windows

X WINDOW

Vol. 1: Xlib Programming Manual
Vol. 2: Xlib Reference Manual
Vol. 3M: X Window System
    User's Guide, Motif Edition
Vol. 4M: X Toolkit Intrinsics Programming
    Manual, Motif Edition
Vol. 5: X Toolkit Intrinsics Reference Manual
Vol. 6A: Motif Programming Manual
Vol. 6B: Motif Reference Manual
Vol. 8 : X Window System
    Administrator's Guide

PROGRAMMING

Access Database Design and Programming
Advanced Oracle PL/SQL Programming
    with Packages
Applying RCS and SCCS
BE Developer's Guide
BE Advanced Topics
C++: The Core Language
Checking C Programs with lint
Developing Windows Error Messages
Developing Visual Basic Add-ins
Guide to Writing DCE Applications
High Performance Computing, 2nd Edition
Inside the Windows 95 File System
Inside the Windows 95 Registry
lex & yacc, 2nd Edition
Linux Device Drivers
Managing Projects with make
Oracle8 Design Tips
Oracle Built-in Packages
Oracle Design
Oracle PL/SQL Programming, 2nd Edition
Oracle Scripts
Oracle Security
Palm Programming: The Developer's Guide
Porting UNIX Software
POSIX Programmer's Guide
POSIX.4: Programming for the Real World
Power Programming with RPC
Practical C Programming, 3rd Edition
Practical C++ Programming
Programming Python
Programming with curses
Programming with GNU Software
Pthreads Programming
Python Pocket Reference
Software Portability with imake, 2nd Edition
UML in a Nutshell
Understanding DCE
UNIX Systems Programming for SVR4
VB/VBA in a Nutshell: The Languages
Win32 Multithreaded Programming
Windows NT File System Internals
Year 2000 in a Nutshell

USING WINDOWS

Excel97 Annoyances
Office97 Annoyances
Outlook Annoyances
Windows Annoyances
Windows98 Annoyances
Windows95 in a Nutshell
Windows98 in a Nutshell
Word97 Annoyances

OTHER TITLES

PalmPilot: The Ultimate Guide

International Distributors

UK, EUROPE, MIDDLE EAST AND NORTHERN AFRICA (EXCEPT FRANCE, GERMANY, SWITZERLAND, & AUSTRIA)

INQUIRIES
International Thomson Publishing Europe
Berkshire House
168-173 High Holborn
London WC1V 7AA
United Kingdom
Tel: 44-1-71-497-1422
Fax: 44-1-71-497-1426

ORDERS
International Thomson Publishing Services, Ltd.
Cheriton House, North Way
Andover, Hampshire SP10 5BE
United Kingdom
Tel: 44-1-264-342-832 (UK)
Tel: 44-1-264-342-806 (outside UK)
Fax: 44-1-264-364-418 (UK)
Fax: 44-1-264-342-761 (outside UK)
Email: itpint@itps.co.uk

FRANCE

GEODIF
61, Bd Saint-Germain
75240 Paris Cedex 05, France
Tel: 33-1-44-41-46-16 (French books)
Tel: 33-1-44-41-11-87 (English books)
Fax: 33-1-44-41-11-44
Email: distribution@eyrolles.com

ORDERS
SODIS
128, av.du Mal de Lattre de Tassigny
77403 Lagny Cédex, France
Tel: 33-1-60-07-82-00
Fax: 33-1-64-30-32-27

INQUIRIES
Éditions O'Reilly
18 rue Séguier
75006 Paris, France
Tel: 33-1-40-51-52-30
Fax: 33-1-40-51-52-31
Email: france@editions-oreilly.fr

GERMANY, SWITZERLAND, AUSTRIA

INQUIRIES
O'Reilly Verlag
Balthasarstr. 81
D-50670 Köln, Germany
Tel: 49-221-973160-0
Fax: 49-221-973160-8
Email: anfragen@oreilly.de

ORDERS
International Thomson Publishing
Königswinterer Straße 418
53227 Bonn, Germany
Tel: 49-228-970240
Fax: 49-228-441342
Email: order@oreilly.de

CANADA (FRENCH LANGUAGE BOOKS)

Les Éditions Flammarion ltée
375, Avenue Laurier Ouest
Montréal (Québec) H2V 2K3
Tel: 00-1-514-277-8807
Fax: 00-1-514-278-2085
Email: info@flammarion.qc.ca

HONG KONG

City Discount Subscription Service, Ltd.
Unit D, 3rd Floor, Yan's Tower
27 Wong Chuk Hang Road
Aberdeen, Hong Kong
Tel: 852-2580-3539
Fax: 852 2580-6463
Email: citydis@ppn.com.hk

KOREA

Hanbit Media, Inc.
Sonyoung Bldg. 202
Yeksam-dong 736-36
Kangnam-ku
Seoul, Korea
Tel: 822-554-9610
Fax: 822-556-0363
Email: hant93@chollian.dacom.co.kr

SINGAPORE, MALAYSIA, THAILAND

Addison-Wesley Longman Singapore Pte., Ltd.
25 First Lok Yang Road
Singapore 629734
Tel: 65-268-2666
Fax: 65-268-7023
Email: Daniel.Loh@awl.com.sg

PHILIPPINES

Mutual Books, Inc.
429-D Shaw Boulevard
Mandaluyong City, Metro
Manila, Philippines
Tel: 632-725-7538
Fax: 632-721-3056
Email: mbikikog@mnl.sequel.net

TAIWAN

O'Reilly Taiwan
No. 3, Lane 131
Hang-Chow South Road
Section 1, Taipei, Taiwan
Tel: 886-2-23968990
Fax: 886 2 23968916
Email: benh@oreilly.com

CHINA

China National Publishing
Industry Trading Corporation
504 AnHuiLi, AnDingMenWai
P.O. Box 782
Beijing 100011, China P.R.
Tel: 86-10-6424-0483
Fax: 86-10-6421-4540
Email: frederic@oreilly.com

INDIA

Computer Bookshop (India) Pvt. Ltd.
190 Dr. D.N. Road, Fort
Bombay 400 001 India
Tel: 91-22-207-0989
Fax: 91-22-262-3551
Email: cbsbom@giasbm01.vsnl.net.in

JAPAN

O'Reilly Japan, Inc.
Kiyoshige Building 2F
12-Bancho, Sanei-cho
Shinjuku-ku
Tokyo 160-0008 Japan
Tel: 81-3-3356-5227
Fax: 81-3-3356-5261
Email: japan@oreilly.com

ALL OTHER ASIAN COUNTRIES

O'Reilly & Associates, Inc.
101 Morris Street
Sebastopol, CA 95472 USA
Tel: 707-829-0515
Fax: 707-829-0104
Email: order@oreilly.com

AUSTRALIA

WoodsLane Pty., Ltd.
7/5 Vuko Place
Warriewood NSW 2102
Australia
Tel: 61-2-9970-5111
Fax: 61-2-9970-5002
Email: info@woodslane.com.au

NEW ZEALAND

Woodslane New Zealand, Ltd.
21 Cooks Street (P.O. Box 575)
Waganui, New Zealand
Tel: 64-6-347-6543
Fax: 64-6-345-4840
Email: info@woodslane.com.au

SOUTH AFRICA

International Thomson South Africa
Building 18, Constantia Park
138 Sixteenth Road
(P.O. Box 2459)
Halfway House, 1685 South Africa
Tel: 27-11-805-4819
Fax: 27-11-805-3648

LATIN AMERICA

McGraw-Hill Interamericana
Editores, S.A. de C.V.
Cedro No. 512
Col. Atlampa
06450, Mexico, D.F.
Tel: 52-5-547-6777
Fax: 52-5-547-3336
Email: mcgraw-hill@infosel.net.mx

O'REILLY®

TO ORDER: **800-998-9938** • **order@oreilly.com** • **http://www.oreilly.com/**
OUR PRODUCTS ARE AVAILABLE AT A BOOKSTORE OR SOFTWARE STORE NEAR YOU.
FOR INFORMATION: **800-998-9938** • **707-829-0515** • **info@oreilly.com**